Chicago —

Also available from Macmillan U. S. A.

The Unofficial Guide to Ethnic Cuisine & Dining in America, by Eve Zibart, Muriel Stevens, and Terrell Vermont

The Unofficial Guide to Dining in Atlanta, by Terrell Vermont

The Unofficial Guide to Dining in Miami and Southeastern Florida, by Lucy Cooper

The Unofficial Guide to Dining in Washington, D. C., by Eve Zibart

The Unofficial Guide to Atlanta, by Fred Brown and Bob Sehlinger

The Unofficial Guide to Branson, Missouri, by Eve Zibart

The Unofficial Guide to Disneyland, by Bob Sehlinger

The Unofficial Guide to Euro Disneyland, by Bob Sehlinger

The Unofficial Guide to Las Vegas, by Bob Sehlinger

The Unofficial Guide to Miami and the Keys, by Bob Sehlinger and Joe Surkiewicz

The Unofficial Guide to the Great Smoky and Blue Ridge Mountains, by Bob Sehlinger and Joe Surkiewicz

The Unofficial Guide to Walt Disney World & EPCOT, by Bob Sehlinger

The Unofficial Guide to Washington, D.C., by Bob Sehlinger and Joe Surkiewicz

Contents

List of Illustrations

Acknowledgments

A special thank you to the many people who assisted with the research and compilation of this book, including sharing their restaurant experiences.

Special thanks to the crack team of Medill School of Journalism students and recent graduates who assisted with gathering the current restaurant data: Meg McGinity assisted with American and seafood restaurants; Greg Henkin especially researched steak and German restaurants; Andrea Sachs, whose experience in France and as a vegetarian helped with relevant restaurants; Sarah Stirland from Hong Kong, whose special help with Asian cuisines and many others was key; and especially Rummana Hussain, whose Indian heritage and knowledge of Middle Eastern cuisines proved helpful in those categories, and whose journalistic skills and interest in various cuisines were invaluable as she worked with me to the final deadline.

Thanks to Joan Hersh, owner of "A Matter of Course" catering; Robert Rohden, president of Laser List Chicago, wine consultant, and computer consultant, for his dedication and invaluable assistance; John Davis, owner and president of several companies including "A Taste of California," a wine mail-order business, for his office support; Lucia de la Cruz, a bilingual friend who lived in Spain, for her late-night assistance calls with Spanish vocabulary; Lowell Komie, for his counsel; and Toshihiko Sawada, director of the Japan National Tourist Organization, for sharing his expertise on his native cuisine.

And a very special thank you to my dining companions, including my mother, Jeanette

Stagg, who instilled in me a love of food and cooking; Jim White, Chicago, San Francisco, and Dallas broadcaster, voice actor, media consultant, and connoisseur, whose articulate critiques and sense of humor breathed new life into this project; Ed Jarratt, who is without food prejudices and is willing to try anything once—even czarnina; and to B. C. Kent, who goes on annual fishing trips, and whose knowledge of fish (and penchant for catfish) and fondness for desserts helped immeasurably.

And gratitude to publisher Bob Sehlinger and his cheerful staff at Menasha Ridge Press, especially Executive Editor Molly Burns and Editorial Assistant Holly Brown, for their continuing support and teamwork.

*— The Unofficial Guide®
to Dining in Chicago —*

Skinning the Cat

A lot of thought went into this guide. While producing a dining guide may appear to be a straightforward endeavor, I can assure you that it is fraught with peril. I have read dining guides by authors who turn up their noses at anything except four-star French restaurants (of which there are a whole lot fewer than people think). Likewise, I have seen a guide that totally omits Thai and Indian restaurants—among others—because the author did not understand those cuisines. I have read guides absolutely devoid of criticism, written by "experts" unwilling to risk offending the source of their free meals. Finally, I've seen those books that were based on surveys and write-ins from diners whose credentials for evaluating fine dining were mysterious at best and questionable at least.

How, then, do you go about developing a truly excellent dining guide? What is the best way to skin the cat?

If dining guides are among the most idiosyncratic of reference books, it is primarily because the background, taste, integrity, and personal agenda of each author are problematical. The authors of most dining guides are vocational or avocational restaurant or food critics. Some of these critics are schooled professionals, with palates refined by years of practical experience and culinary study; others are journalists, often with no background in food criticism or cooking, who are arbitrarily assigned the job of reviewing restaurants by their newspaper or magazine publisher. (Although it *is* occasionally possible to find journalists who are also culinary professionals.) The worst cases are the legions of self-proclaimed food critics who mooch their way from restaurant to restaurant, growing fat on free meals in exchange for writing glowing reviews.

Ignorance of ethnic cuisine or old assumptions about what makes for haute cuisine particularly plague authors in cities without much ethnic variety in restaurants, or authors who have been writing for years about the same old, white-linen, expense account tourist traps. Many years ago in Lexington, Kentucky, for example, there was only one Chinese restaurant in town and it was wildly successful—in spite of the fact that it was Chinese in name only. Its specialty dishes, which were essentially American vegetable casseroles smothered in corn starch, were happily gobbled up by loyal patrons who had never been exposed to real Chinese cooking. The food was not bad, but it was not Chinese either. Visitors from out of town, inquiring about a good local Chinese restaurant, were invariably directed to this place. As you would expect, they were routinely horrified by the fare.

And, while you might argue that American diners are more sophisticated and knowledgeable nowadays than at the time of the Lexington pavilion, the evidence suggests otherwise. In Las Vegas, for instance, a good restaurant town with a number of excellent Italian eateries, the local Olive Garden (a chain restaurant) is consistently voted the city's best Italian restaurant in a yearly newspaper poll. There is absolutely nothing wrong with the Las Vegas Olive Garden, but to suggest that it is the best Italian restaurant in the city is ludicrous. In point of fact, the annual survey says much more about the relative sophistication of Las Vegas diners than it does about the quality of Italian cooking.

But if you pick up a guide that reflects the views of many survey respondents, a *vox populi* or reader's choice compendium, that is exactly the problem. You are dependent upon the average restaurant-goer's capacity to make sound, qualitative judgments—judgments almost always impaired by extraneous variables. How many times have you had a wonderful experience at a restaurant, only to be disappointed on

2

a subsequent visit? Trying to reconcile the inconsistency, you recall that on your previous visit, you were in the company of someone particularly stimulating, and that perhaps you had enjoyed a couple of drinks before eating. What I am getting at is that our reflections on restaurant experiences are often colored by variables having little or nothing to do with the restaurant itself. And while I am given to the democratic process in theory, I have my doubts about depending entirely on survey forms that reflect such experiences.

There are more pragmatic arguments to be made about such eaters' guides as well. If you cannot control or properly qualify your survey respondents, you cannot assure their independence, knowledge, or critical sensitivity. And, since literally anyone can participate in such surveys, the ratings can be easily slanted by those with vested interests. How many bogus responses would it take to dramatically upgrade a restaurant's rating in a survey-based, big city dining guide? Forty or even fewer. Why? Because the publisher receives patron reports (survey responses, readers' calls) covering more restaurants than can be listed in the book. Thus the "voting" is distributed over such a large number of candidate restaurants that the median number of reports for the vast majority of establishments is 120 or fewer. A cunning restaurant proprietor who is willing to stuff the ballot box, therefore, could easily improve his own rating—or lower that of a competitor.

So my mission in the *Unofficial Dining Guides* is to provide you with the most meaningful, useful, and accessible restaurant evaluations possible. Weighing the alternatives, I have elected to work with culinary experts, augmenting their opinions with a carefully qualified survey population of totally independent local diners of demonstrated culinary sophistication. The experts I have sought to author the *Unofficial Dining Guides* are knowledgeable, seasoned professionals; they have studied around the world, written cookbooks or columns, and closely followed the development of restaurants in their cities. They are well versed in ethnic dining, many having studied cuisines in their native lands. And they have no prejudice about high or low cuisine. They are as at home in a Tupelo, Mississippi, catfish shack as in an exclusive French restaurant on New York's Upper East Side.

Equally important, I have sought experts who make every effort to conduct their reviews anonymously, and who always pay full menu prices for their meals. We are "unofficial" because we are independent.

You, the reader of this *Unofficial Dining Guide,* are the inspiration for and, we hope, the beneficiary of our diligence and methodology. Though we cannot evaluate your credentials as a restaurant critic, your opinion as a consumer— of this guide and the restaurants within—is very important to us. A clip-out survey of the restaurants in this guide can be found at the back of the book; please tell us about your dining experiences and let us know whether you agree with our reviews.

Eat well. Be happy.

Bob Sehlinger

Dining in Chicago

Chicago, in my opinion, is the dining mecca of the United States—certainly in terms of ethnic diversity. This is not "Second City" anymore. Even a well-known New York critic wrote several years ago that "Chicago was the most exciting city for dining." Most experts agree that it is one of the best places for quality and wide variety of cuisines.

For many years, my travel assignments on cuisine and culture have taken me around the world. I consider myself fortunate to have dined quite extensively both abroad and in the major United States cities. Two decades ago, New York, New Orleans, and San Francisco were considered the best dining cities, and they're still great, but now others such as Chicago, Los Angeles, Washington, D.C., Atlanta, Dallas, Houston, Miami, and Philadelphia have developed well in the restaurant realm. New York, still deemed number one by many, excels especially in the vast number of excellent French, Italian, Chinese, and American restaurants, and is a melting pot overall. Many New Yorkers admit, however, that dining in Chicago is less of a hassle—not as crowded and certainly less costly, making it more pleasant. This heartland city, like New York, has evolved from ethnic communities complete with churches, shops, and restaurants. It is my belief that it has not only caught up, but has surpassed most other key cities in the dining arena.

O'Hare International Airport, the busiest airport in the world, is one main reason why Chicago gets the best fresh seafood and other products flown in regularly from around the globe. It has a bigger assortment of fresh seafood than coastal cities, although it's in the Midwest. And because Chicago is a key convention town, it features lots of restaurants and hotels for diners demanding the best quality.

At last count, Chicago had just under 6,000 restaurants in the city, and 2,000 of those have liquor licenses. Including Chicago, Cook County, has 9,000 food service establishments, according to the Illinois Restaurant Association. No one can give a specific count of restaurants in this vast suburbia. To have selected just 225 or so of the best of these was no easy task. My decision was based on many criteria, including my own experiences and reports from other frequent diners whose judgment I trust. I tried to maintain a balance of cuisines, styles, geographic locations, price, and the popular as well as the hidden gems. Numerous fine restaurants are not included here, but that doesn't mean they are unworthy. Some are quite new, and I'd rather give them a chance to settle in before visiting. Others were in the process of change at press time. Some of these will be covered in subsequent editions.

Burgeoning Neighborhoods

Particularly hot neighborhoods for new restaurants are River North, with its art galleries and antique shops; the gentrified diagonal Near North Clybourn Corridor; the booming United Center neighborhood (Madison from the stadium to Halsted Street); Navy Pier (undergoing development); Randolph Market and Wicker Park/Bucktown (one of the top three artist communities in the United States). Halsted Street, which was called First Street in earlier times, continues to be "restaurant row" with several good dining spots on the same block, especially north from North Avenue. Printer's Row in the south downtown area developed several years ago and seems well anchored with some stable restaurants. Some restaurants recently opened in Chinatown, and several years ago Greektown got a few new faces. The "Little Saigon or "New Asia" area at North Argyle Street and Sheridan

Road is a neighborhood with a few good storefront restaurants and ethnic shops. And West Devon Avenue has several special street signs designating its diverse ethnicity: some of the best Indian restaurants are found from 2300–2600 West Devon Avenue, and new ones keep popping up.

The southwest Naperville suburban area has developed in the past several years, and a lot of restaurant activity has recently occurred in the west, north, and northwest suburbs. Except for the bastions of old Italian neighborhoods such as the Heart of Italy and Taylor Street, and several fine restaurants here and there, the South Side is sparse as a dining zone. There is a great area of Italian shops and restaurants on West Harlem Avenue, and Highwood in the North Shore, anchored by generations-old Italian establishments, has diversified and now supposedly boasts more restaurants per capita than almost any suburb in the country.

The Rosemont area near O'Hare offers a good assortment of restaurants since many conventions and business meetings are held there, and amazingly, downtown Chicago continues to build and develop areas such as Cityfront, Navy Pier, and the North Pier Terminal. Hotel dining is better than ever; executive chefs have large budgets for the best ingredients and can concentrate on their kitchens, unlike the owner/chefs running independent places. Also, since hotels must attract a local clientele to survive and since competition is fierce, they've really improved their dining act in the past several years. Hotel dining has become a destination, and it's usually complemented by live music in a nearby lounge.

Celebrity Restaurants

This is a big sports city, so naturally there are athletes, coaches, and announcers who have restaurants. Some, like Ditka's (which was overpriced) and Red Kerr's (which was good) have closed. Others such as Harry Caray's and Michael Jordan's are listed in this guide because they offer good food and service. There are numerous restaurant hangouts around the ball-parks, and some of the food service within the parks is noteworthy. Food service at both Comiskey Park, home of the Chicago White Sox, and Wrigley Field, home of the Chicago Cubs, is managed by the Levy Restaurants, and it is excellent. Entertainment celebrities, political figures, and other VIPs have their favored haunts as well, and many are included in this guide and so noted. The Pump Room, Cape Cod Room, and Spiaggia are just three examples.

New-Age Cuisine

Diners are more sophisticated and health conscious, and restaurant cooking has evolved to satisfy their demands and needs. Food is more enlightened today—lighter, with flavoring coming from fresh herbs, spices, infused oils, vinaigrettes and wines, and from healthful cooking methods like grilling and roasting in wood-burning ovens. Sure, restaurant icons still offer some old-guard, flour-thickened sauces with cream and butter, and they are period pieces to be regarded as historical and enjoyed occasionally. Most day-to-day eating is geared to feeling fine, and that means lower fat (less meat and fried fare), higher carbohydrates (grains, veggies, and fruit), and less sodium and sugar. New-age cuisine has leaned in the direction of natural foods, chemical-free ingredients, and more vegetarian fare. Chefs are proud to promote their vegetarian specialties and menus, and more business men and women are ordering these items for lunch with mineral water instead of the steaks and martinis they downed years ago.

New-Age Dining Style

There is a tendency for restaurant interiors to be casual and homey these days, bringing some comfort and a nurturing environment to our dining-out experiences—much needed in our fast-paced, high-stressed lives. The food at these places is appropriately simple and homestyle.

Smoking recently has become a more important health and social issue, and in Chicago all restaurants must set aside a minimum of 30% of their active dining room for non-smokers. Restaurants that wish to establish larger non-smoking sections have the option of certifying a minimum of 50% of their space as non-smoking. Once a minimum is decided upon, it must be maintained until the next license renewal. Establishments may also select to be 100% smoke free. The designated non-smoking area must be contiguous. Bars and meeting rooms for private functions are exempt. Sign postings with specific wording designated by the city are required.

I hope that legislation will give us a smoke-free environment, especially for dining. The recent wave of "cigar dinners" is, I hope, just an ignorant, short-lived fad.

Trends

Spanish cuisine made a splash here as a result of 1992, Spain's legendary year, which commemorated the 500th anniversary of the discovery of America, the summer Olympic Games in Barcelona, and Expo '92 in Seville. Spain's tapas and the sampling or "tasting" style has spread from the host cuisine to others, so we now see southwestern, American, and eclectic tapas. Restaurants are giving customers more options, and many offer half portions when possible. Some places even offer half glasses of wine so people can try more types.

In the heartland, chefs take pride in seeking out small, quality purveyors and changing their menus to utilize the freshest of seasonal ingredients. Wine lists have improved dramatically, and many have become user-friendly, with more options by the glass and half bottle.

Touristy Places

There are many places that tourists, for one reason or another, have heard about and want to try. Some, like the Pump Room and Michael Jordan's, are excellent or very good. Others are less

9

so, and many are overpriced. Some of the following might offer good food and unique atmosphere, but overall they did not merit full profiles:

Dick's Last Resort
435 East Illinois Street
This North Pier spot gets tourists who shop in the building and see the riverfront. It's OK for simple American fare, but not a dining destination.

Ed Debevic's Short Order Deluxe
640 North Wells Street
Typical diner American food.

Gene & Georgetti
500 North Franklin Street
Considered by many steak-lovers to be a great place, but inconsistent food and service, crowded conditions, and dated decor prevent a recommendation.

Greek Islands Restaurant
200 South Halsted Street
A popular, large Greektown favorite that is attractive and serves decent Greek food. Unfortunately, much of it is kept on a steam table. Several other nearby restaurants are in this guide.

Hardrock Cafe
63 West Ontario Street
Good American / ethnic and glitzy presentations; decibel level has been lowered to a comfortable level.

Planet Hollywood
633 North Wells Street
Flashy decor and mediocre American fare.

Three Happiness
2130 South Wentworth Avenue, Chinatown
Bustling, popular Cantonese and dim sum place; good, very authentic food, if you don't mind crowds. Reservations accepted weekdays.

New and Changing Restaurants

Here are just a few of the new places that opened in the past 18 months or so. They show great promise for future editions:

Restaurant	Cuisine
Cafe Absinthe	Eclectic
Carmine's Clam House	Italian seafood
Chez Delphonse	Caribbean
The Daily Bar & Grill	Home-style American
Emilio's Tapas	Spanish tapas
erwin, an american cafe & bar	New American
Grappa	New Italian
I Tre Merli	Northern Italian
Jaxx, Park Hyatt Hotel	Continental/ American with British specialties
Julie Mai's Le Bistro	French/Vietnamese
Le Margaux	French
Madison's	Italian Steakhouse
Marche	French/American brasserie
Mare	Italian seafood
Russian Palace	Russian
Seasons of Long Grove	American seasonal
Toulouse on the Park	French
Triple Crown Seafood	Cantonese/seafood
Tuscany in Oakbrook	Tuscan Italian
Vidalia on Park	New American
Woodland of Madras	South Indian/ vegetarian
Yvette North, Wheeling	French
Zealous	Contemporary

Understanding the Ratings

We have developed detailed profiles for the best restaurants (in our opinion) in town. Each profile features an easily scanned heading which allows you, in just a second, to check out the restaurant's name, cuisine, star rating, cost, quality rating, and value rating.

Star Rating. The star rating is an overall rating which encompasses the entire dining experience, including style, service, and ambience in addition to the taste, presentation, and quality of the food. Five stars is the highest rating possible and connotes the best of everything. Four-star restaurants are exceptional and three-star restaurants are well above average. Two-star restaurants are good. One star is used to connote an average restaurant which demonstrates an unusual capability in some area of specialization, for example, an otherwise unmemorable place which has great barbecued chicken.

Cost. To the right of the star rating is an expense description which provides a comparative sense of how much a complete meal will cost. A complete meal for our purposes consists of an entree with vegetable or side dish, and choice of soup or salad. Appetizers, desserts, drinks, and tips are excluded.

Inexpensive	$14 and less per person
Moderate	$15–25 per person
Expensive	$26–39 per person
Very Expensive	Over $40 per person

Quality Rating. Below the cost rating appears a number and a letter. The number is a quality rating based on a scale of 0–100, with 100 being the highest (best) rating attainable. The quality rating is based expressly on the taste, freshness of ingredients, preparation, presentation, and creativity of food served. There is no consideration of price. If you are a person who wants the best food available, and cost is not an issue, you need look no further than the quality ratings.

Value Rating. If on the other hand you are looking for both quality and value, then you should check the value rating, expressed in letters. The value ratings are defined as follows:

A	Exceptional value, a real bargain
B	Good value
C	Fair value, you get exactly what you pay for
D	Somewhat overpriced
F	Significantly overpriced

— *Locating the Restaurant*

Just below the restaurant address and phone number is a designation for geographic zone. This zone description will give you a general idea of where the restaurant described is located. For ease of use, we divide Chicago into 11 geographic zones.

Zone 1.	North Side
Zone 2.	North Central/O'Hare
Zone 3.	Near North
Zone 4.	The Loop
Zone 5.	South Loop
Zone 6.	South Central/Midway
Zone 7.	South Side
Zone 8.	Southern Suburbs
Zone 9.	Western Suburbs
Zone 10.	Northwest Suburbs
Zone 11.	Northern Suburbs

If you are in The Loop area and intend to walk or take a cab to dinner, you may want to choose a restaurant from among those located in Zone 4. If you have a car, you might include restaurants from contiguous zones in your consideration. (See pages 14–37 for detailed zone maps.)

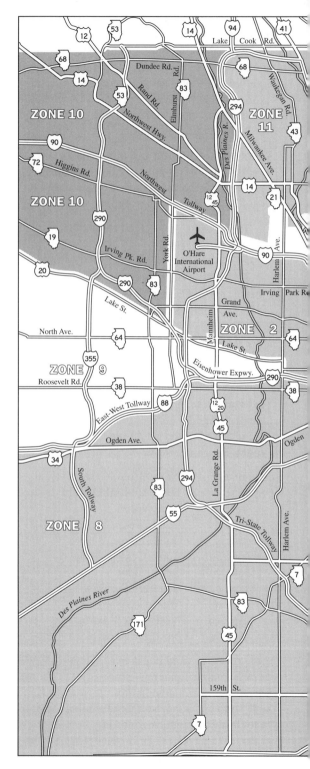

14

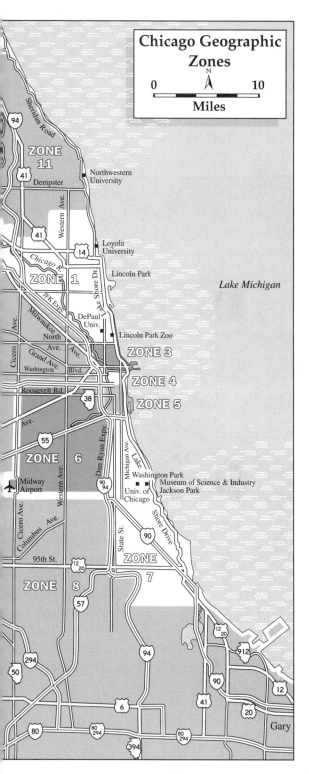

Chicago Geographic Zones

0   N   10
         ↑
       Miles

ZONE 11

Sheridan Road

94
41
Dempster

■ Northwestern University

Western Ave.

41

14

■ Loyola University

Chicago R.

Lincoln Park

ZONE 1

JFK Expy.

Lake Shore Dr.

Milwaukee Ave.

Cicero Ave.

North Ave.

■ DePaul Univ.

Grand Ave.

Ave.

■ Lincoln Park Zoo

Washington

Blvd.

ZONE 3

Roosevelt Rd

ZONE 4

38

ZONE 5

Ave.

55

ZONE 6

Dan Ryan Expy.

Michigan Ave.

Lake

✈ Midway Airport

Western Ave.

90
94

■ Washington Park

■ ■ Museum of Science & Industry

Univ. of Chicago

Jackson Park

Columbus Ave.

Cicero Ave.

State St.

90

Shore Drive

95th St.

12
20

ZONE 7

ZONE 8

57

94

12
20

294

50

90

912

41

12

6

80

80
294

20

80
294

Gary

394

Lake Michigan

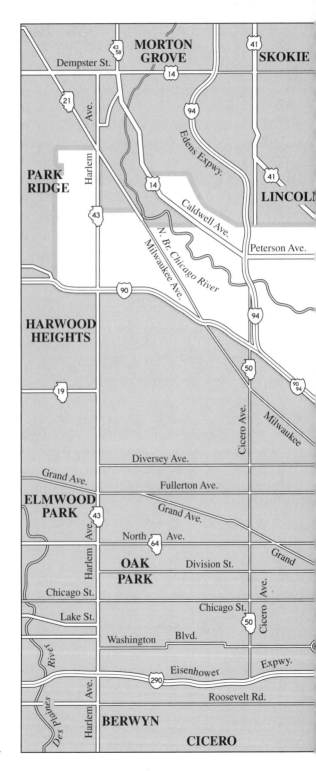

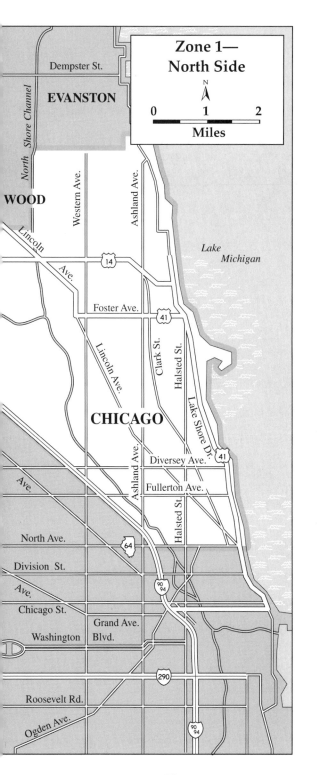

Zone 1—
North Side

N

0   1   2
Miles

Dempster St.

EVANSTON

North Shore Channel

WOOD

Western Ave.

Ashland Ave.

Lincoln

Ave.

14

Foster Ave.

41

Lincoln Ave.

Lake Michigan

Clark St.

Halsted St.

CHICAGO

Lake Shore Dr.

Ashland Ave.

Diversey Ave.

41

Fullerton Ave.

Ave.

Halsted St.

North Ave.

64

Division St.

Ave.

90
94

Chicago St.

Grand Ave.
Blvd.

Washington

290

Roosevelt Rd.

Ogden Ave.

90
94

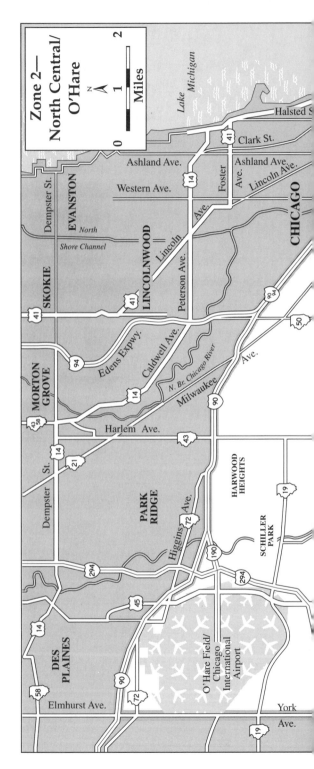

Zone 2—
North Central/O'Hare

N

Miles

0   1   2

Lake Michigan

Halsted St.

Clark St.

Ashland Ave.

Foster Ave.

Ashland Ave.

Lincoln Ave.

Western Ave.

Lincoln Ave.

Dempster St.

EVANSTON

North
Shore Channel

LINCOLNWOOD

Peterson Ave.

CHICAGO

SKOKIE

Edens Expwy.

Caldwell Ave.

N. Br. Chicago River

Milwaukee Ave.

MORTON
GROVE

Harlem Ave.

Dempster St.

PARK
RIDGE

HARWOOD
HEIGHTS

SCHILLER
PARK

Higgins Ave.

DES
PLAINES

O'Hare Field/
Chicago
International
Airport

Elmhurst Ave.

York
Ave.

18

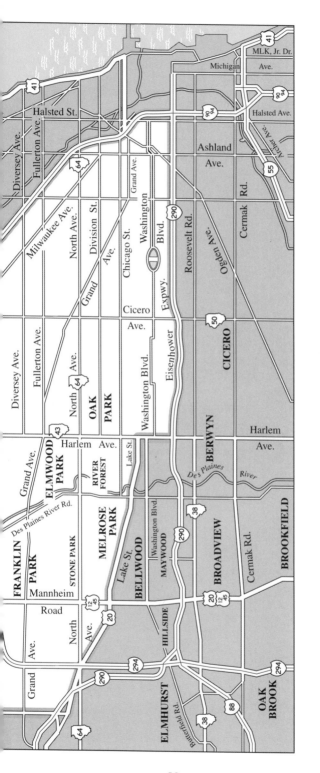

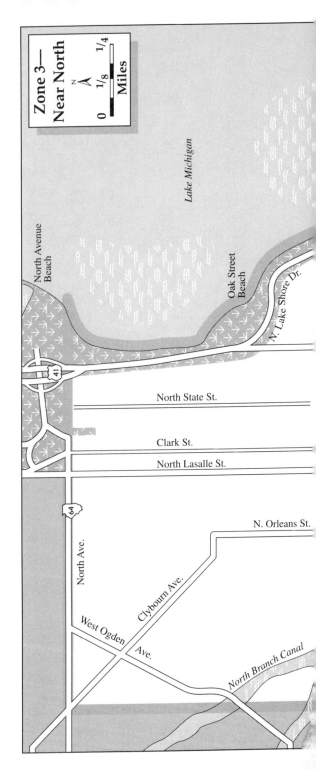

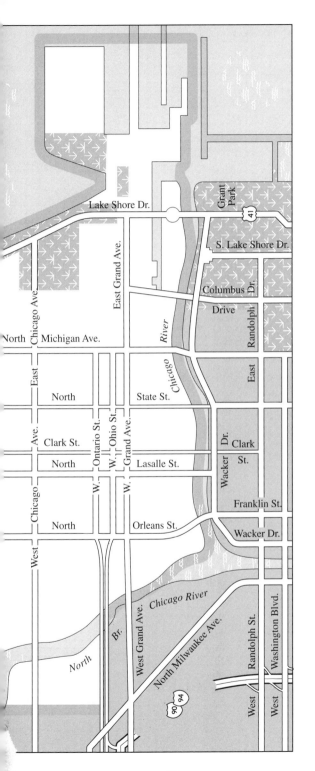

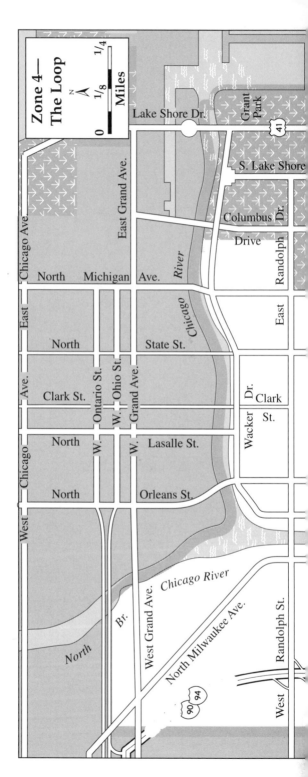

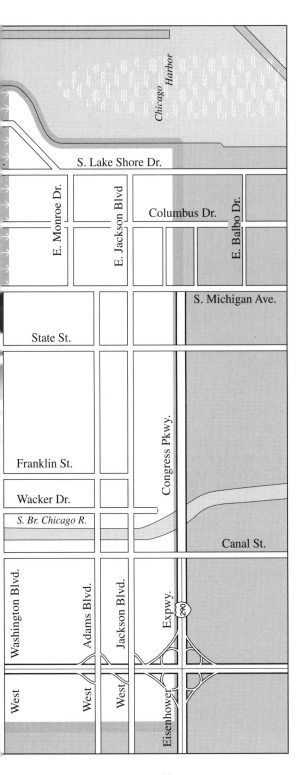

Chicago Harbor

S. Lake Shore Dr.

E. Monroe Dr.

E. Jackson Blvd

Columbus Dr.

E. Balbo Dr.

S. Michigan Ave.

State St.

Congress Pkwy.

Franklin St.

Wacker Dr.

S. Br. Chicago R.

Canal St.

Washington Blvd.

Adams Blvd.

Jackson Blvd.

Expwy.

290

West

West

West

Eisenhower

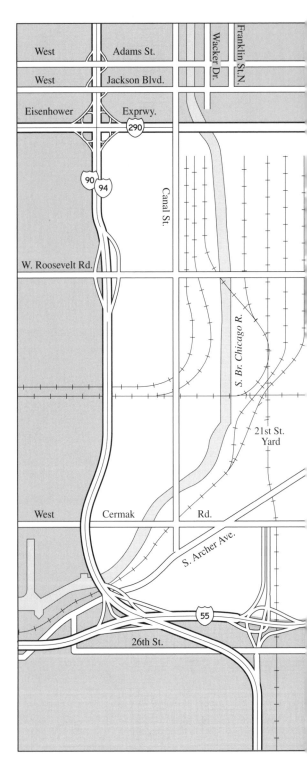

West   Adams St.

West   Jackson Blvd.

Eisenhower   Exprwy.

290

90 94

Canal St.

W. Roosevelt Rd.

S. Br. Chicago R.

21st St.
Yard

West   Cermak   Rd.

S. Archer Ave.

55

26th St.

Wacker Dr.

Franklin St.N.

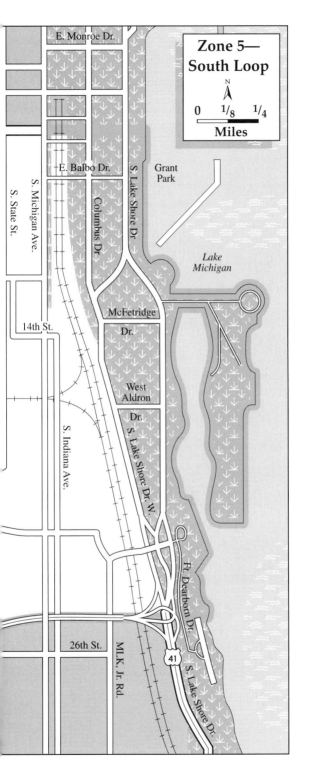

Zone 5—
South Loop

N

0   1/8   1/4

Miles

E. Monroe Dr.

E. Balbo Dr.

Grant
Park

S. Michigan Ave.

S. State St.

Columbus Dr.

S. Lake Shore Dr

Lake
Michigan

14th St.

McFetridge

Dr.

West
Aldron

Dr.

S. Lake Shore Dr. W.

S. Indiana Ave.

Ft. Dearborn Dr.

26th St.

MLK. Jr. Rd.

41

S. Lake Shore Dr.

W. Washington Blvd.

Garfield Park

Eisenhower Expwy.

W. Roosevelt Rd.

Douglas Park

W. Cermak R.

S. Cicero Ave.

S. Pulaski Rd.

Chicago Drainage Canal

Adlai E. Stevenson Expwy.

West 47th St.

West 55th St.

Chicago Midway Airport

West 59th St.

West 63rd St.

Marquette Park

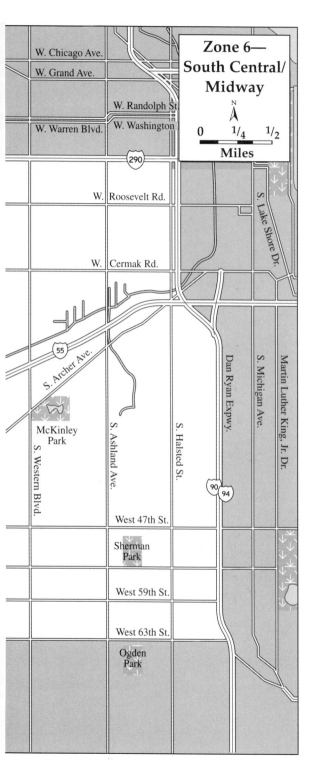

**Zone 6—
South Central/
Midway**

N

0   1/4   1/2

Miles

W. Chicago Ave.

W. Grand Ave.

W. Randolph St.

W. Warren Blvd.   W. Washington

290

W. Roosevelt Rd.

W. Cermak Rd.

55

S. Archer Ave.

McKinley
Park

S. Western Blvd.

S. Ashland Ave.

S. Halsted St.

Dan Ryan Expwy.

S. Michigan Ave.

Martin Luther King, Jr. Dr.

S. Lake Shore Dr.

90 94

West 47th St.

Sherman
Park

West 59th St.

West 63rd St.

Ogden
Park

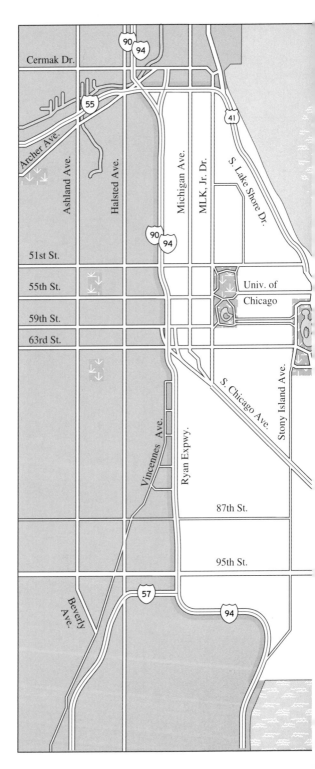

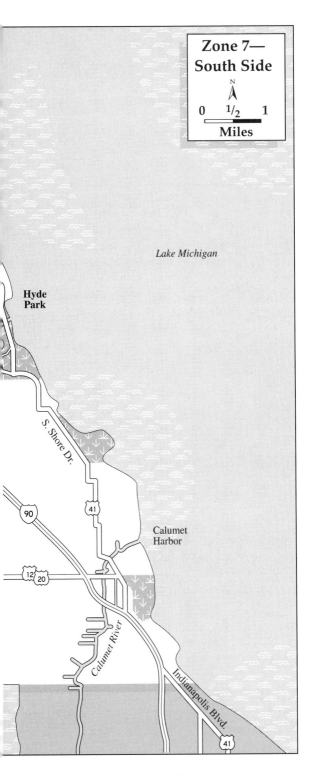

Zone 7—
South Side

N

0   1/2   1

Miles

Lake Michigan

Hyde
Park

S. Shore Dr.

90

41

Calumet
Harbor

12 20

Calumet River

Indianapolis Blvd

41

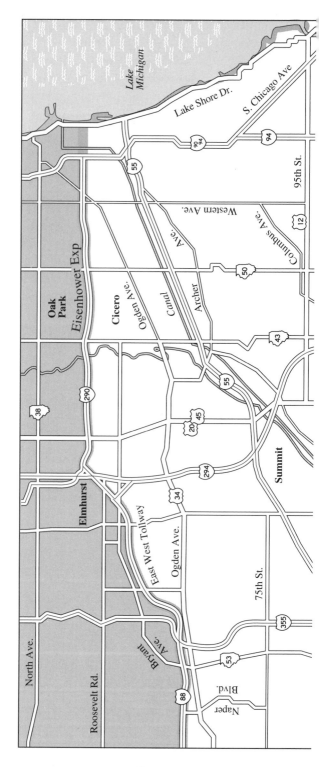

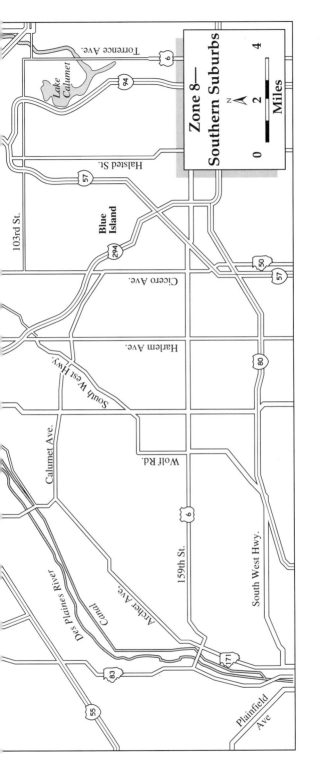

Zone 8—
Southern Suburbs

N

0   2   4

Miles

Torrence Ave.

Lake Calumet

Halsted St.

103rd St.

Blue Island

Cicero Ave.

Harlem Ave.

South West Hwy.

Calumet Ave.

Wolf Rd.

Des Plaines River

Canal

Archer Ave.

159th St.

South West Hwy.

Plainfield Ave.

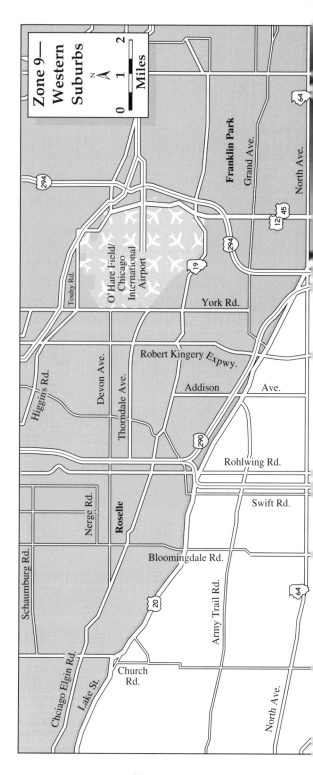

**Zone 9—
Western
Suburbs**

N

0 1 2
Miles

Franklin Park

Grand Ave.

North Ave.

64

294

12 45

294

19

O'Hare Field/
Chicago
International
Airport

Touhy Rd.

York Rd.

Robert Kingery Expwy.

Higgins Rd.

Devon Ave.

Thorndale Ave.

Addison

Ave.

290

Rohlwing Rd.

Swift Rd.

Nerge Rd.

Roselle

Schaumburg Rd.

Bloomingdale Rd.

Army Trail Rd.

64

20

Chciago Elgin Rd.

Lake St.

Church
Rd.

North Ave.

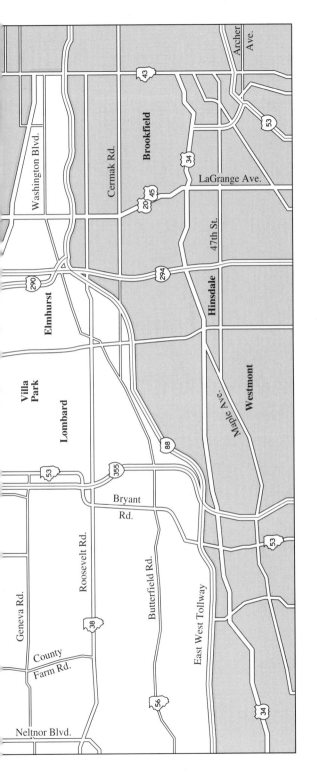

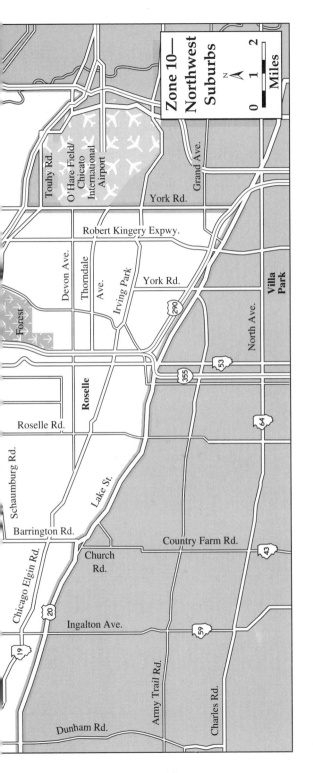

35

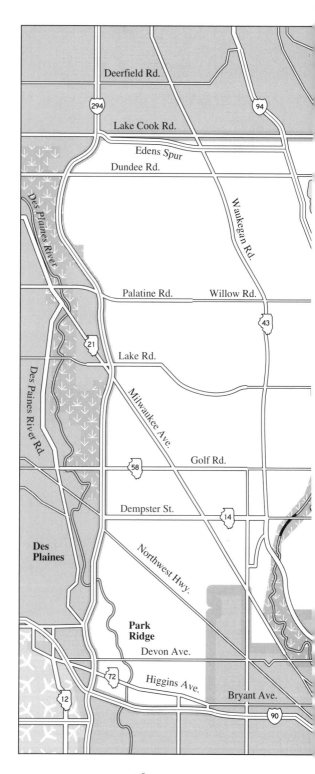

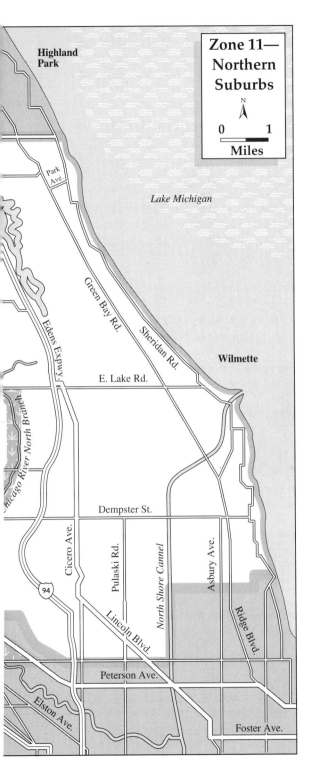

Our Pick of the Best Chicago Restaurants

Because restaurants are opening and closing all the time in Chicago, we have tried to confine our list to establishments—or chefs—with a proven track record over a fairly long period of time. Those newer or changed establishments which demonstrate staying power and consistency will be profiled in subsequent editions.

Also, the list is highly selective. Non-inclusion of a particular place does not necessarily indicate that the restaurant is not good, but only that it was not ranked among the best or most consistent in its genre. Detailed profiles of each restaurant follow in alphabetical order at the end of this chapter.

A Note About Spelling

Most diners who enjoy ethnic restaurants have noticed subtle variations in the spelling of certain dishes and preparations from one menu to the next. A noodle dish found on almost all Thai menus, for example, appears in one restaurant as *pad thai*, in another as *Phat Thai*, and in a third as *Phad Thai*.

This and similar inconsistencies arise from attempts to derive a phonetic English spelling from the name of a dish as pronounced in its country of origin. While one particular English spelling might be more frequently used than others, there is usually no definitive correct spelling for the names of many dishes. In this guide, we have elected to use the spelling most commonly found in authoritative ethnic cookbooks and other reference works.

We call this to your attention because the spelling we use in this guide could be different than that which you encounter on the menu in a certain restaurant. We might say, for instance, that the *tabbouleh* is good at the Pillars of Lebanon, while at the restaurant itself the dish is listed on the menu as *tabouli*.

Chicago Restaurants by Cuisine

Type of Restaurant	Star Rating
Afghani	
The Helmand	★★★¹/₂
American (see also New American)	
Seasons Restaurant at the Four Seasons Hotel	★★★★¹/₂
The Pump Room	★★★★
The Greenery	★★★¹/₂
Oceanique	★★★¹/₂
Walker Bros. Original Pancake House	★★★¹/₂
Harry Caray's	★★★¹/₂
The Mity Nice Grill	★★★¹/₂
Relish	★★★¹/₂
Harry Caray's (Wheeling)	★★★¹/₂
Michael Jordan's Restaurant	★★★¹/₂
Wild Onion	★★★¹/₂
Don Roth's in Wheeling	★★★
Pappagallo's	★★★
Binyon's	★★★
The Big Bowl Cafe	★★★
Big Shoulders	★★★
Jerome's	★★★
R. J. Grunts	★★★
Eccentric	★★¹/₂
foodlife	★★¹/₂
Armenian	
Sayat Nova	★★★¹/₂
Bakery Cafe	
St. Germain Restaurant/Bakery Cafe	★★★¹/₂
The Corner Bakery	★★★
Barbecue	
Dixie Que	★★★¹/₂
N. N. Smokehouse	★★★
Bones	★★¹/₂
Burmese	
Mandalay	★★★
Cajun/Creole	
Maple Tree Inn	★★★¹/₂
Heaven on Seven	★★★¹/₂

NOTE: Profiles follow in alphabetical order in the next chapter.

Price	Quality Rating	Value Rating	Zone
Inexpensive	80	B	1
Mod/Exp	97	C	3
Expensive	92	C	3
Mod/Exp	88	C	10
Moderate	88	C	11
Inexpensive	88	B	10, 11
Mod/Exp	86	C	4
Inexp/Mod	86	C	3
Inexp/Mod	86	C	1
Moderate	85	C	10
Inexp/Mod	85	C	3
Inexp/Mod	85	B	1
Moderate	84	C	10
Inexp/Mod	84	B	11
Inexp/Mod	83	C	4
Inexpensive	82	B	3
Inexpensive	82	B	1
Inexp/Mod	82	C	1
Inexpensive	81	A	1
Moderate	79	C	3
Inexpensive	79	B	3
Inexp/Mod	88	C	10
Inexp/Mod	88	C	3
Inexp/Mod	82	C	4, 8
Inexpensive	87	B	1
Inexpensive	82	B	1
Inexp/Mod	78	C	11
Inexp/Mod	83	B	6
Inexp/Mod	88	C	8
Inexpensive	86	B	4

Restaurants by Cuisine (continued)

Type of Restaurant	Star Rating

Caribbean
    Julio's Latin Cafe   ★★★
    El Dinamico Dallas   ★★¹/₂

Chinese
    Szechwan House   ★★★★
    Emperor's Choice   ★★★¹/₂
    Mandar Inn   ★★★¹/₂
    Mei-Shung Chinese Restaurant   ★★★¹/₂
    T'ang Dynasty   ★★★
    Hong Min Restaurant   ★★★
    Hunan Cafe   ★★★

Continental
    The Pump Room   ★★★★
    Biggs   ★★★★
    Kenessey's Cypress   ★★★¹/₂
    Skardarlija   ★★★

Cuban
    Tania's   ★★★¹/₂

Ethiopian
    Mama Desta's Red Sea Ethiopian   ★★★¹/₂
      Restaurant
    Addis Abeba   ★★★

Filipino
    Pampanga Restaurant   ★★¹/₂

Fondue
    Geja's Cafe   ★★★¹/₂

French (see also New French and French Bistro)
    Everest   ★★★★★
    Le Français   ★★★★★
    Carlos'   ★★★★¹/₂
    Le Vichyssois   ★★★★¹/₂
    The Cottage   ★★★★
    Biggs   ★★★★
    Entre Nous   ★★★¹/₂
    Oceanique   ★★★¹/₂
    Amourette   ★★★

French Bistro
    Kiki's Bistro   ★★★★

NOTE: Profiles follow in alphabetical order in the next
      chapter.

Price	Quality Rating	Value Rating	Zone
Moderate	83	C	10
Inexpensive	79	B	1
Moderate	92	C	4
Inexp/Mod	88	B	5
Moderate	88	C	5
Inexpensive	87	B	1
Moderate	86	C	3
Inexpensive	85	B	5, 8
Inexp/Mod	83	C	3
Expensive	92	C	3
Moderate	90	C	3
Moderate	86	C	9
Moderate	84	B	1
Moderate	86	B	2
Inexpensive	88	B	1
Inexpensive	84	C	1
Inexpensive	77	B	1
Moderate	88	B	1
Expensive	98	C	4
Expensive	97	C	10
Mod/Exp	96	C	11
Moderate	95	B	10
Moderate	92	B	8
Moderate	90	C	3
Mod/Exp	88	C	4
Moderate	88	C	11
Inexp/Mod	83	B	10
Inexp/Mod	94	C	3

Restaurants by Cuisine *(continued)*

Type of Restaurant	Star Rating
French Bistro (cont'd.)	
Un Grand Cafe	★★★★
St. Germain Restaurant/Bakery Cafe	★★★¹/₂
Bistro 110	★★★¹/₂
Yvette	★★★¹/₂
Taylor Street Bistro	★★★
Le Bouchon	★★¹/₂
French/Asian	
Jackie's	★★★★
French/Italian	
Costa D'Oro	★★★★
Gabriel's Restaurant	★★★★
Cuisines	★★★★
Oo-La-La!	★★
Fusion	
Trio	★★★★★
German/American	
Golden Ox	★★★★
The Berghoff	★★★¹/₂
Mirabell Restaurant	★★★
Hans' Bavarian Lodge	★★★
Global/Eclectic	
Pastiche	★★★¹/₂
Greek	
The Parthenon	★★★★¹/₂
Mykonos	★★★★
Papagus Greek Taverna	★★★★
Roditys	★★★¹/₂
Santorini	★★★¹/₂
Aegean Isles	★★★
Pegasus Restaurant and Taverna	★★★
Guatemalan	
El Tinajon	★★★
Hungarian	
Kenessey's Cypress	★★★¹/₂
Indian	
Klay Oven	★★★★
Viceroy of India	★★★

NOTE: Profiles follow in alphabetical order in the next chapter.

Price	Quality Rating	Value Rating	Zone
Moderate	92	C	1
Inexp/Mod	88	C	3
Moderate	86	C	3
Inexp/Mod	85	C	3
Inexp/Mod	81	B	5
Moderate	80	B	1
Mod/Exp	90	C	1
Mod/Exp	93	C	3
Moderate	93	C	11
Inexp/Mod	91	B	4
Inexp/Mod	74	C	1
Expensive	98	C	11
Moderate	90	C	1
Inexpensive	88	B	4
Inexp/Mod	82	C	2
Inexpensive	80	B	10
Inexp/Mod	87	B	1
Inexp/Mod	95	B	4
Inexp/Mod	92	B	11
Moderate	90	C	3
Inexp/Mod	89	B	4
Inexp/Mod	89	C	4
Inexp/Mod	84	C	11
Inexp/Mod	83	C	4
Inexpensive	82	B	1
Moderate	86	C	9
Moderate	91	B	4
Inexp/Mod	84	B	1, 9

Restaurants by Cuisine (continued)

Type of Restaurant	Star Rating
Indian (cont'd.)	
Sher-A-Punjab	★★★
Bukhara	★★★
Chowpatti Vegetarian Restaurant	★★★
Kanval Palace	★★½
Irish Pub	
Kitty O'Shea's	★★★
Italian (see also New Italian)	
Carlucci	★★★★½
Va Pensiero	★★★★½
Vivere (Italian Village)	★★★★½
Spiaggia	★★★★
Cuisines	★★★★
Coco Pazzo	★★★½
Cafe Angelo	★★★½
Carlucci (Rosemont)	★★★½
Luciano's	★★★½
Bice Ristorante	★★★½
La Strada	★★★½
Trattoria Gianni	★★★½
Harry Caray's	★★★½
Harry Caray's (Wheeling)	★★★½
Da Nicola Ristorante	★★★
La Bocca Della Verita	★★★
Pappagallo's	★★★
Tuscany	★★★
Del Rio	★★★
Francesco's Hole in the Wall	★★★
Rosebud Cafe	★★★
Avanzare	★★★
Filippo's	★★★
Mia Francesca	★★★
Tucci Milan	★★★
Maggiano's Little Italy	★★★
Bruna's Ristorante	★★★
Alfo's Ristorante	★★½
Red Tomato	★★½
Cafe Borgia	★★½
Tufano's (Vernon Park Tap)	★★½
Japanese	
Kuni's	★★★★½

NOTE: Profiles follow in alphabetical order in the next chapter.

Price	Quality Rating	Value Rating	Zone
Inexpensive	82	B	1
Moderate	80	C	3
Inexpensive	80	B	10
Inexpensive	76	B	1
Inexpensive	81	B	5
Moderate	95	C	1
Moderate	95	C	11
Moderate	95	C	4
Mod/Exp	93	C	3
Inexp/Mod	91	B	4
Moderate	89	C	4
Inexp/Mod	88	B	4
Moderate	88	C	2
Inexp/Mod	88	B	3, 9, 11
Mod/Exp	87	D	3
Mod/Exp	87	C	4
Inexp/Mod	87	C	1
Mod/Exp	86	C	4
Moderate	85	C	10
Inexp/Mod	84	B	1
Inexpensive	84	B	1
Inexp/Mod	84	B	11
Moderate	84	C	5
Inexp/Mod	83	B	11
Inexp/Mod	83	B	11
Inexp/Mod	83	C	5
Moderate	82	C	3
Inexp/Mod	82	C	1
Inexp/Mod	82	B	1
Inexp/Mod	82	C	4
Moderate	81	C	4, 8
Inexp/Mod	80	B	5
Inexpensive	79	B	5
Inexpensive	79	B	1
Inexp/Mod	78	B	8
Inexp/Mod	76	B	5
Inexp/Mod	96	C	11

Restaurants by Cuisine *(continued)*

Type of Restaurant	Star Rating
Japanese (cont'd.)	
Benkay	★★★★¹/₂
Katsu Japanese Restaurant	★★★¹/₂
Akai Hana	★★★¹/₂
Honda	★★★¹/₂
Shilla	★★★¹/₂
Hatsuhana	★★¹/₂
Korean	
Shilla	★★★¹/₂
Bando	★★★
Lebanese	
Uncle Tannous	★★★
Mediterranean	
Tuttaposto	★★★★
Chez 'D	★★★
Mexican	
Frontera Grill/Topolobampo	★★★★
Twisted Lizard	★★★¹/₂
Don Juan	★★★
El Tipico	★★¹/₂
Middle Eastern	
Ishtar Inn	★★★¹/₂
Pars Cove	★★★¹/₂
Sayat Nova	★★★¹/₂
Reza's	★★★
Uncle Tannous	★★★
Midwestern	
Prairie	★★★★¹/₂
Moroccan/Mediterranean	
L'Olive	★★★¹/₂
Natural	
The Organic Tomato	★★★
New American	
Charlie Trotter's	★★★★★
Printer's Row	★★★★¹/₂
Gordon	★★★★
The Cottage	★★★★

NOTE: Profiles follow in alphabetical order in the next chapter.

Price	Quality Rating	Value Rating	Zone
Mod/Exp	95	D	4
Inexp/Mod	90	B	1
Inexp/Mod	88	C	11
Moderate	88	C	4
Moderate	86	C	1
Inexp/Mod	76	C	3
Moderate	86	C	1
Inexp/Mod	83	C	1
Inexp/Mod	84	B	1
Inexp/Mod	91	C	3
Inexp/Mod	82	B	1
Inexp/Mod	93	C	4
Inexpensive	87	B	1
Inexp/Mod	84	C	1
Inexpensive	79	B	1, 11
Inexpensive	90	B	3
Inexp/Mod	89	C	1
Inexp/Mod	88	C	10
Inexp/Mod	84	C	1, 3
Inexp/Mod	84	B	1
Mod/Exp	95	C	5
Inexpensive	91	A	1
Inexpensive	83	B	3
Very Expensive	98	C	1
Moderate	95	B	5
Moderate	93	C	4
Moderate	92	B	8

Type of Restaurant	Star Rating

New American (cont'd.)
- Melange American Eatery ★★★★
- The Signature Room at the Ninety-Fifth ★★★★
- Winnetka Grill ★★★★
- The Marc ★★★¹/₂
- 302 West ★★★¹/₂
- Jilly's Cafe ★★★¹/₂
- Blackhawk Lodge ★★★
- Hubbard Street Grill ★★★

New French
- Le Titi de Paris ★★★★¹/₂
- Yoshi's Cafe ★★★★¹/₂
- The Dining Room ★★★★¹/₂
- Tallgrass Restaurant ★★★★¹/₂
- Ambria ★★★★
- Jimmy's Place ★★★★
- La Boheme ★★★★
- Montparnasse ★★★¹/₂
- Yvette ★★★¹/₂
- Yvette Wintergarden ★★★¹/₂
- Froggy's French Cafe ★★★

New Italian
- Bella Vista ★★★¹/₂
- Via Veneto ★★★¹/₂
- Pazzo's Pizza and Pasta Kitchen ★★¹/₂

Pan Asian
- Lulu's ★★¹/₂

Persian
- Pars Cove ★★★¹/₂
- Cy's Crab House ★★★
- Reza's ★★★

Peruvian
- Machu Picchu ★★

Polish
- Lutnia Continental Cafe ★★★¹/₂
- Pierogi Inn ★★¹/₂
- Home Bakery ★★¹/₂
- Miska's ★★¹/₂

NOTE: Profiles follow in alphabetical order in the next chapter.

Price	Quality Rating	Value Rating	Zone
Inexp/Mod	91	C	11
Mod/Exp	90	C	3
Moderate	90	C	11
Moderate	87	C	3
Moderate	87	C	9
Inexp/Mod	85	B	11
Moderate	82	C	3
Inexp/Mod	81	C	4
Mod/Exp	97	C	10
Mod/Exp	96	C	1
Mod/Exp	95	C	3
Very expensive	95	C	8
Mod/Exp	93	C	1
Mod/Exp	90	C	1
Moderate	90	C	11
Mod/Exp	89	C	8
Inexp/Mod	85	C	3
Inexp/Mod	85	C	4
Moderate	84	B	11
Inexp/Mod	86	C	1
Inexpensive	85	B	1
Inexpensive	79	B	2, 4, 9
Inexpensive	80	B	11
Inexp/Mod	89	C	1
Inexpensive	84	B	1
Inexp/Mod	84	C	1, 3
Inexpensive	74	B	1
Moderate	87	C	2
Inexpensive	79	B	2
Inexpensive	77	B	2
Inexpensive	77	B	2

Type of Restaurant	Star Rating
Prime Rib	
Lawry's The Prime Rib	★★★★
Russian	
Russian Tea Cafe	★★★¹/₂
Seafood	
Nick's Fishmarket	★★★★¹/₂
Shaw's Crab House and Shaw's Blue Crab Lounge & Oyster Bar	★★★★¹/₂
Cape Cod Room	★★★★
Catch 35	★★★★
Don's Fishmarket and Tavern	★★★★
The Old Carolina Crab House	★★★★
My Place For?	★★★¹/₂
Palm Restaurant	★★★¹/₂
That Steak Joynt	★★★¹/₂
Cy's Crab House	★★★
Bob Chinn's Crab House	★★★
Shaw's Seafood Grill	★★★
Serbian/Continental	
Skadarlija	★★★
Southern	
Army & Lou's	★★★★
Stanley's Kitchen & Tap	★★¹/₂
Southwestern	
Blue Mesa	★★★★
Twisted Lizard	★★★¹/₂
The Original A-1	★★★
Santa Fe Tapas	★★★
Spanish	
Emilio's Tapas Bar Restaurant	★★★★
Cafe Iberico Tapas Bar	★★★¹/₂
Cafe-Ba-Ba-Reeba!	★★★¹/₂
Tania's	★★★¹/₂
Gypsy's Cove	★★★
Emilio's Meson Sabika Tapas Bar Restaurant	★★★
Little Spain	★★★
La Paella	★★★

NOTE: Profiles follow in alphabetical order in the next chapter.

Price	Quality Rating	Value Rating	Zone
Moderate	90	B	3
Moderate	88	C	4
Mod/Exp	95	D	2, 4
Moderate	95	C	4
Mod/Exp	95	C	3
Mod/Exp	93	C	4
Inexp/Mod	93	B	11
Inexp/Mod	92	B	4
Inexp/Mod	89	B	1
Mod/Exp	87	C	3
Mod/Exp	85	C	1
Inexpensive	84	B	1
Moderate	82	B	10
Moderate	80	C	11
Moderate	84	B	1
Inexp/Mod	90	B	7
Inexpensive	79	A	1
Inexp/Mod	89	B	1
Inexpensive	87	B	1
Inexpensive	83	B	4
Inexp/Mod	82	C	1
Moderate	91	C	9
Inexp/Mod	87	B	3
Moderate	87	C	1
Moderate	86	B	2
Inexp/Mod	83	B	1
Moderate	82	C	8
Moderate	82	B	2
Moderate	81	C	1

Type of Restaurant	Star Rating
Steak	
Gibson's Steakhouse	★★★★¹/₂
Chicago Chop House	★★★★
Morton Steak House	★★★★
Ruth's Chris Steakhouse	★★★★
Kinzie Street Chophouse	★★★★
The Saloon	★★★¹/₂
Palm Restaurant	★★★¹/₂
That Steak Joynt	★★★¹/₂
Swedish/American	
Ann Sather	★★★
Tapas	
Emilio's Tapas Bar Restaurant	★★★★
Cafe Iberico Tapas Bar	★★★¹/₂
Cafe-Ba-Ba-Reeba!	★★★¹/₂
Gypsy's Cove	★★★
Emilio's Meson Sabika Tapas Bar Restaurant	★★★
Thai	
Arun's	★★★★¹/₂
Thai Touch	★★★★
Thai Borrahn	★★★★
P. S. Bangkok	★★★
Siam Cafe	★★★
Ukrainian	
Galans	★★
Vegetarian	
Cafe Voltaire	★★★
Chowpatti Vegetarian Restaurant	★★★
Blind Faith Cafe	★★¹/₂
The Bread Shop	★★¹/₂
Vietnamese/Chinese	
Hoang Mai	★★★¹/₂
Song Huong	★★★¹/₂

NOTE: Profiles follow in alphabetical order in the next chapter.

Price	Quality Rating	Value Rating	Zone
Mod/V. Exp	94	C	3
Moderate	94	C	3
Expensive	93	C	2, 3, 8
Mod/Exp	93	B	4
Moderate	91	B	4
Mod/Exp	89	C	3
Mod/Exp	87	C	3
Mod/Exp	85	C	1
Inexpensive	83	B	1
Moderate	91	C	9
Inexp/Mod	87	B	3
Moderate	87	C	1
Inexp/Mod	83	B	1
Moderate	82	C	8
Mod/Exp	95	C	1
Inexpensive	91	B	1
Inexpensive	90	B	3
Inexpensive	84	A	1
Inexpensive	84	A	1
Inexp/Mod	74	C	2
Inexpensive	83	B	1
Inexpensive	80	B	10
Inexpensive	79	B	11
Inexpensive	79	B	1
Inexpensive	89	A	1
Inexpensive	86	A	1

Chicago Restaurants by Star Rating

Name of Restaurant	Cuisine

Five-Star Restaurants

Charlie Trotter's	New American
Everest	French
Trio	Fusion
Le Français	French

Four-Star Restaurants

Le Titi de Paris	New French
Seasons Restaurant at the Four Seasons Hotel	American
Carlos'	French
Kuni's	Japanese
Yoshi's Cafe	New French
Arun's	Thai
Benkay	Japanese
Carlucci	Italian
The Dining Room	New French
Le Vichyssois	French
Nick's Fishmarket	Seafood
The Parthenon	Greek
Prairie	Midwestern
Printer's Row	New American
Shaw's Crab House and Shaw's Blue Crab Lounge & Oyster Bar	Seafood
Tallgrass Restaurant	New French
Va Pensiero	Italian
Vivere (Italian Village)	Italian
Gibson's Steakhouse	Steak
Cape Cod Room	Seafood
Chicago Chop House	Steak
Kiki's Bistro	French Bistro
Ambria	New French
Catch 35	Seafood
Costa D'Oro	French/Italian
Don's Fishmarket and Tavern	Seafood
Frontera Grill/Topolobampo	Mexican
Gabriel's Restaurant	French/Italian
Gordon	New American
Morton Steak House	Steak
Ruth's Chris Steakhouse	Steak
Spiaggia	Italian
The Cottage	New American/ French

NOTE: Profiles follow in alphabetical order in the next chapter.

Star Rating	Price	Quality Rating	Value Rating	Zone
★★★★★	Very Expensive	98	C	1
★★★★★	Expensive	98	C	4
★★★★★	Expensive	98	C	11
★★★★★	Expensive	97	C	10
★★★★$^{1}/_{2}$	Mod/Exp	97	C	10
★★★★$^{1}/_{2}$	Mod/Exp	97	C	3
★★★★$^{1}/_{2}$	Mod/Exp	96	C	11
★★★★$^{1}/_{2}$	Inexp/Mod	96	C	11
★★★★$^{1}/_{2}$	Mod/Exp	96	C	1
★★★★$^{1}/_{2}$	Mod/Exp	95	C	1
★★★★$^{1}/_{2}$	Mod/Exp	95	D	4
★★★★$^{1}/_{2}$	Moderate	95	C	1
★★★★$^{1}/_{2}$	Mod/Exp	95	C	3
★★★★$^{1}/_{2}$	Moderate	95	B	10
★★★★$^{1}/_{2}$	Mod/Exp	95	D	2, 4
★★★★$^{1}/_{2}$	Inexp/Mod	95	B	4
★★★★$^{1}/_{2}$	Mod/Exp	95	C	5
★★★★$^{1}/_{2}$	Moderate	95	B	5
★★★★$^{1}/_{2}$	Moderate	95	C	4
★★★★$^{1}/_{2}$	Very Expensive	95	C	8
★★★★$^{1}/_{2}$	Moderate	95	C	11
★★★★$^{1}/_{2}$	Moderate	95	C	4
★★★★$^{1}/_{2}$	Mod/V. Exp	94	C	3
★★★★	Mod/Exp	95	C	3
★★★★	Moderate	94	C	3
★★★★	Inexp/Mod	94	C	3
★★★★	Mod/Exp	93	C	1
★★★★	Mod/Exp	93	C	4
★★★★	Mod/Exp	93	C	3
★★★★	Inexp/Mod	93	B	11
★★★★	Inexp/Mod	93	C	4
★★★★	Moderate	93	C	11
★★★★	Moderate	93	C	4
★★★★	Expensive	93	C	2, 3, 8
★★★★	Mod/Exp	93	B	4
★★★★	Mod/Exp	93	C	3
★★★★	Moderate	92	B	8

Name of Restaurant	Cuisine

Four-Star Restaurants (cont'd.)

Mykonos	Greek
The Old Carolina Crab House	Seafood
The Pump Room	American/ Continental
Szechwan House	Chinese
Un Grand Cafe	French Bistro
Cuisines	French/Italian
Emilio's Tapas Bar Restaurant	Spanish/Tapas
Kinzie Street Chophouse	Steak
Klay Oven	Indian
Melange American Eatery	New American
Thai Touch	Thai
Tuttaposto	Mediterranean
Army & Lou's	Southern/ Soul Food
Biggs	Continental/French
Golden Ox	German/ American
Jackie's	French/Asian
Jimmy's Place	New French
La Boheme	New French
Lawry's The Prime Rib	Prime Rib
Papagus Greek Taverna	Greek
The Signature Room at the Ninety-Fifth	New American
Thai Borrahn	Thai
Winnetka Grill	New American
Blue Mesa	Southwestern

Three-Star Restaurants

L'Olive	Moroccan/ Mediterranean
Ishtar Inn	Middle Eastern
Katsu Japanese Restaurant	Japanese
Coco Pazzo	Italian
Hoang Mai	Vietnamese/ Chinese
Montparnasse	New French
My Place For?	Seafood
Pars Cove	Persian
Roditys	Greek
The Saloon	Steak

NOTE: Profiles follow in alphabetical order in the next chapter.

Star Rating	Price	Quality Rating	Value Rating	Zone
★★★★	Inexp/Mod	92	B	11
★★★★	Inexp/Mod	92	B	4
★★★★	Expensive	92	C	3
★★★★	Moderate	92	C	4
★★★★	Moderate	92	C	1
★★★★	Inexp/Mod	91	B	4
★★★★	Moderate	91	C	9
★★★★	Moderate	91	B	4
★★★★	Moderate	91	B	4
★★★★	Inexp/Mod	91	C	11
★★★★	Inexpensive	91	B	1
★★★★	Inexp/Mod	91	C	3
★★★★	Inexp/Mod	90	B	7
★★★★	Moderate	90	C	3
★★★★	Moderate	90	C	1
★★★★	Mod/Exp	90	C	1
★★★★	Mod/Exp	90	C	1
★★★★	Moderate	90	C	11
★★★★	Moderate	90	B	3
★★★★	Moderate	90	C	3
★★★★	Mod/Exp	90	C	3
★★★★	Inexpensive	90	B	3
★★★★	Moderate	90	C	11
★★★★	Inexp/Mod	89	B	1
★★★½	Inexpensive	91	A	1
★★★½	Inexpensive	90	B	3
★★★½	Inexp/Mod	90	B	1
★★★½	Moderate	89	C	4
★★★½	Inexpensive	89	A	1
★★★½	Mod/Exp	89	C	8
★★★½	Inexp/Mod	89	B	1
★★★½	Inexp/Mod	89	C	1
★★★½	Inexp/Mod	89	B	4
★★★½	Mod/Exp	89	C	3

Restaurants by Star Rating (continued)

Name of Restaurant	Cuisine

Three-Star Restaurants (cont'd.)

Name of Restaurant	Cuisine
Santorini	Greek
Akai Hana	Japanese
The Berghoff	German/ American
Cafe Angelo	Italian
Carlucci (Rosemont)	Tuscan Italian
Emperor's Choice	Chinese
Entre Nous	French
Geja's Cafe	Fondue
The Greenery	American
Honda	Japanese
Luciano's	Italian
Mama Desta's Red Sea Ethiopian Restaurant	Ethiopian
Mandar Inn	Chinese
Maple Tree Inn	Cajun/Creole
Oceanique	French/American
Russian Tea Cafe	Russian
Sayat Nova	Armenian
St. Germain Restaurant/ Bakery Cafe	French Bistro
Walker Bros. Original Pancake House	American
Bice Ristorante	Italian
Cafe Iberico Tapas Bar	Spanish/Tapas
Cafe-Ba-Ba-Reeba!	Spanish/Tapas
Dixie Que	Barbecue
La Strada	Italian
Lutnia Continental Cafe	Polish/Continental
The Marc	New American
Mei-Shung Chinese Restaurant	Chinese/Taiwanese
Palm Restaurant	Steak/Seafood
Pastiche	Global/Eclectic
302 West	New American
Trattoria Gianni	Italian
Twisted Lizard	Southwestern/ Mexican
Bella Vista	New Italian
Bistro 110	French
Harry Caray's	American/Italian
Heaven on Seven	Cajun/Creole

NOTE: Profiles follow in alphabetical order in the next chapter.

Star Rating	Price	Quality Rating	Value Rating	Zone
★★★½	Inexp/Mod	89	C	4
★★★½	Inexp/Mod	88	C	11
★★★½	Inexpensive	88	B	4
★★★½	Inexp/Mod	88	B	4
★★★½	Moderate	88	C	2
★★★½	Inexp/Mod	88	B	5
★★★½	Mod/Exp	88	C	4
★★★½	Moderate	88	B	1
★★★½	Mod/Exp	88	C	10
★★★½	Moderate	88	C	4
★★★½	Inexp/Mod	88	B	3, 9, 11
★★★½	Inexpensive	88	B	1
★★★½	Moderate	88	C	5
★★★½	Inexp/Mod	88	C	8
★★★½	Moderate	88	C	11
★★★½	Moderate	88	C	4
★★★½	Inexp/Mod	88	C	10
★★★½	Inexp/Mod	88	C	3
★★★½	Inexpensive	88	B	10, 11
★★★½	Mod/Exp	87	D	3
★★★½	Inexp/Mod	87	B	3
★★★½	Moderate	87	C	1
★★★½	Inexpensive	87	B	1
★★★½	Mod/Exp	87	C	4
★★★½	Moderate	87	C	2
★★★½	Moderate	87	C	3
★★★½	Inexpensive	87	B	1
★★★½	Mod/Exp	87	C	3
★★★½	Inexp/Mod	87	B	1
★★★½	Moderate	87	C	9
★★★½	Inexp/Mod	87	C	1
★★★½	Inexpensive	87	B	1
★★★½	Inexp/Mod	86	C	1
★★★½	Moderate	86	C	3
★★★½	Mod/Exp	86	C	4
★★★½	Inexpensive	86	B	4

Name of Restaurant	Cuisine

Three-Star Restaurants (cont'd.)

Kenessey's Cypress	Continental/ Hungarian
The Mity Nice Grill	American
Relish	American
Shilla	Korean/Japanese
Song Huong	Vietnamese/ Chinese
Tania's	Cuban/Spanish
Harry Caray's (Wheeling)	American/Italian
Jilly's Cafe	New American
Michael Jordan's Restaurant	American
That Steak Joynt	Steak/Seafood
Via Veneto	New Italian
Wild Onion	American
Yvette	New French
Yvette Wintergarden	New French
The Helmand	Afghani
T'ang Dynasty	Chinese
Hong Min Restaurant	Chinese/Dim Sum
Addis Abeba	Ethiopian
Aegean Isles	Greek
Cy's Crab House	Seafood/Persian
Da Nicola Ristorante	Italian
Don Juan	Mexican
Don Roth's in Wheeling	American
Froggy's French Cafe	New French
La Bocca Della Verita	Italian
P. S. Bangkok	Thai
Pappagallo's	Italian/American
Reza's	Persian
Siam Cafe	Thai
Skadarlija	Serbian/ Continental
Tuscany	Italian
Uncle Tannous	Lebanese
Viceroy of India	Indian
Amourette	French
Ann Sather	Swedish/American
Bando	Korean
Binyon's	American
Cafe Voltaire	Vegetarian
Del Rio	Italian

NOTE: Profiles follow in alphabetical order in the next chapter.

Star Rating	Price	Quality Rating	Value Rating	Zone
★★★¹/₂	Moderate	86	C	9
★★★¹/₂	Inexp/Mod	86	C	3
★★★¹/₂	Inexp/Mod	86	C	1
★★★¹/₂	Moderate	86	C	1
★★★¹/₂	Inexpensive	86	A	1
★★★¹/₂	Moderate	86	B	2
★★★¹/₂	Moderate	85	C	10
★★★¹/₂	Inexp/Mod	85	B	11
★★★¹/₂	Inexp/Mod	85	C	3
★★★¹/₂	Mod/Exp	85	C	1
★★★¹/₂	Inexpensive	85	B	1
★★★¹/₂	Inexp/Mod	85	B	1
★★★¹/₂	Inexp/Mod	85	C	3
★★★¹/₂	Inexp/Mod	85	C	4
★★★¹/₂	Inexpensive	80	B	1
★★★	Moderate	86	C	3
★★★	Inexpensive	85	B	5, 8
★★★	Inexpensive	84	C	1
★★★	Inexp/Mod	84	C	11
★★★	Inexpensive	84	B	1
★★★	Inexp/Mod	84	B	1
★★★	Inexp/Mod	84	C	1
★★★	Moderate	84	C	10
★★★	Moderate	84	B	11
★★★	Inexpensive	84	B	1
★★★	Inexpensive	84	A	1
★★★	Inexp/Mod	84	B	11
★★★	Inexp/Mod	84	C	1, 3
★★★	Inexpensive	84	A	1
★★★	Moderate	84	B	1
★★★	Moderate	84	C	5
★★★	Inexp/Mod	84	B	1
★★★	Inexp/Mod	84	B	1, 9
★★★	Inexp/Mod	83	B	10
★★★	Inexpensive	83	B	1
★★★	Inexp/Mod	83	C	1
★★★	Inexp/Mod	83	C	4
★★★	Inexpensive	83	B	1
★★★	Inexp/Mod	83	B	11

Restaurants by Star Rating (continued)

Name of Restaurant	Cuisine

Three-Star Restaurants (cont'd.)

Name of Restaurant	Cuisine
Francesco's Hole in the Wall	Italian
Gypsy's Cove	Spanish/Tapas
Hunan Cafe	Chinese
Julio's Latin Cafe	Caribbean
Mandalay	Burmese
The Organic Tomato	Natural
The Original A-1	Southwestern
Pegasus Restaurant and Taverna	Greek
Rosebud Cafe	Italian
Avanzare	Italian
The Big Bowl Cafe	American
Big Shoulders	American
Blackhawk Lodge	New American
Bob Chinn's Crab House	Seafood
Chez 'D	Mediterranean
The Corner Bakery	Bakery Cafe
El Tinajon	Guatemalan
Emilio's Meson Sabika Tapas Bar Restaurant	Spanish/Tapas
Filippo's	Italian
Jerome's	American
Little Spain	Spanish
Mia Francesca	Italian
Mirabell Restaurant	German/American
N. N. Smokehouse	Barbecue/Filipino
Santa Fe Tapas	Southwestern
Sher-A-Punjab	Indian
Tucci Milan	Italian
Hubbard Street Grill	New American
Kitty O'Shea's	Irish Pub
La Paella	Spanish
Maggiano's Little Italy	Italian
R. J. Grunts	American
Taylor Street Bistro	French Bistro
Bruna's Ristorante	Italian
Bukhara	Indian
Chowpatti Vegetarian Restaurant	Indian/Vegetarian
Hans' Bavarian Lodge	German/American
Shaw's Seafood Grill	Seafood

NOTE: Profiles follow in alphabetical order in the next chapter.

Star Rating	Price	Quality Rating	Value Rating	Zone
★★★	Inexp/Mod	83	B	11
★★★	Inexp/Mod	83	B	1
★★★	Inexp/Mod	83	C	3
★★★	Moderate	83	C	10
★★★	Inexp/Mod	83	B	6
★★★	Inexpensive	83	B	3
★★★	Inexpensive	83	B	4
★★★	Inexp/Mod	83	C	4
★★★	Inexp/Mod	83	C	5
★★★	Moderate	82	C	3
★★★	Inexpensive	82	B	3
★★★	Inexpensive	82	B	1
★★★	Moderate	82	C	3
★★★	Inexp/Exp	82	B	10
★★★	Inexp/Mod	82	B	1
★★★	Inexp/Mod	82	C	4, 8
★★★	Inexpensive	82	B	1
★★★	Moderate	82	C	8
★★★	Inexp/Mod	82	C	1
★★★	Inexp/Mod	82	C	1
★★★	Moderate	82	B	2
★★★	Inexp/Mod	82	B	1
★★★	Inexp/Mod	82	C	2
★★★	Inexpensive	82	B	1
★★★	Inexp/Mod	82	C	1
★★★	Inexpensive	82	B	1
★★★	Inexp/Mod	82	C	4
★★★	Inexp/Mod	81	C	4
★★★	Inexpensive	81	B	5
★★★	Moderate	81	C	1
★★★	Moderate	81	C	4, 8
★★★	Inexpensive	81	A	1
★★★	Inexp/Mod	81	B	5
★★★	Inexp/Mod	80	B	5
★★★	Moderate	80	C	3
★★★	Inexpensive	80	B	10
★★★	Inexpensive	80	B	10
★★★	Moderate	80	C	11

Name of Restaurant	Cuisine

Two-Star Restaurants

Le Bouchon	French Bistro
Lulu's	Pan Asian
Alfo's Ristorante	Italian
Blind Faith Cafe	Vegetarian
The Bread Shop	Vegetarian
Eccentric	American
El Dinamico Dallas	Caribbean
El Tipico	Mexican
foodlife	American
Pazzo's Pizza and Pasta Kitchen	New Italian
Pierogi Inn	Polish
Red Tomato	Italian
Stanley's Kitchen & Tap	Southern
Bones	Barbecue
Cafe Borgia	Italian
Home Bakery	Polish/European
Miska's	Polish
Pampanga Restaurant	Filipino
Hatsuhana	Japanese
Kanval Palace	Indian
Tufano's (Vernon Park Tap)	Italian
Galans	Ukrainian
Machu Picchu	Peruvian
Oo-La-La!	French/Italian

NOTE: Profiles follow in alphabetical order in the next chapter.

Star Rating	Price	Quality Rating	Value Rating	Zone
★★½	Moderate	80	B	1
★★½	Inexpensive	80	B	11
★★½	Inexpensive	79	B	5
★★½	Inexpensive	79	B	11
★★½	Inexpensive	79	B	1
★★½	Moderate	79	C	3
★★½	Inexpensive	79	B	1
★★½	Inexpensive	79	B	1, 11
★★½	Inexpensive	79	B	3
★★½	Inexpensive	79	B	2, 4, 9
★★½	Inexpensive	79	B	2
★★½	Inexpensive	79	B	1
★★½	Inexpensive	79	A	1
★★½	Inexp/Mod	78	C	11
★★½	Inexp/Mod	78	B	8
★★½	Inexpensive	77	B	2
★★½	Inexpensive	77	B	2
★★½	Inexpensive	77	B	1
★★½	Inexp/Mod	76	C	3
★★½	Inexpensive	76	B	1
★★½	Inexp/Mod	76	B	5
★★	Inexp/Mod	74	C	2
★★	Inexpensive	74	B	1
★★	Inexp/Mod	74	C	1

Chicago Restaurants by Geographic Zone

Type of Restaurant	Star Rating

Zone 1—North Side

Afghani
The Helmand ★★★¹/₂

American
Relish ★★★¹/₂
Wild Onion ★★★¹/₂
Big Shoulders ★★★
Jerome's ★★★
R. J. Grunts ★★★

Barbecue
Dixie Que ★★★¹/₂
N. N. Smokehouse ★★★

Caribbean
El Dinamico Dallas ★★¹/₂

Chinese/Taiwanese
Mei-Shung Chinese Restaurant ★★★¹/₂

Ethiopian
Mama Desta's Red Sea ★★★¹/₂
Ethiopian Restaurant
Addis Abeba ★★★

Filipino
Pampanga Restaurant ★★¹/₂

Fondue
Geja's Cafe ★★★¹/₂

French Bistro
Un Grand Cafe ★★★★
Le Bouchon ★★¹/₂

French/Asian
Jackie's ★★★★

French/Italian
Oo-La-La! ★★

German/American
Golden Ox ★★★★

Global/Eclectic
Pastiche ★★★¹/₂

NOTE: Profiles follow in alphabetical order in the next chapter.

Price	Quality Rating	Value Rating
Inexpensive	80	B
Inexp/Mod	86	C
Inexp/Mod	85	B
Inexpensive	82	B
Inexp/Mod	82	C
Inexpensive	81	A
Inexpensive	87	B
Inexpensive	82	B
Inexpensive	79	B
Inexpensive	87	B
Inexpensive	88	B
Inexpensive	84	C
Inexpensive	77	B
Moderate	88	B
Moderate	92	C
Moderate	80	B
Mod/Exp	90	C
Inexp/Mod	74	C
Moderate	90	C
Inexp/Mod	87	B

Restaurants by Zone (continued)

Type of Restaurant	Star Rating

Zone 1—North Side (continued)

Guatemalan
   El Tinajon ★★★

Indian
   Viceroy of India ★★★
   Sher-A-Punjab ★★★
   Kanval Palace ★★½

Italian
   Carlucci ★★★★½
   Trattoria Gianni ★★★½
   Da Nicola Ristorante ★★★
   La Bocca Della Verita ★★★
   Filippo's ★★★
   Mia Francesca ★★★
   Red Tomato ★★½

Japanese
   Katsu Japanese Restaurant ★★★½

Korean
   Shilla ★★★½
   Bando ★★★

Lebanese
   Uncle Tannous ★★★

Mediterranean
   Chez 'D ★★★

Mexican
   Don Juan ★★★
   El Tipico ★★½

Moroccan/Mediterranean
   L'Olive ★★★½

New American
   Charlie Trotter's ★★★★★

New French
   Yoshi's Cafe ★★★★½
   Ambria ★★★★
   Jimmy's Place ★★★★

NOTE: Profiles follow in alphabetical order in the next chapter.

Price	Quality Rating	Value Rating
Inexpensive	82	B
Inexp/Mod	84	B
Inexpensive	82	B
Inexpensive	76	B
Moderate	95	C
Inexp/Mod	87	C
Inexp/Mod	84	B
Inexpensive	84	B
Inexp/Mod	82	C
Inexp/Mod	82	B
Inexpensive	79	B
Inexp/Mod	90	B
Moderate	86	C
Inexp/Mod	83	C
Inexp/Mod	84	B
Inexp/Mod	82	B
Inexp/Mod	84	C
Inexpensive	79	B
Inexpensive	91	A
Very Expensive	98	C
Mod/Exp	96	C
Mod/Exp	93	C
Mod/Exp	90	C

Restaurants by Zone *(continued)*

Type of Restaurant	Star Rating

Zone 1—North Side (continued)

New Italian
Bella Vista — ★★★½
Via Veneto — ★★★½

Persian
Pars Cove — ★★★½
Reza's — ★★★

Peruvian
Machu Picchu — ★★

Seafood
My Place For? — ★★★½
Cy's Crab House — ★★★

Serbian/Continental
Skadarlija — ★★★

Southern
Stanley's Kitchen & Tap — ★★½

Southwestern
Blue Mesa — ★★★★
Twisted Lizard — ★★★½
Santa Fe Tapas — ★★★

Spanish
Cafe-Ba-Ba-Reeba! — ★★★½
Gypsy's Cove — ★★★
La Paella — ★★★

Steak/Seafood
That Steak Joynt — ★★★½

Swedish/American
Ann Sather — ★★★

Thai
Arun's — ★★★★½
Thai Touch — ★★★★
P. S. Bangkok — ★★★
Siam Cafe — ★★★

Vegetarian
Cafe Voltaire — ★★★
The Bread Shop — ★★½

NOTE: Profiles follow in alphabetical order in the next chapter.

Price	Quality Rating	Value Rating
Inexp/Mod	86	C
Inexpensive	85	B
Inexp/Mod	89	C
Inexp/Mod	84	C
Inexpensive	74	B
Inexp/Mod	89	B
Inexpensive	84	B
Moderate	84	B
Inexpensive	79	A
Inexp/Mod	89	B
Inexpensive	87	B
Inexp/Mod	82	C
Moderate	87	C
Inexp/Mod	83	B
Moderate	81	C
Mod/Exp	85	C
Inexpensive	83	B
Mod/Exp	95	C
Inexpensive	91	B
Inexpensive	84	A
Inexpensive	84	A
Inexpensive	83	B
Inexpensive	79	B

Type of Restaurant	Star Rating

Zone 1—North Side (continued)

Vietnamese/Chinese
    Hoang Mai   ★★★¹/₂
    Song Huong   ★★★¹/₂

Zone 2—North Central/O'Hare

Cuban
    Tania's   ★★★¹/₂

German/American
    Mirabell Restaurant   ★★★

Italian
    Carlucci (Rosemont)   ★★★¹/₂

New Italian
    Pazzo's Pizza and Pasta Kitchen   ★★¹/₂

Polish
    Lutnia Continental Cafe   ★★★¹/₂
    Pierogi Inn   ★★¹/₂
    Home Bakery   ★★¹/₂
    Miska's   ★★¹/₂

Seafood
    Nick's Fishmarket   ★★★★¹/₂

Spanish
    Little Spain   ★★★

Steak
    Morton Steak House   ★★★★

Ukrainian
    Galans   ★★

Zone 3—Near North

American
    Seasons Restaurant at the Four Seasons Hotel   ★★★★¹/₂
    The Pump Room   ★★★★
    The Mity Nice Grill   ★★★¹/₂
    Michael Jordan's Restaurant   ★★★¹/₂
    The Big Bowl Cafe   ★★★

NOTE: Profiles follow in alphabetical order in the next chapter.

Price	Quality Rating	Value Rating
Inexpensive	89	A
Inexpensive	86	A
Moderate	86	B
Inexp/Mod	82	C
Moderate	88	C
Inexpensive	79	B
Moderate	87	C
Inexpensive	79	B
Inexpensive	77	B
Inexpensive	77	B
Mod/Exp	95	D
Moderate	82	B
Expensive	93	C
Inexp/Mod	74	C
Mod/Exp	97	C
Expensive	92	C
Inexp/Mod	86	C
Inexp/Mod	85	C
Inexpensive	82	B

Type of Restaurant	Star Rating

Zone 3—Near North (continued)

American (cont'd.)
   Eccentric ★★½
   foodlife ★★½

Chinese
   T'ang Dynasty ★★★
   Hunan Cafe ★★★

French
   Kiki's Bistro ★★★★
   Biggs ★★★★
   St. Germain Restaurant/Bakery Cafe ★★★½
   Bistro 110 ★★★½

French/Italian
   Costa D'Oro ★★★★

Greek
   Papagus Greek Taverna ★★★★

Indian
   Bukhara ★★★

Italian
   Spiaggia ★★★★
   Luciano's ★★★½
   Bice Ristorante ★★★½
   Avanzare ★★★

Japanese
   Hatsuhana ★★½

Mediterranean
   Tuttaposto ★★★★

Middle Eastern
   Ishtar Inn ★★★½

Natural
   The Organic Tomato ★★★

New American
   The Signature Room at the Ninety-Fifth ★★★★
   The Marc ★★★½
   Blackhawk Lodge ★★★

NOTE: Profiles follow in alphabetical order in the next chapter.

Price	Quality Rating	Value Rating
Moderate	79	C
Inexpensive	79	B
Moderate	86	C
Inexp/Mod	83	C
Inexp/Mod	94	C
Moderate	90	C
Inexp/Mod	88	C
Moderate	86	C
Mod/Exp	93	C
Moderate	90	C
Moderate	80	C
Mod/Exp	93	C
Inexp/Mod	88	B
Mod/Exp	87	D
Moderate	82	C
Inexp/Mod	76	C
Inexp/Mod	91	C
Inexpensive	90	B
Inexpensive	83	B
Mod/Exp	90	C
Moderate	87	C
Moderate	82	C

Type of Restaurant	Star Rating
Zone 3—Near North (continued)	
New French	
The Dining Room	★★★★¹/₂
Yvette	★★★¹/₂
Prime Rib	
Lawry's The Prime Rib	★★★★
Seafood	
Cape Cod Room	★★★★
Spanish/Tapas	
Cafe Iberico Tapas Bar	★★★¹/₂
Steak	
Gibson's Steakhouse	★★★★¹/₂
Chicago Chop House	★★★★
Morton Steak House	★★★★
The Saloon	★★★¹/₂
Palm Restaurant	★★★¹/₂
Thai	
Thai Borrahn	★★★★

Zone 4—The Loop

American	
Harry Caray's	★★★¹/₂
Binyon's	★★★
Bakery Cafe	
The Corner Bakery	★★★
Cajun/Creole	
Heaven on Seven	★★★¹/₂
Chinese	
Szechwan House	★★★★
French	
Everest	★★★★★
Entre Nous	★★★¹/₂
German/American	
The Berghoff	★★★¹/₂

NOTE: Profiles follow in alphabetical order in the next chapter.

Price	Quality Rating	Value Rating
Mod/Exp	95	C
Inexp/Mod	85	C
Moderate	90	B
Mod/Exp	95	C
Inexp/Mod	87	B
Mod/V. Exp	94	C
Moderate	94	C
Expensive	93	C
Mod/Exp	89	C
Mod/Exp	87	C
Inexpensive	90	B
Mod/Exp	86	C
Inexp/Mod	83	C
Inexp/Mod	82	C
Inexpensive	86	B
Moderate	92	C
Expensive	98	C
Mod/Exp	88	C
Inexpensive	88	B

Type of Restaurant	Star Rating

Zone 4—The Loop (continued)

Greek
    The Parthenon ★★★★¹/₂
    Roditys ★★★¹/₂
    Santorini ★★★¹/₂
    Pegasus Restaurant and Taverna ★★★

Indian
    Klay Oven ★★★★

Italian
    Vivere (Italian Village) ★★★★¹/₂
    Coco Pazzo ★★★¹/₂
    Cafe Angelo ★★★¹/₂
    La Strada ★★★¹/₂
    Tucci Milan ★★★
    Maggiano's Little Italy ★★★

Italian/French
    Cuisines ★★★★

Japanese
    Benkay ★★★★¹/₂
    Honda ★★★¹/₂

Mexican
    Frontera Grill/Topolobampo ★★★★

New American
    Gordon ★★★★
    Hubbard Street Grill ★★★

New French
    Yvette Wintergarden ★★★¹/₂

New Italian
    Pazzo's Pizza and Pasta Kitchen ★★¹/₂

Russian
    Russian Tea Cafe ★★★¹/₂

Seafood
    Nick's Fishmarket ★★★★¹/₂
    Shaw's Crab House and Shaw's ★★★★¹/₂
      Blue Crab Lounge & Oyster Bar

NOTE: Profiles follow in alphabetical order in the next chapter.

Price	Quality Rating	Value Rating
Inexp/Mod	95	B
Inexp/Mod	89	B
Inexp/Mod	89	C
Inexp/Mod	83	C
Moderate	91	B
Moderate	95	C
Moderate	89	C
Inexp/Mod	88	B
Mod/Exp	87	C
Inexp/Mod	82	C
Moderate	81	C
Inexp/Mod	91	B
Mod/Exp	95	D
Moderate	88	C
Inexp/Mod	93	C
Moderate	93	C
Inexp/Mod	81	C
Inexp/Mod	85	C
Inexpensive	79	B
Moderate	88	C
Mod/Exp	95	D
Moderate	95	C

Type of Restaurant	Star Rating

Zone 4—The Loop (continued)

Seafood (cont'd.)
| Catch 35 | ★★★★ |
| The Old Carolina Crab House | ★★★★ |

Southwestern
| The Original A-1 | ★★★ |

Steak
| Ruth's Chris Steakhouse | ★★★★ |
| Kinzie Street Chophouse | ★★★★ |

Zone 5—South Loop

Chinese
Emperor's Choice	★★★¹/₂
Mandar Inn	★★★¹/₂
Hong Min Restaurant	★★★

French Bistro
| Taylor Street Bistro | ★★★ |

Irish Pub
| Kitty O'Shea's | ★★★ |

Italian
Tuscany	★★★
Rosebud Cafe	★★★
Bruna's Ristorante	★★★
Alfo's Ristorante	★★¹/₂
Tufano's (Vernon Park Tap)	★★¹/₂

Midwestern
| Prairie | ★★★★¹/₂ |

New American
| Printer's Row | ★★★★¹/₂ |

Zone 6—South Central/Midway

Burmese
| Mandalay | ★★★ |

NOTE: Profiles follow in alphabetical order in the next chapter.

Price	Quality Rating	Value Rating
Mod/Exp	93	C
Inexp/Mod	92	B
Inexpensive	83	B
Mod/Exp	93	B
Moderate	91	B
Inexp/Mod	88	B
Moderate	88	C
Inexpensive	85	B
Inexp/Mod	81	B
Inexpensive	81	B
Moderate	84	C
Inexp/Mod	83	C
Inexp/Mod	80	B
Inexpensive	79	B
Inexp/Mod	76	B
Mod/Exp	95	C
Moderate	95	B
Inexp/Mod	83	B

Type of Restaurant	Star Rating

Zone 7—South Side

Southern
    Army & Lou's   ★★★★

Zone 8—Southern Suburbs

Bakery Cafe
    The Corner Bakery   ★★★

Cajun/Creole
    Maple Tree Inn   ★★★$^1/_2$

Chinese/Dim Sum
    Hong Min Restaurant   ★★★

Italian
    Maggiano's Little Italy   ★★★
    Cafe Borgia   ★★$^1/_2$

New American/French
    The Cottage   ★★★★

New French
    Tallgrass Restaurant   ★★★★$^1/_2$
    Montparnasse   ★★★$^1/_2$

Spanish/Tapas
    Emilio's Meson Sabika Tapas   ★★★
      Bar Restaurant

Steak
    Morton Steak House   ★★★★

Zone 9—Western Suburbs

Continental/Hungarian
    Kenessey's Cypress   ★★★$^1/_2$

Indian
    Viceroy of India   ★★★

Italian
    Luciano's   ★★★$^1/_2$

New American
    302 West   ★★★$^1/_2$

NOTE: Profiles follow in alphabetical order in the next
      chapter.

Price	Quality Rating	Value Rating
Inexp/Mod	90	B
Inexp/Mod	82	C
Inexp/Mod	88	C
Inexpensive	85	B
Moderate	81	C
Inexp/Mod	78	B
Moderate	92	B
Very expensive	95	C
Mod/Exp	89	C
Moderate	82	C
Expensive	93	C
Moderate	86	C
Inexp/Mod	84	B
Inexp/Mod	88	B
Moderate	87	C

Type of Restaurant	Star Rating

Zone 9—Western Suburbs (continued)

New Italian
Pazzo's Pizza and Pasta Kitchen ★★½

Spanish/Tapas
Emilio's Tapas Bar Restaurant ★★★★

Zone 10—Northwest Suburbs

American
The Greenery ★★★½
Walker Bros. Original Pancake House ★★★½
Harry Caray's (Wheeling) ★★★½
Don Roth's in Wheeling ★★★

Armenian
Sayat Nova ★★★½

Caribbean
Julio's Latin Cafe ★★★

French
Le Français ★★★★★
Le Vichyssois ★★★★½
Amourette ★★★

German/American
Hans' Bavarian Lodge ★★★

Indian/Vegetarian
Chowpatti Vegetarian Restaurant ★★★

New French
Le Titi de Paris ★★★★½

Seafood
Bob Chinn's Crab House ★★★

Zone 11—Northern Suburbs

American
Walker Bros. Original Pancake House ★★★½

NOTE: Profiles follow in alphabetical order in the next chapter.

Price	Quality Rating	Value Rating
Inexpensive	79	B
Moderate	91	C
Mod/Exp	88	C
Inexpensive	88	B
Moderate	85	C
Moderate	84	C
Inexp/Mod	88	C
Moderate	83	C
Expensive	97	C
Moderate	95	B
Inexp/Mod	83	B
Inexpensive	80	B
Inexpensive	80	B
Mod/Exp	97	C
Inexp/Exp	82	B
Inexpensive	88	B

Restaurants by Zone *(continued)*

Type of Restaurant	Star Rating

Zone 11—Northern Suburbs (continued)

Barbecue
Bones ★★¹/₂

French
Carlos' ★★★★¹/₂
Oceanique ★★★¹/₂

French/Italian
Gabriel's Restaurant ★★★★

Fusion
Trio ★★★★★

Greek
Mykonos ★★★★
Aegean Isles ★★★

Italian
Va Pensiero ★★★★¹/₂
Luciano's ★★★¹/₂
Pappagallo's ★★★
Del Rio ★★★
Francesco's Hole in the Wall ★★★

Japanese
Kuni's ★★★★¹/₂
Akai Hana ★★★¹/₂

Mexican
El Tipico ★★¹/₂

New American
Melange American Eatery ★★★★
Winnetka Grill ★★★★
Jilly's Cafe ★★★¹/₂

New French
La Boheme ★★★★
Froggy's French Cafe ★★★

Pan Asian
Lulu's ★★¹/₂

NOTE: Profiles follow in alphabetical order in the next
chapter.

Price	Quality Rating	Value Rating
Inexp/Mod	78	C
Mod/Exp	96	C
Moderate	88	C
Moderate	93	C
Expensive	98	C
Inexp/Mod	92	B
Inexp/Mod	84	C
Moderate	95	C
Inexp/Mod	88	B
Inexp/Mod	84	B
Inexp/Mod	83	B
Inexp/Mod	83	B
Inexp/Mod	96	C
Inexp/Mod	88	C
Inexpensive	79	B
Inexp/Mod	91	C
Moderate	90	C
Inexp/Mod	85	B
Moderate	90	C
Moderate	84	B
Inexpensive	80	B

Type of Restaurant	Star Rating

Zone 11—Northern Suburbs (continued)

Seafood
| Don's Fishmarket and Tavern | ★★★★ |
| Shaw's Seafood Grill | ★★★ |

Vegetarian
| Blind Faith Cafe | ★★½ |

NOTE: Profiles follow in alphabetical order in the next chapter.

Price	Quality Rating	Value Rating
Inexp/Mod	93	B
Moderate	80	C
Inexpensive	79	B

Recommended for Late Night Dining

Name of Restaurant	Cuisine
Bando	Korean
Bella Vista	New Italian
Bistro 110	French
Cafe-Ba-Ba-Reeba!	Spanish/Tapas
The Dining Room	New French
Emperor's Choice	Chinese
Hong Min Restaurant	Chinese/Dim Sum
The Marc	New American
Morton Steak House	Steak
Nick's Fishmarket	Seafood
The Parthenon	Greek
Reza's	Persian
Ruth's Chris Steakhouse	Steak
The Saloon	Steak
Santorini	Greek
Seasons Restaurant at the Four Seasons Hotel	American
Skadarlija	Serbian/Continental
Stanley's Kitchen & Tap	Southern
Tania's	Cuban/Spanish
That Steak Joynt	Steak/Seafood
Twisted Lizard	Southwestern/Mexican
Uncle Tannous	Lebanese

Recommended for Quiet & Romantic Dining

Name of Restaurant	Cuisine
Ambria	New French
Amourette	French
Arun's	Thai
Biggs	Continental/French
Blue Mesa	Southwestern
Costa D'Oro	French/Italian
The Cottage	New American/French
The Dining Room	New French
Emilio's Tapas Bar Restaurant	Spanish/Tapas
Entre Nous	French
Everest	French
Geja's Cafe	Fondue
Gordon	New American
The Greenery	American

Star Rating	Price	Quality Rating	Value Rating	Zone
★★★	Inexp/Mod	83	C	1
★★★½	Inexp/Mod	86	C	1
★★★½	Moderate	86	C	3
★★★½	Moderate	87	C	1
★★★★½	Mod/Exp	95	C	3
★★★½	Inexp/Mod	88	B	5
★★★	Inexpensive	85	B	5, 8
★★★½	Moderate	87	C	3
★★★★	Expensive	93	C	2, 3, 8
★★★★½	Mod/Exp	95	D	2, 4
★★★★½	Inexp/Mod	95	B	4
★★★	Inexp/Mod	84	C	1, 3
★★★★	Mod/Exp	93	B	4
★★★½	Mod/Exp	89	C	3
★★★½	Inexp/Mod	89	C	4
★★★★½	Mod/Exp	97	C	3
★★★	Moderate	84	B	1
★★½	Inexpensive	79	A	1
★★★½	Moderate	86	B	2
★★★½	Mod/Exp	85	C	1
★★★½	Inexpensive	87	B	1
★★★	Inexp/Mod	84	B	1

Star Rating	Price	Quality Rating	Value Rating	Zone
★★★★	Mod/Exp	93	C	1
★★★	Inexp/Mod	83	B	10
★★★★½	Mod/Exp	95	C	1
★★★★	Moderate	90	C	3
★★★★	Inexp/Mod	89	B	1
★★★★	Mod/Exp	93	C	3
★★★★	Moderate	92	B	8
★★★★½	Mod/Exp	95	C	3
★★★★	Moderate	91	C	9
★★★½	Mod/Exp	88	C	4
★★★★★	Expensive	98	C	4
★★★½	Moderate	88	B	1
★★★★	Moderate	93	C	4
★★★½	Mod/Exp	88	C	10

Name of Restaurant	Cuisine
Jackie's	French/Asian
Jilly's Cafe	New American
La Bocca Della Verita	Italian
Le Français	French
Le Titi de Paris	New French
Le Vichyssois	French
Little Spain	Spanish
Lutnia Continental Cafe	Polish
The Pump Room	American/Continental
Russian Tea Cafe	Russian
Sayat Nova	Armenian
Seasons Restaurant at the Four Seasons Hotel	American
That Steak Joynt	Steak/Seafood
Trio	Fusion
Vivere (Italian Village)	Italian
Yoshi's Cafe	New French
Yvette	New French
Yvette Wintergarden	New French

Recommended for Business Dining

Name of Restaurant	Cuisine
Avanzare	Italian
Binyon's	American
Cape Cod Room	Seafood
Carlucci	Italian
Chicago Chop House	Steak
Gibson's Steakhouse	Steak
Harry Caray's	American/Italian
Kinzie Street Chophouse	Steak
La Strada	Italian
Lawry's The Prime Rib	Prime Rib
Michael Jordan's Restaurant	American
Morton Steak House	Steak
Nick's Fishmarket	Seafood
Palm Restaurant	Steak/Seafood
Prairie	Midwestern
Printer's Row	New American
Ruth's Chris Steakhouse	Steak
The Saloon	Steak

Star Rating	Price	Quality Rating	Value Rating	Zone
★★★★	Mod/Exp	90	C	1
★★★½	Inexp/Mod	85	B	11
★★★	Inexpensive	84	B	1
★★★★★	Expensive	97	C	10
★★★★½	Mod/Exp	97	C	10
★★★★½	Moderate	95	B	10
★★★	Moderate	82	B	2
★★★½	Moderate	87	C	2
★★★★	Expensive	92	C	3
★★★½	Moderate	88	C	4
★★★½	Inexp/Mod	88	C	10
★★★★½	Mod/Exp	97	C	3
★★★½	Mod/Exp	85	C	1
★★★★★	Expensive	98	C	11
★★★★½	Moderate	95	C	4
★★★★½	Mod/Exp	96	C	1
★★★½	Inexp/Mod	85	C	3
★★★½	Inexp/Mod	85	C	4

Star Rating	Price	Quality Rating	Value Rating	Zone
★★★	Moderate	82	C	3
★★★	Inexp/Mod	83	C	4
★★★★	Mod/Exp	95	C	3
★★★★½	Moderate	95	C	1
★★★★	Moderate	94	C	3
★★★★½	Mod/V. Exp	94	C	3
★★★½	Mod/Exp	86	C	4
★★★★	Moderate	91	B	4
★★★½	Mod/Exp	87	C	4
★★★★	Moderate	90	B	3
★★★½	Inexp/Mod	85	C	3
★★★★	Expensive	93	C	2, 3, 8
★★★★½	Mod/Exp	95	D	2, 4
★★★½	Mod/Exp	87	C	3
★★★★½	Mod/Exp	95	C	5
★★★★½	Moderate	95	B	5
★★★★	Mod/Exp	93	B	4
★★★½	Mod/Exp	89	C	3

— More Recommendations

Here are a few quick recommendations for special interest groups:

The Best Bagels

Bruegger's Bagel Bakery   (708) 475-1056
711 Church Street, Evanston
This is a growing national chain, and Evanston is the first store in Illinois. Bruegger's also has outlets in Naperville and Elmhurst.

Chicago Bagel Authority   (312) 248-9606
953 West Armitage Avenue

Kaufman's Bagel and Delicatessen
(708) 677-9880 / 4905 Dempster Street, Skokie

Pastiche, A Global Cafe   (312) 296-4999
4343 North Clarendon
The best bagels are available here on Sunday mornings for brunch. They're boiled and par-baked, then baked to order.

The Organic Tomato   (312) 664-7783
22 West Maple Street

The Best Bakeries

Konditorei   (312) 565-0565
Swissotel Chicago, 323 East Wacker Drive

The Corner Bakery
(312) 644-8100 / 516 North Clark Street
(312) 441-0821 / Union Station, Adams Street
  Concourse, 210 South Canal Street
(312) 335-3663 / Water Tower Place, Mezzanine,
  835 North Michigan Avenue
(708) 368-0505 / Oakbrook Center, Route 83 at
  22nd Street, Oak Brook

St. Germain Restaurant/Bakery Cafe
(312) 266-9900 / 1210 North State Parkway

Bernhardt's Bakery   (708) 362-2355
336 North Milwaukee Avenue, Libertyville
Gourmet horns with various fillings are especially good.

Foodstuffs
(708) 328-7704 / 2106 Central Avenue, Evanston
(708) 835-5105 / 338 Park Avenue, Glencoe

The Organic Tomato   (312) 664-7783
22 West Maple Street

The Bread Shop   (312) 528-8108
3400 North Halsted Street

Great Harvest Bread Co.   (708) 866-8609
2120 Central Street, Evanston

Blind Faith Cafe and Bakery   (708) 328-6875
525 Dempster Street, Evanston

Ambrosia Euro-American Patisserie
(708) 304-8278 / 710 West Northwest Highway,
   Barrington

The Best Barbecue and Ribs

Hecky's BBQ   (708) 492-1182
1902 Green Bay Road, Evanston
Rib tips, chicken wings.

Gayle Street Inn   (312) 725-1300
4914 North Milwaukee Avenue
Baby backs.

Robinson's No. 1 Ribs   (312) 337-1399
655 West Armitage Avenue
Ribs and chicken.

N. N. Smokehouse   (312) TNT-4700
1465-67 West Irving Park Road

Dixie Que   (312) 252-5600
2001 West Fullerton Avenue
St. Louis ribs and Cajun ribs.

Leon's Bar-B-Q
(312) 488-4556 / 8259 South Cottage Grove
   Avenue
(312) 778-7828 / 1158 West 59th Street
(312) 731-1454 / 1640 East 79th Street

Miller's Pub   (312) 645-5377
134 South Wabash Avenue

Twin Anchors Restaurant and Tavern
(312) 266-1616 / 1655 North Sedgwick Street
In business for over 60 years.

Bones   (708) 677-3350
7110 North Lincoln Avenue, Lincolnwood

The Best Beer Lists

Big Bar, Hyatt Regency   (312) 565-1234
151 East Wacker Drive

Jameson's Tavern   (312) 876-0016
118 South Clinton Street

Ranalli's   (312) 642-4700
1925 North Lincoln Avenue

Goose Island Brewing Company
(312) 915-0071 / 1800 North Clybourn Avenue

Millrose Brewing Company   (708) 382-7673
45 South Barrington Road, South Barrington

Cork & Carry   (312) 445-2675
10614 South Western Avenue
Seventy varieties, 12 on tap.

Joe Bailly's   (312) 238-1313
10854 South Western Avenue

Resi's Bierstube   (312) 472-1749
2034 West Irving Park Road
Perhaps the oldest beergarden in the city—over
28 years at press time; 60 imports and 6 on tap.

Red Lion Pub   (312) 348-2695
2446 North Lincoln Avenue
One of the best selections for English beers.

The Best Breakfasts

Lou Mitchell's   (312) 939-3111
565 West Jackson Boulevard

Egg Harbor Cafe   (708) 295-3449
512 North Western Avenue, Lake Forest

City Tavern   (312) 280-2740
33 West Monroe Street

3rd Coast
(312) 664-7225 / 29 East Delaware Place
(312) 649-0730 / 1260 North Dearborn Street
The Dearborn location is the original 3rd Coast.
The two are owned by brothers, but are separate
businesses, however similar. Dearborn location
open 24 hours.

Ina's Kitchen   (312) 525-1116
934 West Webster Avenue

Army & Lou's   (312) 483-3100
422 East 75th Street

Ann Sather's
(312) 348-2378 / 929 West Belmont Avenue
(312) 271-6677 / 5207 North Clark Street

The Best Burgers and Sandwiches

Bigsby's Bar & Grill   (312) 642-5200
1750 North Clark Street
Home of the Raging Bull Burger (blackened beef
with Cajun spices, guacamole, and Monterey
Jack cheese). A place to watch Bulls games.

John Barleycorn Memorial Pub, Inc.
(312) 348-8899 / 658 West Belden Avenue
Bar food, good burgers and sandwiches, salads;
classical music and art slides. Nice garden.

Hackney's
(708) 724-7171 / 1514 East Lake Avenue,
  Glenview
(708) 724-5577 / 1241 Harms Road, Glenview
Known for burgers and fried onion loaf.

Hamburger Hamlet
(708) 918-0505 / 1000 Lakeview Parkway,
  Vernon Hills
(708) 998-6900 / 1432 Waukegan Road,
  Glenview

Moody's   (312) 275-2696
5910 North Broadway
Specialties include the Moody Burger with
various cheeses. Great garden.

The Best Coffee and Dessert Places

Lutz's Continental Cafe and Pastry Shop
(312) 478-7785 / 2458 West Montrose Avenue

Cafe Express   (708) 864-1868
615 Dempster Street, Evanston

Cafe Express South   (708) 328-7940
500 Main Street, Evanston

Kenessey's Cypress   (708) 323-2727
500 East Ogden Avenue, Hinsdale

St. Germain Restaurant/Bakery Cafe
(312) 266-9900 / 1210 North State Parkway

The Best Delis

D. B. Kaplan's   (312) 280-2700
845 North Michigan Avenue

Bagel Restaurant and Deli
(312) 477-0300 / 3107 North Broadway
(708) 677-0100 / 50 Old Orchard Shopping
  Center, Skokie

Winklestein's   (312) 642-3354
1120 North State Street

The Best Hot Dogs

Gold Coast Dogs
(312) 527-1222 / 418 North State Street
(312) 327-8887 / 2100 North Clark Street
(312) 939-2624 / 325 South Franklin Street
Vienna beef dogs; friendly, accommodating
service, including curbside; also great burgers
and other sandwiches. Call about other locations
in Northwestern Atrium.

The Best Pizza

Bertucci's Brick Oven Pizza   (312) 266-3400
675 North LaSalle Street
Three other new locations in suburbs. More
thick-crust pizza pie.

California Pizza Kitchen   (312) 222-9030
414 North Orleans Street
Call about other locations. Thin-crust/gourmet.

The Original Gino's East   (708) 364-6644
1321 West Golf Road, Rolling Meadows
Award-winning pizza, rated Number One in the
nation by *People* magazine.

Pizzeria Uno   (312) 321-1000
29 East Ohio Street

Pizzeria Due   (312) 943-2400
619 North Wabash Avenue
Both Uno and Due serve Chicago-style, deep-
dish pizza.

Lou Malnati's
(312) 828-9800 / 439 North Wells Street
(708) 673-0800 / 6649 North Lincoln Avenue,
   Lincolnwood
Gourmet deep-dish and thin-crust.

Bino's   (708) 433-1231
581 Elm Street, Highland Park

Giovanni's Pizza   (708) 795-7171
6823 West Roosevelt Road, Berwyn

Edwardo's Natural Pizza Restaurant
(312) 337-4490 / 1212 North Dearborn Street
(312) 939-3366 / 521 South Dearborn Street
Call for other locations in the city and suburbs.
Some stuffed pizza versions are recommended;
Edwardo's grows its own basil.

Suparossa   (708) 867-4611
7309 West Lawrence Avenue, Harwood Heights
Call for other locations in the city and suburbs.
Original stuffed pizza (ricotta-spinach is award-
winning), pan pizza, and wood-fired oven pizza.

The Best Wine Bars

Pops for Champagne,
Champagne and Jazz Club
(312) 472-1000 / 2934 North Sheffield Avenue
Sunday jazz brunch. Adjacent Star Bar does
monthly tastings. Call (312) 472-7272.

Gypsy Restaurant and Wine Bar
(312) 644-9779 / 215 East Ohio Street

Geja's Cafe   (312) 281-9101
340 West Armitage Avenue

I Tre Merli   (312) 266-3100
316 West Erie Street
Northern Italian cuisine; late night dining.

Madison's   (312) 455-0099
1330 West Madison Street
More than 20 wines by the glass.

Restaurant Profiles

Addis Abeba

Ethiopian	★★★	Inexpensive

3521 North Clark Street
(312) 929-9383
Zone 1   North Side

Quality	Value
84	**C**

Reservations: Recommended on weekends
When to go: Weekdays are less crowded
Entree range: $7.50–9.25
Payment: All major credit cards
Service rating: ★★★
Friendliness rating: ★★★
Parking: Street, three garages nearby
Bar: Full service
Wine selection: Italian, American, and Ethiopian
Dress: Casual
Disabled access: Yes, including rest rooms
Customers: Mostly local, ethnics, and a few tourists
Dinner: Monday–Thursday, 5–10 P.M.; Friday and
    Saturday, 5–11 P.M.; Sunday, 4–10 P.M.

Atmosphere / setting: Clean, well-lit setting filled
with exotic artifacts of Ethiopia, including paintings
and handwoven straw baskets. African tablecloths with
ivory and black batik prints add to the ethnic aura.

House specialities: Fosolia (string beans, onions, and
carrots cooked in tomato sauce) is exceptional; other
vegetarian dishes of lentil, chickpeas, and mushrooms,
seasoned with exotic spices, are equally zesty; savory
doro tibs (breast of chicken stir-fried in Ethiopian herb
butter and garlic) comes mild or spicy, as do many
other entrees.

Other recommendations: Spicy appetizers such as
the sambussa, jalapeño, and lentil "egg roll" will tingle
your taste buds; katenya (spinach and cheese blended
with spiced butter and cardamom, rolled up in injera,
the spongy sour bread) is another superb tangy treat.

Summary & comments: Ethiopian dishes, most of
which are saucy, are served on communal platters,
from which customers "dip" them with injera. If eating
with friends, it is a great idea to order the vegetarian,
meat, veg-meat, or seafood and meat combinations so
you can sample the wide array of succulent dishes
available at Addis Abeba.

Aegean Isles

Greek	★★★	Inexpensive/Moderate

561 Roger Williams Avenue, (Ravinia) Highland Park

Quality	Value
84	C

(708) 433-5620
Zone 11   Northern Suburbs

Reservations: Recommended for large parties
When to go: Weekdays
Entree range: $6.95–14.95
Payment: VISA, MC, D
Service rating: ★★★★
Friendliness rating: ★★★★¹/₂
Parking: Lot
Bar: Full service
Wine selection: Extensive Greek wines
Dress: Casual
Disabled access: Wheelchair access, rest rooms
Customers: International, diverse
Dinner: Monday–Friday, 4:30–10 P.M.; Saturday and Sunday, 4:30–11 P.M.

Atmosphere / setting: Small and cozy with an open kitchen; very Greek, including wall hangings and other decor.

House specialities: Fresh fish; shrimp Aegean (sautéed with feta, flambéed with dry vermouth); ethnic Greek specialties such as dolmades (stuffed vine leaves); moussaka (layered eggplant, beef, potato, and cheese casserole); baby lamb chops; baked chicken with oregano sauce.

Other recommendations: Spinach pie appetizer; shrimp D'Angelo; chicken Aegean; roasted sweet red peppers stuffed with feta; bougatsa (pastry-custard blend) flambéed with Greek brandy.

Entertainment & amenities: Thursday, 7:30 P.M., belly dancing.

Summary & comments: The place is so small that it's almost like stepping into a home, and the service is just as personal. The menu is limited compared to other Greek tavernas, but high quality has been maintained over the years because of the caring, spirited owner. Since the restaurant is near Ravinia Park, where outdoor concerts are given in summer, Greek picnic baskets are available during the season.

Akai Hana

Japanese   ★★★½   **Inexpensive/Moderate**

	Quality	Value
3217 West Lake Avenue, Wilmette (708) 251-0384 Zone 11 Northern Suburbs	88	C

Reservations: Accepted for 6 or more
When to go: Any time
Entree range: $11–20; sushi combination boxes: lunch, $6.75–11.25; dinner, $11.75–13.50
Payment: All major credit cards
Service rating: ★★★½
Friendliness rating: ★★★★
Parking: Free
Bar: Wine and beer
Wine selection: Average for Japanese restaurant: limited—saké, some American
Dress: Casual
Disabled access: Yes
Customers: Local, including Japanese businessmen who settled in the area
Lunch: Every day, 11:30 A.M.–2 P.M.
Dinner: Monday–Thursday, 5–10 P.M.; Friday and Saturday, 5–10:20 P.M.; Sunday, 4:30–9:20 P.M.

Atmosphere / setting: Bright and bustling; white tablecloths with wooden accents.

House specialities: Sushi combination boxes; sautéed giant clam. Salmon teriyaki is one of the best dishes. Extensive appetizer list includes some very native Japanese items, such as fried shrimp heads.

Other recommendations: Teriyaki preparations; combo plates. Green tea ice cream is a refreshing finish.

Summary & comments: This restaurant grew from a grocery and became an instant success. The North Shore was lacking a good Japanese restaurant, and this place filled the niche. Suburbia overall lacks the rich, assorted ethnic dining available in the city. The success of Akai Hana is a good start toward expanding suburban culinary horizons beyond French, Italian, and American.

Alfo's Ristorante

Italian	★★½	Inexpensive

**2512 South Oakley Avenue,
Heart of Italy neighborhood**
(312) 523-6994
Zone 5   South Loop

Quality	Value
79	B

Reservations: Recommended
When to go: Any time for lunch and dinner
Entree range: $8.50–15.95
Payment: VISA, MC, AMEX, DC
Service rating: ★★★½
Friendliness rating: ★★★★½
Parking: Adjacent lot
Bar: Full service
Wine selection: Italian, some Californian
Dress: Casual
Disabled access: Yes
Customers: Diverse
Lunch: Tuesday–Friday, 11 A.M.–3 P.M.
Dinner: Tuesday–Friday, 4:30–10 P.M.; Saturday,
4:30–11 P.M.; Sunday, 2–9 P.M.

Atmosphere / setting: Cozy, intimate setting; homey
and dimly lit. Large private booths.

House specialities: Fried calamari (some of the best);
veal saltimbocca; beef braggiole.

Other recommendations: Chicken Vesuvio;
homemade ravioli; lasagna; linguini with clam sauce.

Summary & comments: This longtime establishment
is one of the anchors in this Heart of Italy neighborhood brimming with Italian eateries. Owner Josette
Pieroni is motherly and nurturing. Service takes a cue
from her direction and is caring and friendly. Food
might be more old-fashioned in style, but it's prepared
well and served with love. Very Italian and comforting.

Ambria

New French   ★★★★   **Moderate/Expensive**

Beldon Stratford Hotel, 2300 North Lincoln Park West

Quality	Value
93	C

(312) 472-0076
Zone 1   North Side

Reservations: Required
When to go: Early on weeknights; late on weekends
Entree range: $19.50–29.95
Payment: All major credit cards
Service rating: ★★★★
Friendliness rating: ★★★★
Parking: Valet, $4
Bar: Full-service, dining bar for customers only
Wine selection: Award-winning list of 570 international wines; $10–1,500 per bottle; 5 by the glass, $7–12. Sommelier is skilled at suggesting appropriate wines to go with the food and personal tastes.
Dress: Dressy; jacket required, tie optional—no denim or sneakers
Disabled access: Wheelchair accessible; call ahead for special accommodations
Customers: Sophisticated, selective clientele; international and upscale local
Dinner: Monday–Thursday, 6–9:30 P.M.; Friday and Saturday, 6–10:30 P.M.

Atmosphere / setting: Deep-toned woods, ultra suede banquettes and crystalline-etched glass with art nouveau architectural touches; tiny shaded lamps on each table; massive flower-filled urns. This place resembles an old mansion or an old club from the 1900s; murals and elegant fixtures; fashionable decor and ambiance.

House specialities: Roasted New York state foie gras with caramelized apples; loin of lamb with sweet mini-peppers and rosemary infusion; fillet of Casco Bay cod in rice paper with lobster-paprika sauce; mango parfait with berries.

Other recommendations: Baby pheasant, foie gras, wild mushrooms, and thyme broth; a symphony of market vegatables and grains; soufflé du jour.

Summary & comments: Well-established (15-plus years) crème de la crème of French restaurants and one of the top-shelf places within the Lettuce Entertain

You Enterprises group. Managing partner Gabino Sotelino maintains quality here, and Chef Takashi Yagihashi uses his innovative culinary skills to produce French cuisine légère with Italian, Spanish, and Oriental influences. Menu was recently simplified. Lovely presentations. Some flaws occasionally in food and service, but overall, a reliable place.

Honors / Awards: Four-star rating from *Chicago* magazine, *Chicago Tribune,* and *Mobil Travel Guide;* 5 diamonds from AAA; Award of Excellence for its wine celler from *Wine Spectator.*

Amourette

French ★★★ **Inexpensive/Moderate**

2275 Rand Road, Palatine

Quality	Value
83	B

(708) 359-6220

Zone 10   Northwest Suburbs

Reservations: Recommended; necessary on Friday and Saturday
When to go: Weekdays
Entree range: $9.95–22
Payment: All major credit cards
Service rating: ★★★★
Friendliness rating: ★★★★½
Parking: Lot around restaurant
Bar: Full service
Wine selection: International by bottle and glass
Dress: Casual
Disabled access: Yes
Customers: Diverse, business, couples, local, some from other locations
Lunch: Tuesday–Friday, 11:30 A.M.–2 P.M.
Dinner: Tuesday–Sunday, 5–10:30 P.M.

Atmosphere/setting: Romantic French cafe; homey; welcoming.

House specialities: Fromage de chevre sur son lit vert (Caesar salad with romaine lettuce, Parmesan cheese, Dijon mustard, Worcestershire sauce, minced anchovy, olive oil, and croutons topped with sautéed, herb-encrusted goat cheese); assortment of pâtés and fine cheeses; rack of lamb; roast duck with raspberry.

Other recommendations: Sautéed Dover sole meunière-style or almondine, filleted tableside; snapper fillets and herbal Boursin cheese in phyllo, atop fresh spinach; monthly prix-fixe, 4-course dinner, $15, Sunday–Friday.

Summary & comments: The food at this charming suburban place is well-prepared French cuisine that doesn't deviate much from the classics. Chef Michel Coatrieux keeps his cooking simple, and the finished dishes are not fussy. Amourette offers excellent French fare at reasonable prices. Restaurant is available for parties.

Ann Sather

| Swedish/American | ★★★ | Inexpensive |

929 West Belmont Avenue
(312) 348-2378
Zone 1   North Side

Quality	Value
83	**B**

5207 North Clark Street, Andersonville
(312) 271-6677
Zone 1   North Side

Reservations: Accepted for 6 or more
When to go: Any time
Entree range: $6.95–11.95
Payment: VISA, MC, AMEX
Service rating: ★★★★
Friendliness rating: ★★★★½
Parking: Lot (Belmont); access to a lot Wednesday–
    Sunday; call for details (Andersonville)
Bar: Full service, including Swedish beer
Wine selection: American
Dress: Casual
Disabled access: Yes (Belmont); no (Andersonville)
Customers: Neighborhood, family, single, senior
Open: Every day, 7 A.M.–10 P.M.

Atmosphere / setting: Hand-painted Scandinavian murals grace the walls. The original Belmont location has six rooms on two levels. Both places are comfortable and welcoming. Andersonville designates the downstairs non-smoking weekends, 9:30 A.M.–2 P.M.

House specialities: Swedish sampler (roast duck with lingonberry glaze, meatball, potato sausage, sauerkraut, and brown beans); broiled salmon with mustard dill sauce; Swedish pancakes with lingonberries.

Other recommendations: Swedish meatballs; Swedish potato sausage; large cinnamon rolls; hot peach cobbler with ice cream; Swedish spritzer.

Summary & comments: The only restaurant serving Swedish specialties other than breakfast. Community-minded, family-run business with a caring staff. Very comfortable for dining alone. Friendly staffers welcome customers of any age—kids get complimentary kiddy cocktails and rainbow sherbet.

Honors / Awards: Voted best breakfast in the Midwest, January 1994, by CBS *This Morning*.

Army & Lou's

Southern   ★★★★   **Inexpensive/Moderate**

---

422 East 75th Street
(312) 483-3100
Zone 7   South Side

Quality	Value
90	**B**

Reservations: Accepted any time for any size group
When to go: Weekdays after lunch rush
Entree range: $6.95–22.95
Payment: VISA, MC, AMEX; no checks
Service rating: ★★★★
Friendliness rating: ★★★★
Parking: Lot next door
Bar: Full service
Wine selection: About 12 selections by the glass
  only; reasonably priced; mostly Californian
Dress: Casual
Disabled access: Yes
Customers: From all over area; many out-of-state
  visitors
Open: Wednesday–Monday, 9 A.M.–10 P.M.;
  Tuesday, closed.

Atmosphere / setting: Bright, cheerful, and comfortable with light-colored sponged walls and a rotating art exhibit from the gallery across the street—African and Haitian art. Tablecloths and flowers. Non-smoking dining room.

House specialities: Fresh farm-raised catfish steaks and catfish fillet; half a fried chicken (juicy, not greasy); award-winning seafood gumbo; U.S. prime kosher short ribs of beef jardiniere; meaty baby back ribs with zesty barbecue sauce.

Other recommendations: Chicken gumbo; New England clam chowder; fried jumbo oysters; fried jumbo shrimp; cornbread stuffing; peach cobbler; sweet potato pie.

Summary & comments: This South Side restaurant is celebrating its 50th anniversary in 1995. Original recipes are used, but have been adjusted to be lower in sodium and fat. The food is excellent, the servers charming and friendly, the place comfortable, and the regulars keep returning. The place swells on Sundays after church, and politicians and community groups keep the private room busy. Children's menu.

Arun's

Thai ★★★★½ **Moderate/Expensive**

	Quality	Value
4156 North Kedzie Avenue	**95**	**C**

4156 North Kedzie Avenue
(312) 539-1909
Zone 1   North Side

Reservations: Recommended
When to go: Dinner
Entree range: $13.95–23.95
Payment: Major credit cards
Service rating: ★★★★½
Friendliness rating: ★★★★½
Parking: Street
Bar: Full service, including Thai and Japanese beers
Wine selection: International—about 2 dozen Austrian, French, Italian, and Californian wines; bottles, $18–46; 3 by the glass
Dress: Casual
Disabled access: Yes
Customers: Local and out-of-town, business, couples
Dinner: Tuesday–Saturday, 5–10 P.M.; Sunday, 5–9 P.M.; Monday, closed.

Atmosphere / setting: Colorful exterior. Beautifully appointed, multi-level interior with a small, museum-like front alcove devoted to antiques and exquisite art. The narrow upper dining area has open windows with a view into the lower dining room. Colorful authentic art and other Thai artifacts adorn the intimate rooms. Owner's brother, an artist/architect, did much of the work, and the owner's paintings decorate the rest rooms.

House specialities: Khao kriab (steamed rice dumplings filled with Dungeness crabmeat, shrimp, chicken, peanuts, garlic, and a tangy sweet-sour vinaigrette); picturesque golden baskets (flower-shaped, bite-sized pastries filled with a mixture of shrimp, chicken, sweet corn, and shiitake mushrooms, garnished with intricately carved vegetable baskets); three-flavored red snapper (crisply fried whole fish with traditional Bangkok-style three-flavored tamarind sauce: spicy, sweet, and sour); three-combination curry (country-style yellow curry with shrimp quenelle, chicken, squash, and fuzzy melon in a sauce that's hot, spicy, and peppery).

Other recommendations: Hoy tord (crusty golden mussel pancake topped with bean sprouts, garlic chive, and hot chili and sweet chili-garlic sauces); Siamese dumplings (delicate rice dumplings with minced shrimp, chicken, sweet daikon turnips, peanuts, chopped chilies, cilantro, and lettuce); chicken coconut soup; summer salad (seasonal) with mint, sprouts, and fish cake slices; gingery veal with lemongrass and miso (no veal in Thai history—the owner created this); meefun delight (soft-fried noodles with shrimp, chicken, and scallion). Desserts are delightful: seven-layer rice custard (alternating colors of white, pink, and pale green) steamed from a mixture of rice flour and coconut milk. And while poetic license was employed with the next, it's great nonetheless: poached pear in red wine with bite-sized chocolate cakes and strawberry-ginger sauce. End with a wonderful elixir of lemongrass, water, and tiny fruit balls, which is purifying and serves as a digestive.

Summary & comments: This magnificently decorated restaurant serves appropriately exquisite food. Chef/owner Arun Sampanthavivat has refined traditional Thai cuisine and elevated Thai cooking to a new fine dining plateau. The menu reveals the use of chilies, but the food doesn't cause burns and tears if you're cautious about eating the peppers. The flavor nuances are more herbal, spicy, sweet, and sour. Arun loves to carve the intricate vegetable baskets that garnish plates, and spends about two hours daily on this task. To be able to spend more time managing the business, he's appointed a Thai chef, Rang San Sutzharit, to run the kitchen. At press time, a party room was being built and the kitchen was being enlarged. The higher prices here are understandable once you taste the results of this labor-intensive cuisine.

Honors / Awards: The chef was recently named 1994 Culinary Master by the Food and Beverage Federation.

Avanzare

Italian ★★★ **Moderate**

---

161 East Huron Street
(312) 337-8056
Zone 3   Near North

Quality	Value
82	**C**

Reservations: Strongly recommended
When to go: Lunch and dinner; avoid peak times for dinner, around 7–8 P.M.
Entree range: Lunch, $10–17; dinner, $12–26
Payment: All major credit cards
Service rating: ★★★
Friendliness rating: ★★★
Parking: Ask about the discounted lot across the street at Radisson Hotel
Bar: Full service; no beer on tap
Wine selection: Wide variety of Italian and domestics; several nice choices by the glass
Dress: Upscale casual to dressy
Disabled access: Yes—call first
Customers: Local, professionals, business, travelers
Lunch: Monday–Friday, 11:30 A.M.–2 P.M.
Dinner: Monday–Thursday, 5:30–10 P.M.; Friday and Saturday, 5–11 P.M.; Sunday, 5–9:30 P.M.

Atmosphere/setting: Large and stately; beautiful display of Italian foodstuffs. Some banquettes are close together; second level has more seating. Lovely sidewalk cafe is rimmed with shrubs and a divider.

House specialities: Daily specials, including risotto (e.g., with pan-seared diver scallops, squash blossoms, and Parmesan; flavorful but with a very soft consistency); creative pastas (e.g., butternut squash ravioli with walnuts); antipasto; salmon alla griglia in port wine; delicate sautéed snapper with a mustard crust on a bed of angelhair pasta; veal chop with grilled portobello mushrooms in porcini sauce.

Other recommendations: Roasted free-range chicken with spring vegetable crisp and marsala syrup. One dessert was a crumble with an oat granola–like mixture that seemed a far cry from Italy.

Summary & comments: Chef changes left the food a bit inconsistent for awhile, but the last dinner proved hopeful, although there was room for improvement.

Bando

Korean ★★★ **Inexpensive/Moderate**

2200 Lawrence Avenue
(312) 728-7400
Zone 1   North Side

Quality	Value
83	**C**

Reservations: Accepted
When to go: Any time
Entree range: $9.95–12.95
Payment: VISA, MC, AMEX
Service rating: ★★★
Friendliness rating: ★★$^{1}/_{2}$
Parking: Free indoor parking
Bar: Full service
Wine selection: American and French
Dress: Dressy
Disabled access: Yes
Customers: Local ethnic and American
Open: Every day, 11 A.M.–11 P.M.

Atmosphere / setting: Spacious, splashy, split-level dining room with bottom-vented, built-in grills at the tables.

House specialities: Bulgoki (barbecue beef), gahl-bee (barbecue-beef short ribs), dahk bulgoki (sliced, boneless barbecue chicken), and spicy barbecue pork, all marinated, with grilled onions and mushrooms; kim chee; pan-fried, egg-battered oysters and butterfly shrimp.

Other recommendations: Spicy seafood casserole with noodles; catfish and red snapper, each prepared two ways; buckwheat noodles with sliced beef, cucumber, and a mild sauce.

Entertainment & amenities: Grilling your own dinner at your table.

Summary & comments: This Korean restaurant with large banquet facilities is popular with the Korean community. At times, there seems to be a language problem: some staffers speak and understand minimal English. The food is mainly authentic, although certain dishes are milder for American tastes. Japanese tempura and some Chinese-influenced dishes are on the menu too. Included with dinners are soup, rice, and numerous sides, Korean-style. Fresh fruit and ginseng tea make a nice finish.

Bella Vista

New Italian ★★★½ **Inexpensive/Moderate**

	Quality	Value
1001 West Belmont Avenue (312) 404-0111 Zone 1 North Side	86	C

Reservations: Recommended
When to go: Weeknights
Entree range: $6.95–15.95
Payment: All major credit cards
Service rating: ★★★½
Friendliness rating: ★★★★
Parking: Valet, $4
Bar: Yes
Wine selection: 300 international selections, $19–150; substantial Italian; 10 by the glass, $4.50–6.50
Dress: Casual
Disabled access: Yes
Customers: Younger professional, affluent, couples, families with young children
Lunch: Monday–Saturday, 11:30 A.M.–5 P.M.
Dinner: Monday–Thursday, 5 P.M.–midnight; Friday and Saturday, 5 P.M.–2 A.M.; Sunday, 5–10 P.M.

Atmosphere / setting: The name "beautiful view" says it well—a stunning interior and elegant, award-winning architecture in the former Belmont Trust and Savings Bank from 1929, a historic landmark building; beaux-arts motif with exquisite hand-painted walls, walk-through wine cellar, inlaid Italian marble floor, and wood-fire stove; copper- and glass–enclosed pizza kitchen; 30-foot ceiling. Seats 300 on 5 levels. Every table has a good view.

House specialities: Antipasto del Giorno with seasonal oak-roasted vegetables, seafood salad, oak-roasted potato salad, and two other selections; gourmet wood-fire pizzas (e.g., fresh basil pesto, tomatoes, pine nuts, and fresh mozzarella; or roasted potato, grilled eggplant, olives, spicy tomato sauce, and fresh Parmesan); black pepper linguini with shiitake and portobello mushrooms, and baby artichokes in a mushroom-rosemary broth; free-form lamb and potato torta (grilled loin of lamb layered with potato "sheets," bacon, spinach, caramelized onions, and fresh mint).

Other recommendations: Oak-roasted calamari marinated in lemon and fresh rosemary with plum tomatoes and wilted arugula; Gorgonzola salad with endive, watercress, pears, peppered pecans, and red wine vinaigrette.

Entertainment & amenities: Architectural tours of the restaurant are a "must see."

Summary & comments: The architecture and interior design are a feast for the eyes, and the dishes are colorful and intricately presented. The former chef's philosophy was to create food to outshine the decor, and at times this was confusing to the palate. There was a lot happening on most plates—a panoply of garnishes and little sides; however, the flavors tended to complement the main ingredients. The new chef, David Kasuh, is making his mark in the kitchen and is already simplifying presentations. At this writing, the restaurant hired a top wine consultant, Robert Rohden, to assist with the wine program.

Benkay

Japanese ★★★★¹/₂ **Moderate/Expensive**

	Quality	Value
Hotel Nikko, 320 North Dearborn Street	95	D

(312) 836-5490
Zone 4   The Loop

Reservations: Accepted
When to go: Busiest times are dinner hours
Entree range: $7.50–25
Payment: All major credit cards
Service rating: ★★★★¹/₂
Friendliness rating: ★★★★¹/₂
Parking: Valet
Bar: Full service
Wine selection: International, some Japanese
Dress: Business
Disabled access: Yes
Customers: Business, including Japanese, family, tourist
Breakfast: Tuesday–Saturday, 7–10 A.M.
Lunch: Tuesday–Saturday, 11:30 A.M.–2 P.M.
Dinner: Tuesday–Saturday, 5:30–10 P.M.

Atmosphere / setting: Exquisite, authentic Japanese decor. Main dining room has the Chicago River and the hotel's Japanese gardens as a backdrop. Six tatami rooms provide private environments: 1 room for 2 people; 3 rooms seating 2 to 6 people; and 2 rooms seating up to 18 people. Guests are seated upon tatami mats, with their backs supported in comfortable chairs and their feet in recessed floor wells. Waitresses wear kimonos. Sensational Japanese table settings.

House specialities: Authentic Japanese breakfast served in a beautiful lacquered box holding assorted delicacies, $24; sushi and sashimi available a la carte; also sushi dinners, $25–35; special dinner sets offering various specialties, from teriyaki and tempura to nabeyaki udon with sushi, udon noodles, and shrimp tempura, $22.50–38.50. All dinners are served with an appetizer, miso soup, salad, Japanese pickles, rice, and dessert. Grilled salmon with crispy, dried, seasoned seaweed; an assortment of simmered vegetables (squash, carrots, shiitake mushrooms, and pea pods); steamed rice; soybean paste soup; pickled Japanese vegetables (red turnip, radish, cucumber, and eggplant); fresh fruit in season and choice of coffee or traditional Japanese green tea.

Other recommendations: Lunch: noodles express menu, $7.30–12; sushi lunch special (assortment with chef's choice of nine sushi pieces); full-course dining menus, including shabu shabu kaiseki, sukiyaki kaiseki, sushi kaiseki, plus three special menus for the connoisseur that require a 24-hour advance reservation, $45–100. And for those with simple tastes, try the bean curd with scallions and ginger or the steamed egg with a thick bonito-flavored sauce and shredded seaweed.

Summary & comments: The Hotel Nikko Chicago, which opened in 1987, is a 20-story, 421-room international luxury hotel which manages its top-notch restaurants carefully and with style. Benkay is the quintessential Japanese restaurant with great attention to proper authentic detail. Dining here may be costly, but it is a memorable cultural experience.

The Berghoff

German/American   ★★★¹/₂   **Inexpensive**

---

17 West Adams Street
(312) 427-3170
Zone 4   The Loop

Quality	Value
88	B

Reservations: Recommended for 5 or more
When to go: Busy at lunchtime and the early dinner hour, so avoid if you're in a rush; generally fast service.
Entree range: Lunch, average $6.95; dinner, $8.25–14.50
Payment: VISA, MC, AMEX, DC
Service rating: ★★★¹/₂
Friendliness rating: ★★★★
Parking: Discount in nearby garages after 4 P.M.
Bar: Full service; The Berghoff's own regular and dark beer is available on tap
Wine selection: Extensive German, French, American, and Italian; inexpensive house wines available by the glass, half and full liter
Dress: Summer, casual; winter tends to be dressier (more suits and ties, although ties are not required)
Disabled access: Yes, including rest rooms
Customers: Local, including a loyal German clientele; some tourists
Lunch/Dinner: Monday–Thursday, 11 A.M.–9:30 P.M.; Friday and Saturday, 11 A.M.–10 P.M.

Atmosphere / setting: Turn-of-the-century building; old paintings; lots of wood in spacious dining room, which is decorated with traditional dried flowers and branches. Rathskeller downstairs serves lunch.

House specialities: Good traditional German specialties: sauerbrauten and Wiener schnitzel; seafood such as fillet of sole with roasted almonds and lemon-parsley butter. Daily specials include some German items, such as schlacht-platte (a combination of bratwurst, "Kasseler Rippchen," and smoked Thuringer with kraut). Creamed herring and chilled smoked salmon are two nice appetizers.

Other recommendations: Seafood de Jonghe; veal medallions in mushroom-sherry wine sauce; chicken schnitzel; broiled swordfish steak; Black Forest torte.

Summary & comments: The menu proudly states, "family operated since 1898," when Herman Joseph Berghoff opened his cafe as a showcase for his celebrated dormunder-style beer. In a day when restaurants' life spans are shorter, this longevity is quite an achievement. The Berghoff is a Chicago landmark due to the good quality German traditional food and many other dishes, fine Berghoff beer and Berghoff bourbon, low prices, old-world atmosphere, and efficient service. The management has modernized the menu to satisfy current desires—lighter fare, including seafood, salads, and light entrees. There are just a few standard German dishes on the regular menu, and several appear among the substantial number of specials each weekday along with American (e.g., Southwestern-style salmon) and even Italian entrees (e.g., linguini with angry shrimp). The delicious, textured bread here is made from the brewery side-products (hops, etc.), and loaves are sold to carry home. Accomodating waiters wear old-world black trousers, white shirts, and aprons. This place is a great success story, serving 2,000 a day in the street-level dining room and downstairs for lunch. Private parties and catering are available.

Bice Ristorante

Italian   ★★★¹/₂   **Moderate/Expensive**

---

158 East Ontario Street
(312) 664-1474
Zone 3   Near North

Quality	Value
87	**D**

Reservations: Recommended
When to go: Wednesday, Thursday, and Sunday
Entree range: Lunch, $10–17; dinner, $11–21
Payment: All major credit cards except Discover
Service rating: ★★★¹/₂
Friendliness rating: ★★★
Parking: Valet
Bar: Full service
Wine selection: On the costly end; 110 selections, mostly Italian with touch of American and French; $25–300 a bottle; 8 by the glass, exclusively Italian and California cabernet, $10
Dress: Moderately casual to upscale; shorts discouraged except in the garden in summer
Disabled access: Wheelchair; no rest room access
Customers: Diverse, business, Italian; sophisticated
Lunch: Monday–Saturday, 11:30 A.M.–2:30 P.M.
Dinner: Monday–Thursday, 5:30–10:30 P.M.; Friday and Saturday, 5:30–11:30 P.M.; Sunday, 5:30–10 P.M.

Atmosphere / setting: Upscale, contemporary Italian, art deco; well-lit, fun, and lively atmosphere. Bar area in front opens onto sidewalk via large doors. Outdoor cafe on the side and sidewalk cafe, weather permitting.

House specialities: Menu changes daily. Fresh pastas; tuna carpaccio on a bed of frisse with a citronette dressing (appetizer); risotto fruitti di mare; panesotti stuffed with wild game and topped with a white truffle–butter sauce; orange cake glazed with bitter-sweet chocolate.

Other recommendations: Veal Milanese; tiramisu; homemade ice creams and sorbets in several flavors.

Summary & comments: A chic place with prices to match, but the steady crowds here don't seem to care. It's a gathering spot for many of the Italian foodies. Excellent, very Italian food and comprehensive menu, but pricey, even for a pasta dish. Service is professional and attentive.

The Big Bowl Cafe

American ★★★ **Inexpensive**

159-1/2 West Erie Street
(312) 787-8297
Zone 3   Near North

Quality	Value
82	B

Reservations: Not accepted
When to go: Avoid busiest times: peak lunchtime and
dinnertime, around 7 P.M.
Entree range: $4.95–8.95
Payment: All credit cards accepted
Service rating: ★★★¹/₂
Friendliness rating: ★★★¹/₂
Parking: Valet at the adjacent Eccentric
Bar: Full service; good selection of beers
Wine selection: 5 Californian and 1 Italian by glass or
bottle; modestly priced
Dress: Casual
Disabled access: Yes
Customers: Mixed locals including business,
professionals, and couples
Open: Monday–Thursday, 11:30 A.M.–10 P.M.;
Friday and Saturday, 11:30 A.M.–11 P.M.;
Sunday, 5–9 P.M.

Atmosphere / setting: Very small, narrow room that
resembles a porch. Casual, non-smoking with 50 seats.

House specialities: Unique creations with strong
Asian and Mexican influences—all served in a bowl.
New-wave pot stickers (ginger chicken, vegetable and
mushroom, shrimp and roasted garlic, with sauces such
as citrus-soy and hot mustard); smoked chicken,
poblano, and goat cheese quesadilla; vegetarian chili;
stir-fried vegetable rice; chicken salad with plum
dressing, cashews, and wontons.

Other recommendations: Small dishes: mango
guacamole and chips; "soup of the moment" is usually
great. Big bowls: roasted corn tortilla stew with grilled
chicken and avocado. "Killer combos" offer a
sampling of the key dishes listed. Brownie cheesecake
with raspberry sauce; caramelized pears.

Summary & comments: The food is very lively in
flavor and texture, although much of it is soothing and
comforting. Whatever you cannot finish can be carried
out in "porta-bowls."

Big Shoulders

American	★★★	Inexpensive

Chicago Historical Society,
  1601 North Clark Street

Quality	Value
82	B

(312) 587-7766
Zone 1   North Side

Reservations: Recommended
When to go: Lunch, dinner, Sunday brunch
Entree range: Lunch, $5.95–7.95; dinner, $8.95–13.95
Payment: VISA, MC, AMEX, DC
Service rating: ★★★½
Friendliness rating: ★★★½
Parking: Street or metered lot in park nearby
Bar: Full service
Wine selection: American
Dress: Casual
Disabled access: Yes
Customers: Locals and visitors to the Chicago Historical Society
Brunch: Sunday, 10:30 A.M.–3 P.M.
Lunch: Every day, 11:30 A.M.–3 P.M.
Dinner: Wednesday–Sunday, 5–8 P.M.

Atmosphere/setting: The restaurant is a semicircle enclosed in glass and resembles a greenhouse. It features murals, a magnificent terra-cotta arch (from the bank at the Union Exchange), and high ceilings. Windows overlook a lovely garden.

House specialities: Grilled chicken Caesar salad; homemade daily soups; Sheboygan-style bratwurst. Signature whole-wheat millet bread and jalapeño corn bread come with selections.

Other recommendations: Wild rice cakes with wild mushroom sauce; sirloin salad with asparagus, pistachios, chevre, and sherry-mustard vinaigrette; apple-streusel pie a la mode.

Entertainment & amenities: Most evenings, live classical guitar, piano, or other music. Occasional poetry slams (contests).

Summary & comments: Named for Carl Sandburg's description of our city in his poem, "Chicago," this lovely restaurant has a special intellectual style befitting the Chicago Historical Society and what it represents. Owner Jerome F. Kliejunas has long been a proponent of additive-free, fresh, natural ingredients and smoke-free dining. He maintains that health consciousness here and states on his menus, "If the selection seems limited, it's because I believe one of the keys to maintaining my standard is to try to do a few things well." His simple fare is attractively presented and freshly prepared with harmonious flavors. The short dinner menu, including pasta, fish, chicken breast sandwiches, and hamburgers, is appropriate for a place that closes early. Catering is available for business meetings of 30 to weddings of 300.

Biggs

Continental/French ★★★★ **Moderate**

1150 North Dearborn Street
(312) 787-0900
Zone 3   Near North

Quality	Value
90	**C**

Reservations: Recommended
When to go: Dinner
Entree range: $11–23
Payment: All major credit cards
Service rating: ★★★½
Friendliness rating: ★★★★
Parking: Valet, $5
Bar: Full service
Wine selection: Intelligently balanced wine cellar holds mostly domestic and numerous French selections, many of note (e.g., 1945 Château Latour, $1,050). Several wines from Spain, Italy, Germany, Austria, New Zealand, and Australia. Bottles from $15.50; several by the glass, from $4.
Dress: Casual elegance
Disabled access: No ramp; stairs to restaurant. If customer can be helped up the stairs, the bathroom is accessible
Customers: Yuppie, business, couples—especially on weekends
Dinner: Every day, 5–10 P.M.

Atmosphere/setting: This romantic restaurant is set in an elegant, historic Victorian mansion (1874) with a paneled foyer, a curved stairway with a wood bannister, parquet floors, Italian marble mantles in the Red Room, and exquisite carved mantles in the library and the original formal dining room. There's also an outdoor cafe.

House specialities: Escargot in curry and mango sauce; classic beef Wellington with truffle sauce; rack of lamb au jus with garlic sauce; sautéed salmon with smoked salmon sauce and caviar; escallop of veal and fresh morels; roast pheasant.

Other recommendations: Lobster and spinach gratin; ballotine of duck with pistachios; sautéed snapper fillet with crayfish and velouté of wild mushrooms; broiled whitefish. Homemade desserts and pastries include browned thin apple tart; white and dark chocolate mousse with fresh raspberries; individual strawberry and blueberry pies. Also a terrace and bar menu with light foods, such as chilled seafood salad and baked quiche Provençal.

Summary & comments: This is one of the few landmark mansions housing a restaurant in the Chicago area, and owner Peter Salchow has preserved the gracious and intimate surroundings. The grey brick mansion was built by John DeKoven and his family. The second owner was Joseph Biggs, who managed his catering business from the coach house and catered the most social parties of the day. Today, Biggs carries on the tradition and caters parties for up to 175 people. The food has maintained a high quality over the years, evolving from modern continental to classic/creative French, to a blend of the two.

Honors / awards: 5 Diamond Award

Binyon's

American　　★★★　　**Inexpensive/Moderate**

327 South Plymouth Court
(312) 341-1155
Zone 4　　The Loop

Quality	Value
83	**C**

Reservations: Recommended
When to go: Lunch and dinner
Entree range: Lunch, $6.95–12.95; dinner, $8.95–18.95
Payment: All major credit cards
Service rating: ★★★½
Friendliness rating: ★★★★
Parking: Street
Bar: Full service
Wine selection: Largely American with a few Italian and French choices; fairly priced; several by the glass
Dress: Casual and business
Disabled access: No
Customers: Lawyers, brokers, bankers
Lunch: Monday–Friday, 11:30 A.M.–4:30 P.M.
Dinner: Monday–Saturday, 4:30–9 P.M.

Atmosphere / setting: Three floors of traditional dining rooms date back to Prohibition days; old-style decor is comfortable with booths and tables.

House specialities: Velvety turtle soup with glass of sherry; crab cakes; shrimp de Jonghe; roast prime ribs; imported English Dover sole; spinach salad. Baked oysters and scallops Binyon de Jonghe are exemplary.

Other recommendations: Sautéed calf's sweetbreads; sautéed veal kidneys; Delmonico steak; lamb and pork chops; Caesar salad (half orders available).

Summary & comments: This bastion of old Chicago dining maintains its quality culinary traditions in a gracious atmosphere. It has been in this Loop location since 1941. The original de Jonghe garlic-butter and breadcrumb preparation was introduced here in the 1940s by an employee; the de Jonghe entrees remain signature items today. The menu is straightforward with simple listings. Entrees include soup or salad, vegetable, and choice of starch. The last sampling of desserts included a coarse, dense rice pudding and an apple strudel that could have been flakier.

Bistro 110

French Bistro ★★★½ **Moderate**

---

110 East Pearson Street
(312) 266-3110
Zone 3   Near North

Quality	Value
86	**C**

Reservations: Recommended for 5 or more
When to go: Any time
Entree range: $10–17
Payment: All major credit cards
Service rating: ★★★½
Friendliness rating: ★★★★½
Parking: Valet
Bar: Full service
Wine selection: Extensive French and domestics
Dress: Casual
Disabled access: Yes
Customers: Neighborhood, local, business, tourist, shoppers, hip urbanites
Brunch: Outdoor seating for Sunday jazz brunch, 11 A.M.–3 P.M.
Lunch/Dinner: Monday–Thursday, 11:30 A.M.–11 P.M.; Friday and Saturday, 11:30 A.M.–midnight; Sunday, 11:30 A.M.–10 P.M.

Atmosphere / setting: Outdoor cafe; inside seats 135 in the dining room, 56 in the cafe; colorful murals.

House specialities: Oven-roasted whole garlic served with fresh crusty French bread; wood-roasted chicken, snapper, and other fish specials usually served with an array of roasted vegetables; onion soup; creative pastas (e.g., linguini with rock shrimp).

Other recommendations: Clafoutis "tutti frutti" berries; apple tarte au chevre pouliguy; crème brûlée.

Entertainment & amenities: Sunday New Orleans–style jazz brunch featuring the Grady Johnson Jazz Trio. Occasional French promotions with exchange chefs.

Summary & comments: Very alive, energetic bistro that is like a scene out of Paris. One of the loveliest views of the historic Water Tower. Food is well-prepared and especially flavorful and healthful from the wood oven. Pastries for savory and sweet tarts are flaky and very French in nature. This place can reach high decibels on a bustling night.

Blackhawk Lodge

New American ★★★ **Moderate**

41 East Superior Street
(312) 280-4080
Zone 3   Near North

Quality	Value
82	**C**

Reservations: Recommended
When to go: Any time
Entree range: Lunch, $7.95–14.95; dinner, $10.95–21.95
Payment: All major credit cards
Service rating: ★★★★
Friendliness rating: ★★★½
Parking: Valet in the evenings; self-park garage in the building
Bar: Full service
Wine selection: Domestic, $16–50 per bottle
Dress: Casual; some business and dressy
Disabled access: Yes
Customers: Neighborhood locals, business, tourists, shoppers
Brunch: Sunday, 11:30 A.M.–3 P.M.
Lunch/Dinner: Monday–Thursday, 11:30 A.M.–10 P.M.; Friday, 11:30 A.M.–11 P.M.; Saturday, 5–11 P.M. (outdoor seating available)

Atmosphere / setting: Rustic yet gracious setting resembles a family vacation home. Warm and welcoming environment designed by restaurant architect Marve Cooper in collaboration with owners Doug Roth and Larry and Mark Levy of Levy Restaurants. The four sections of the restaurant include the entry and bar with dining seats, the main dining room (smoke-free), the porch and the gazebo (with 50 outdoor seats). Indoor decor includes oak floors, knotty pine paneling, timber walls, wicker furniture, tapestries, and textured fabrics. Decorative appointments feature family photos and Audubon prints.

House specialities: Award-winning barbecue ribs; pan-fried Idaho trout; signature cheddar cheese grits with tasso ham; roasted turkey filet with mashed potatoes, rhubarb chutney, and sage cream; Granny Smith apple pie.

Other recommendations: Corn chowder; crabcakes; goat cheese soufflé; applewood-smoked sturgeon and cured salmon; cappuccino ice-cream pie.

Entertainment & amenities: Live jazz at Sunday brunch.

Summary & comments: This place suggests an era when life was easygoing and basic values centered around family and honesty. The back-to-basics cuisine with regional influences focuses on simple preparations with creative touches. Shortly before press time, Charles Weber was named executive chef; his fine reputation and early reports of his minor changes to the menu indicate that the food will be improving.

Honors / Awards: *Chicago* magazine's 1992 Critic's Choice Award; Ribs voted second best in Chicago by the *Chicago Tribune*.

Blind Faith Cafe

Vegetarian	★★½	Inexpensive

---

525 Dempster Street, Evanston
(708) 328-6875
Zone 11   Northern Suburbs

Quality	Value
79	**B**

Reservations: Accepted weekdays only for 4 or more
When to go: Avoid peak mealtimes; any time OK
Entree range: $6.50–8.95
Payment: VISA, MC, AMEX
Service rating: ★★★
Friendliness rating: ★★★★
Parking: Street (metered)
Bar: Wine and beer; juice bar
Wine selection: Organic house red and white wines, $17 average cost per bottle; $4 a glass; different wine featured every 2 weeks
Dress: Casual
Disabled access: No special accommodations, but easy access for disabled
Customers: A lively mix of students and professors from Northwestern University, singles, couples and families, local Blind Faith diehards, visitors from downtown and out of town; the health conscious and the curious
Bakery: Monday–Friday, 8 A.M.–7 P.M.; Saturday and Sunday, 8 A.M.–8 P.M.
Breakfast: Monday–Friday, 10 A.M.–2 P.M.; Saturday and Sunday, 8 A.M.–2 P.M.
Lunch/Dinner: Monday–Saturday, 2–10 P.M.; Sunday, 2–8 P.M.

Atmosphere/setting: The dominating theme is wholesomeness and freshness. The restaurant is divided into two spacious sections, the casual dining room and the self-serve, cafe-style area and juice bar. There's an adjacent bakery. Similar to a gas station, you must decide on full-serve or self-serve dining. Eating areas are airy and spacious, with large windows allowing natural sunlight or moonlight to filter through. The bright, comfortable atmosphere is enhanced by colorful handmade quilts adorning the walls.

House specialities: Breakfast: chilaquiles, eggs, or tofu sautéed with onions, tortilla chips, and salsa, and served with rice, black beans, guacamole, and sour cream; homemade granola with choice of milk, cider, soy milk, or yogurt. Lunch/dinner: broccoli-shoyu-soba stir-fry with pea pods and seitan in a sesame-tamari sauce, on Japanese buckwheat noodles; grilled goat cheese and spinach sandwich on house spinach-feta bread, with brown rice and carrot-cilantro salad; macrobiotic plate (brown rice topped with shiitake mushroom sauce, vegetable and bean of the day, steamed kale vinaigrette, cup of miso soup, and a pickle); fruit smoothie with choice of flavors (e.g., blueberry-banana, raspberry-peach).

Other recommendations: Breakfast: banana-almond pancakes; cinnamon-raisin French toast. Lunch/dinner: pecan scallopini on fresh linguini, marinara, and melted mozzarella; spicy seitan fajitas mixed with sautéed onions, peppers, and tomatoes, with guacamole, refried beans, rice, and tortillas; black bean burrito; peanut-butter-tofu-banana shake.

Summary & comments: Over a decade ago the owner started this cafe considering "the health of the human body as well as health of our planet." Today it is one of Chicago's best known and respected vegetarian restaurants. All the dishes are prepared with fresh, unprocessed, and mostly organic ingredients. Overall, the cooking is straightforward, and some dishes are actually bland. The drinking water, coffee, and tea are carbon filtered. The restaurant also provides dairy-free and low-fat alternatives, offering soy cheese, milk, and yogurt. The menu's glossary describes some of the more unusual and exotic items and may offer further enlightenment (for example, Hajiki is "a black sea vegetable with a distinct 'sweetfood' flavor—very high in calcium and other minerals"). If you want your experience to extend beyond the dining hours, bring home some baked goods. The bakery offers innovative treats such as: potato-dill bread, tofu no-cheesecake, and hippie cookies (with raisins, mixed dried fruit, vanilla soy milk, and honey), as well as such tradition-al fare as banana bread, raisin-bran muffins, and chunky chocolate cookies. Some are pure decadence, but since they're made with all-natural ingredients, you can feel good about indulging.

Blue Mesa

Southwestern ★★★★ **Inexpensive/Moderate**

1729 North Halsted Street
(312) 944-5990
Zone 1   North Side

Quality	Value
89	**B**

Reservations: Accepted
When to go: Any time
Entree range: $8–13
Payment: VISA, MC, AMEX, D, DC
Service rating: ★★★1/2
Friendliness rating: ★★★★1/2
Parking: Valet, $4
Bar: Full service
Wine selection: Limited Spanish and American
Dress: Casual
Disabled access: Yes
Customers: Mixed
Brunch: Sunday, 11 A.M.–2:30 P.M.
Lunch: Monday–Saturday, 11:30 A.M.–2:30 P.M.
Dinner: Monday–Saturday, 5–10:30 P.M.

Atmosphere/setting: Authentic adobe restaurant with kiva fireplaces and large, rounded rooms with dried chilies and native artwork on the white stucco walls. Outdoor patio.

House specialities: Enchilada del Mar, a blend of shrimp, scallops, fish, corn, mushrooms, and leeks in a lobster chipotle sauce, between two blue corn tortillas and topped with cheese. Blue corn enchiladas; some of the best chicken and steak fajitas around; Santa Fe pizza with homemade chorizo. Sopapillas are served with most entrees. Desserts include white chocolate quesadilla and adobe pie cajeta with ice cream and caramel sauce.

Other recommendations: Taste of Santa Fe appetizer includes grilled sirloin with roasted tomatillo sauce, guacamole, barbecue chicken wings, and blackened shrimp with tequila butter. The Grande Platter includes seafood chalupa, chicken enchilada, chili relleno with red chili sauce, posole, and fiesta salad. Crossing the border, there's a Tex-Mex combination with barbecue chicken and blackened shrimp.

Summary & comments: This authentic adobe restaurant is devoted to the unique cuisine of New Mexico, with some creative license. The cooking and atmosphere pay tribute to Santa Fe culture, which is an exciting blend of Indian and Spanish traditions. The Marienthal brothers built this gem after researching it carefully. Enjoy a drink at the lovely bar and then move to the dining room for a meal that gives a taste of historical Santa Fe right in Chicago.

Bob Chinn's Crab House

Seafood ★★★ **Moderate**

---

393 South Milwaukee Avenue, Wheeling

Quality	Value
82	B

(708) 520-3633
Zone 10   Northwest Suburbs

Reservations: Accepted only for 6 or more; number system used
When to go: Any day before 6 P.M. or after 9 P.M.
Entree range: $9.95–34.95
Payment: All major credit cards
Service rating: ★★★
Friendliness rating: ★★★
Parking: Valet, $2
Bar: Full service
Wine selection: Wide range of Californian; approximately 40 wines
Dress: Casual
Disabled access: Yes
Customers: Diverse, international, couples, family, business
Lunch: Monday–Friday, 11 A.M.–2:30 P.M.; Saturday, noon–3 P.M.
Dinner: Monday–Thursday, 4:30–10:30 P.M.; Friday, 4:30–11:30 P.M.; Saturday, 3–11:30 P.M.; Sunday, 3–10 P.M.

Atmosphere / setting: Similar to an old-fashioned crab house, except vaster and bustling, often with fast-moving lines of people. Very casual, no-frills, high-volume, 650-seat eatery. Walls are adorned with memorabilia, kudos, and air-freight receipts as proof of the freshness of the supplies. Sinks are available for rinsing your hands after peeling shrimp and eating lobster and crab.

House specialities: Alaskan Dungeness crab; raw bar; variety of fresh fish.

Other recommendations: Beer-batter fried-fish sampler with dipping sauces; six-way fish special (e.g., Hawaiian onaga prepared different ways; often some Oriental preparations); aged steak dishes including prime New York strip steak on a sizzling platter.

Summary & comments: Early raw bar special offered daily is a great value and a nice appetizer while you wait for a table. Helpful, efficient staff is used to quick service and instructing diners on how to dismember a Dungeness crab. This is an amazingly high-volume place (serving an average of 2,500 people a day!) that maintains its consistently high quality and fair pricing. Owner Bob Chinn and his wife, Marilyn, run this establishment with marketing savvy. Every piece of fish from the trimming of fillets is used in the fish samplers. Although not a relaxed environment, with the loudspeaker booming out numbers and lines of the hungry and the fed coming and going, it's worth it for the good selection of simply prepared seafood.

Honors / Awards: Silver Platter Award; Restaurant and Institutions 1993 "Top Ten Independents" award (served 1,200,000 per year).

Bones

Barbecue ★★¹/₂ **Inexpensive/Moderate**

**7110 North Lincoln Avenue,
  Lincolnwood**
(708) 677-3350
Zone 11   Northern Suburbs

Quality	Value
78	**C**

Reservations: Accepted
When to go: Avoid busy weekends when there might
  be a wait
Entree range: $9.95–17.95
Payment: All major credit cards
Service rating: ★★★¹/₂
Friendliness rating: ★★★★
Parking: Lot
Bar: Full service
Wine selection: Medium-sized list; mostly domestic,
  house wines, and a limited selection of others,
  including Italian
Dress: Casual
Disabled access: Yes
Customers: Mixed locals; weekdays more business;
  weekends more families and couples
Lunch/Dinner: Sunday–Thursday, 11:30 A.M.–
  10:30 P.M.; Friday and Saturday, 11:30
  A.M.–midnight.
Carryout Store: Monday–Thursday, 4–
  10:30 P.M.; Friday and Saturday, 4 P.M.–
  midnight; Sunday, 3–10 P.M. Orders are accepted
  at host stand when carryout store is closed

Atmosphere / setting: Big bar/lounge and adjacent
dining rooms seat 280. Decorated whimsically with
logos of theaters, hotels, radio stations, and the late
Riverview Park, as well as sports memorabilia and
caricatures of Chicago celebrities.

House specialities: Hickory slow-smoked barbecue
baby back ribs and chicken; Sima's whole garlic
chicken; roasted brisket with potato pancakes; center-
cut skirt steak; Lake Superior whitefish and salmon;
shrimp prepared several ways; buffalo chicken wings;
shrimp or chicken Caesar salads.

Other recommendations: Combination platters:
select two items from barbecue, garlic chicken, brisket,
garlic shrimp, and more, served with soup or salad and
potato. Appetizers: spinach fingers, potato skins, garlic

chicken fingers. Chilled poached salmon fillet salad; Mediterranean chicken with pasta; blue-cheese burger; Skoog pie (rich with caramel, chocolate, and nuts); key lime pie.

Entertainment & amenities: Browsing through the art and memorabilia.

Summary & comments: This is one of the oldest Lettuce Entertain You Enterprises places, and the name says what it specializes in. Watch for a menu update with additional vegetarian items soon. Casual and bustling. Private parties accommodated.

The Bread Shop

Vegetarian	★★¹/₂	Inexpensive

3400 North Halsted Street
(312) 528-8108
Zone 1   North Side

Quality	Value
79	**B**

Reservations: Not accepted
When to go: 8–11:30 A.M.
Entree range: $5–10
Payment: VISA, MC
Service rating: ★★¹/₂
Friendliness rating: ★★★¹/₂
Parking: Street (metered)
Bar: None
Wine selection: None
Dress: Casual
Disabled access: No special accommodations;
   entrance is easy; rest rooms around a corner and up a
   step
Customers: All ages, local, visitor, the health-
   conscious, couples, family
Open: Monday–Saturday, 8 A.M.–10 P.M.; Sunday,
   9 A.M.–9 P.M. Same menu day and evening.

Atmosphere / setting: Friendly, lively, and casual;
cafeteria-style setup; outdoor cafe and indoor seating.
They don't cook to order.

House specialities: Whole-wheat focaccia with pesto
and feta; veggie pâté; chili, veggie burgers, and
burritos; specials change daily; baked-on-premise
breads (e.g., cheese herb, millet sesame, multi-grain
sourdough, peach breakfast bread, jalapeño corn,
pumpkin, saffron, and lemon tea); cookies; muffins
(e.g., banana chip, date nut, and pecan orange); scones
(fruit and chocolate chip-mocha); cakes; pies (e.g.,
apricot, mock mincemeat, squash). The regular breads
are not very crusty, such as those that are hearth-baked.

Other recommendations: Falafel; pizza; vegetable
quiche; tofu dips and spreads prepared in various
ethnic ways (e.g., Indian, Mexican, or "deviled").
Standard items such as hummus and tabbouleh.

Entertainment & amenities: Browsing through the
grocery store and bakery attached to the restaurant;
bread-making classes are offered on Sundays.

Summary & comments: This pioneer on busy Halsted has expanded and evolved into a one-stop shopping combination cafe, deli, juice bar, and grocery from the original bakery shop. Very pure vegetarian and natural food, in keeping with owner Kay Stepkin's philosophy about the importance of organically grown products and chemical-free ingredients. She had a vision more than two decades ago, long before the acceptance of natural foods, and had the courage and perseverance to nurture her business while nourishing customers. She says the Bread Shop's mission is to provide the most wholesome and natural foods that are also delicious. The chocolate is sweetened with barley malt, the eggs come from uncaged chickens (free of antibiotics), the oil is unrefined, and most of the grains are organic. All cooking and baking is done with filtered water. Probably the city's largest variety of natural, house-made foods—many of them healthy versions of ethnic specialties. The Bread Shop also makes dishes for special diets. Grocery sells bulk. Big catering and takeout business.

Honors / Awards: Oldest natural food store in Chicago, open since 1971.

Bruna's Ristorante

Italian ★★★ **Inexpensive/Moderate**

2424 South Oakley Avenue

Quality	Value
80	**B**

(312) 254-5550

Zone 5   South Loop

Reservations: Recommended

When to go: Any time for lunch or dinner

Entree range: $8.95–16.95

Payment: VISA, MC, AMEX, DC, CB, D

Service rating: ★★★¹/₂

Friendliness rating: ★★★★¹/₂

Parking: Street; valet on Friday and Saturday evenings

Bar: Full service

Wine selection: Mostly Italian, including restaurant's private label imported from Italy (Vino Nobile di Montepulciano and chianti); some excellent selections, $15.50–95 per bottle; some great choices by the glass, $3.50–4.50

Dress: Casual

Disabled access: No, but wheelchairs could be helped up the two steps

Customers: Diverse, business, especially for lunch; couples and family, especially for dinner

Lunch/Dinner: Monday–Thursday, 11 A.M.–10 P.M.; Friday and Saturday, 11 A.M.–11 P.M.; Sunday, 1–10 P.M.

Atmosphere / setting: Old-world style with original, oil-painted murals; ceramics; casual, warm look.

House specialities: Pastas (e.g., Luciano's fusilli, various ravioli, tortellini alla Bolognese); Bruna's veal scallopini; shrimp fra diavolo; chicken limone.

Other recommendations: Desserts including tiramisu and fruit tart.

Summary & comments: Owner Luciano Silvestri is on hand to direct the operation and has a keen pride in his wine cellar and the recipes he brings back from his biannual trips to Italy. He and his wife, Ilona, bought this restaurant from the original owner in 1981; it has been open since 1933—it's the oldest restaurant in the Heart of Italy, a close-knit Italian community on the near southwest side. The cooking here is full flavored, well prepared, and served with style.

Bukhara

Indian   ★★★   **Moderate**

---

2 East Ontario Street
(312) 943-0188
Zone 3   Near North

Quality	Value
80	**C**

Reservations: Recommended
When to go: Any time
Entree range: $8–25
Payment: All major credit cards
Service rating: ★★★¹/₂
Friendliness rating: ★★★¹/₂
Parking: Discount with validation at nearby garages
Bar: Full service, including Taj Mahal beer
Wine selection: Fairly extensive; mixed
Dress: Moderately casual, business
Disabled access: Yes, including rest rooms
Customers: Diverse, business
Lunch: Monday–Friday (buffet available for $7.95), 11:30 A.M.–2:30 P.M.; Saturday and Sunday, noon–3 P.M.
Dinner: Sunday–Thursday, 5:30–10 P.M.; Friday and Saturday, 5:30–11 P.M.

Atmosphere / setting: Handsomely appointed, classy interior with visible tandoor kitchen. Nice bar area.

House specialities: Marinated fresh seafood, poultry, and meats roasted in tandoors; sikandari raan (whole leg of lamb); tiger prawns Bukhara; dal Bukhara (black lentils); and roti (whole-wheat bread).

Other recommendations: Spiced cottage cheese–stuffed bread; roomali (plain wheat bread); sheekh kebab (skewered, charcoal-grilled, cumin-flavored, minced lamb); flavorful kulfi gulabi dessert; an exotic pudding of dates, almonds, and milk.

Summary & comments: This ancient nomad cooking of the Indian subcontinent was introduced at this restaurant several years ago. To be authentic, no utensils are served. Eating with your hands as the nomads did is sensuous and fun, although they weren't seated in such an elegant atmosphere. There's an Indian saying, "Eating with utensils is like making love through an interpreter." Sauces are well spiced, and, although some tandoori meats can be on the dry side, most are delectable. Catering is available.

Cafe Angelo

Italian   ★★★½   **Inexpensive/Moderate**

225 North Wabash Avenue
(312) 332-3370
Zone 4   The Loop

Quality	Value
88	**B**

Reservations: Recommended
When to go: Busiest 5–8 P.M. on weekdays and
weekends
Entree range: $11–26
Payment: All major credit cards
Service rating: ★★★½
Friendliness rating: ★★★★½
Parking: Garage next door; after 5 P.M., $3.50 with
validation
Bar: Full service, including separate cocktail lounge
Wine selection: Mostly Italian, some Californian,
$16–75 per bottle; several by the glass. Educational
list with nice selection of Italian wines, with regions
and descriptions listed
Dress: Casual, but many dress up for the theater
Disabled access: Yes
Customers: Diverse, largely business, theatergoers
Breakfast: Every day, 7–10:30 A.M.
Lunch: Every day, 11:30 A.M.–4:30 P.M.
Dinner: Every day, 4:30–10 P.M.

Atmosphere / setting: Split-level, intimate retreat;
wood paneling and paintings; very clubbish. Main
dining area resembles a living room with no windows.

House specialities: Lobster with linguini; ravioli
stuffed with ricotta and spinach, tossed with your
choice of sage butter or tomato or pesto sauce;
trimmed, thick veal chop with polenta and artichokes;
striped sea bass or wood-grilled Atlantic swordfish
with honey-ginger glaze, with jicama and mango salsa
(obviously this preparation isn't Italian).

Other recommendations: Antipasto table—a great
assortment or cold salads and vegetables; bruschetta
topped with garlic and chopped tomatoes; wood-
grilled octopus with capers vinaigrette, with
homegrown tomatoes and red onion; cioppino;
homemade sausage with sautéed greens, peppers, and
potatoes.

Summary & comments: Cafe Angelo is well known for its authentic regional Italian cooking, with an emphasis on lower calories and fat. The pre-theater prix-fixe dinner with all-evening parking validation makes this one of the city's best dining-out bargains. Owner Angelo Nicelli added healthful items to his menu long ago, and he keeps changing dishes to avert any boredom for the regulars. He grows his own tomatoes and basil on his farm, so customers share the pleasurable bounty during the summer. This place is a longtime downtown favorite and a good value.

Cafe-Ba-Ba-Reeba!

| Spanish/Tapas | ★★★½ | Moderate |

2024 North Halsted Street
(312) 935-5000
Zone 1   North Side

Quality	Value
87	C

Reservations: Lunch, accepted; dinner, limited; not accepted for outdoor patio

When to go: Early or late

Entree range: Tapas, $1.95–5.95; paella, $10.95; no real entrees

Payment: All major credit cards

Service rating: ★★★½

Friendliness rating: ★★★½

Parking: Valet, $4

Bar: 2 bars—1 horseshoe-shaped in front, another in the back; bars seat 170 people, who can also eat there; true Spanish tapas-style

Wine selection: 120 Spanish selections; a few American, but 99% Spanish; bottles, $8–45; 4 wines by the glass; sangria, sherries, and Spanish liquors available

Dress: Casual, dressy

Disabled access: Wheelchair accessible; call ahead for special accommodations

Customers: Young, lively crowd; many students; a popular hangout

Lunch: Tuesday–Friday, 11 A.M.–2:30 P.M.; Saturday, 11:30 A.M.–3 P.M.; Sunday, closed.

Dinner: Monday–Thursday, 5:30–11 P.M.; Friday and Saturday, 5:30 P.M.–midnight; Sunday, noon–10 P.M.; Friday and Saturday, bar open until 1 A.M.

Atmosphere/setting: Upbeat, vibrant interior with vivid Mediterranean colors; dried garlic, hams, and other foodstuffs hang from the open-service kitchen. Lively murals of different parts of Spain, with a gallery of Spanish artists; 7 different seating areas (seating a total of 360) and a colorful, outdoor garden patio that seats 84.

House specialities: Tapas: patatas con allioli (garlic potato salad); terrine of grilled eggplant and oven-dried tomatoes, cilantro vinaigrette, and goat cheese; bambas a la parrilla (grilled shrimp brochette with sherry vinaigrette); paella Valenciana (Spanish saffron-rice dish of chicken, pork, seafood, green beans, and tomatoes); fideua de mariscos (cazuela of lobster, shrimp, and monkfish baked with saffron broth, angelhair pasta); sautéed octopus, potatoes, tomatoes, and green onions; vieiras a la parrilla (grilled sea scallops with mango-lime vinaigrette and curry lentil salad).

Other recommendations: Tapas: calamares a la plancha (fresh grilled squid, olive oil, garlic, and lemon); champinones rellenos (mushrooms stuffed with spinach, Manchego cheese, and red-pepper sauce); black bean soup with chorizo; flan de la casa; tarta de almen dras y fruta (fresh seasonal fruit and almond pastry cream in an almond-rum crust).

Summary & comments: Before the word "tapas" was really known in Chicago, this was the first Spanish restaurant to introduce the "little plate" concept; it was opened by Lettuce Entertain You Enterprises and Basque chef/partner Gabino Sotelino. The tapas craze spawned several more places, some of which are less costly and about as ambitious in menu and wine list. But this lively place with a large menu has a clientele that seems to grow. The restaurant can accommodate 20–150 customers in its private and semiprivate rooms. Sample several tapas items to create a full meal—it's fun to share—or choose from the traditional Spanish dishes in larger portions.

Cafe Borgia

Italian   ★★¹/₂   **Inexpensive/Moderate**

17923 Torrence Avenue, Lansing
(708) 474-5515
Zone 8   Southern Suburbs

Quality	Value
78	B

Reservations: No
When to go: Weekday evenings often less busy
Entree range: $10–15
Payment: All major credit cards
Service rating: ★★★
Friendliness rating: ★★★¹/₂
Parking: Free lot or street
Bar: None
Wine selection: None, BYOB
Dress: Casual, but dressier on weekends
Disabled access: Entrance, no; rest rooms, yes
Customers: Professional, students, couples, families
Lunch/Dinner: Sunday–Thursday, 11 A.M.–
    11 P.M.; Friday and Saturday, 11 A.M.–midnight;
    Saturday, closed 3–4:30 P.M.

Atmosphere / setting: Informal cafe feel; granite
tables with wrought-iron bases; pastel-colored outdoor
patio with painted flowers on fence around deck.

House specialities: Cream of eggplant and roasted
red pepper soup; linguini pescatore with calamari, bay
scallops, and mussels in a red or white sauce; tender
steamed baby clams in garlic, lemon, and oil sauce;
stuffed eggplant with prosciutto and mozzarella, baked
in a tomato-cream sauce; zuccotto with layered sponge
cake soaked in marsala and brandy, filled with
whipped cream, hazelnuts, and almonds, and topped
with chocolate and raspberry sauces.

Other recommendations: Roasted lamb shank,
rosemary jus, with roasted potatoes and onions; veal-
spinach cannelloni; four cheese–stuffed chicken breast;
tiramisu.

Summary & comments: The simple Roman cooking
here is aggressively flavored by innovative chef/owner
Mike Jesso. Major triumphs are his favorites: cream of
eggplant and roasted red pepper soup and tender baby
clams, above. This well-established place is one of the
best restaurants on the South Side and has its loyal
following.

Cafe Iberico Tapas Bar

Spanish/Tapas ★★★¹/₂ **Inexpensive/Moderate**

---

739 North LaSalle Street
(312) 573-1510
Zone 3   Near North

Quality	Value
87	**B**

Reservations: Recommended for 9 or more
When to go: Before 6:30 P.M. or after 8:30 P.M.
Entree range: $7.50–15.95; tapas, $2.50–4.50
Payment: VISA, MC, D
Service rating: ★★★¹/₂
Friendliness rating: ★★★¹/₂
Parking: Valet
Bar: Full service
Wine selection: Spanish; some nice selections,
    including sangria
Dress: Casual
Disabled access: Yes, including rest rooms
Customers: Diverse, many Latin Americans
Lunch/Dinner: Monday–Thursday, 11 A.M.–
    11 P.M.; Friday, 11 A.M.–1:30 A.M.; Saturday,
    noon–1:30 A.M.; Sunday, noon–11 P.M.

Atmosphere / setting: Authentic touch of Spain: a
tapas bar; a dining room with checkered table cloths,
wall murals and wine bottles on ceiling racks, and the
rustic bodega (wine cellar room) downstairs.

House specialities: Paella estilo Iberico; gazpacho
Andaluz. Tapas include grilled octopus with potatoes
and olive oil; Spanish cured ham, Manchego cheese,
and toasted tomato bread; tortilla Española. Specials
include hard-to-find fish cheeks with baby eels.
Poached pears with wine and ice cream.

Other recommendations: Shrimp with wine and
garlic sauce; croquetas de pollo (chicken croquettes), a
home-style dish; stuffed eggplant with goat cheese;
crema Catalana for dessert.

Summary & comments: Just north of downtown, this
popular place expanded recently by adding a bodega
complete with wood-burning oven. Authentic
atmosphere, cuisine, and wines make this one of the
best tapas places in the city, especially for the prices.
Spanish food conveys passionate regionalism and
culinary traditions, and it's possible to experience a
good sampling of that here.

Cafe Voltaire

Vegetarian	★★★	Inexpensive

3231 North Clark Street
(312) 528-3136
Zone 1   North Side

Quality	Value
83	**B**

Reservations: Not accepted
When to go: Evenings; call to avoid theater rush
   (Underground Performance Space downstairs)
Entree range: $6.95–10.95
Payment: VISA, MC, Transmedia
Service rating: ★★★½
Friendliness rating: ★★★★
Parking: Public garage nearby
Bar: Beer and wine bar; some good imported brews
   and 3 draft beers. The beverage list is comically
   categorized into "liquids that limit the flow of
   oxygen to your brain" and "liquids that don't"
Wine selection: Moderate collection of about 9—
   mostly Californian, some French, some organic,
   $15–70 a bottle; most bottles also offered by the
   glass, $3.25–4.50; 1 half bottle as well
Dress: Casual, can be Bohemian funky
Disabled access: Yes
Customers: Diverse, from punk rockers to 80-year-
   old grandmothers
Breakfast: Sunday, 11 A.M.–3 P.M.
Lunch/Dinner: Sunday–Thursday, 11 A.M.–1 P.M.;
   Friday and Saturday, 11 A.M.–3 A.M.

Atmosphere / setting: Funky, theatrical decor with
plants and high windows. Art on the walls changes
every month and can be a bit avant garde at times.
Theater is truly underground in the lower level.
Comfortable; dim lighting.

House specialities: Menu is changing with new chef.
Some items offered recently include: earthy tomato-
cheese bread (whole grain baguette with tomato,
marinara, chevre, and basil); nachos made with blue
corn chips covered with Jack cheese, vegetarian chili,
guacamole, salsa, and sour cream (this large dish
serves three); Voltaire grinder (big, messy vegetable
sandwich served with more sautéed veggies and brown
rice or blue corn chips); mango frappé (pure, velvety,
frozen mango).

Other recommendations: Russian pie (hearty vegetable-cheese pie with whole-wheat crust); spinach lasagna (organic whole-wheat spinach noodles stuffed with layers of ricotta, spinach, mozzarella, and marinara sauce).

Entertainment & amenities: Every evening; time varies for different performances, including performance art and poetry.

Summary & comments: One of the best vegetarian restaurants, with a varied menu, huge portions, and efficient and knowledgeable service. At press time, a new, very respected chef was appointed with plans to change the menu. Based on a recent dinner before his arrival, the rating was excellent and is only expected to improve. Cafe Voltaire is named, according to the menu, after a legendary gathering spot in Zurich called Cabaret Voltaire, "which was a lightning rod for artistic freedom, expression, and entertainment." The cabaret featured a variety of food, drink, poetry, performance, declaration, music, and debate from many famous patrons. The owner here borrowed the name and spirit, and expresses a declaration that all the food is made from the finest vegetarian, whole, and organic ingredients available. Fine espresso beans are ground to make the house-specialty coffee drinks. Desserts include delicious frappés—just pure, fresh fruit blended and frozen. This is a healthful cultural experience.

Cape Cod Room

Seafood   ★★★★   **Moderate/Expensive**

The Drake Hotel,
  140 Walton Street

Quality	Value
95	**C**

(312) 787-2200
Zone 3   Near North

Reservations: Recommended
When to go: Monday, Tuesday, or Wednesday
Entree range: $15–35, served with potato and salad
  or slaw
Payment: All major credit cards
Service rating: ★★★★
Friendliness rating: ★★★★½
Parking: Valet
Bar: Full service
Wine selection: Good assortment of champagnes and
  sparkling wines; imported and domestic whites and
  reds chosen for the seafood menu. House wines—
  several by the glass; imports include French,
  German, and Italian; bottles range from $23–60. The
  hotel's extensive reserve list also available
Dress: Jackets required
Disabled access: Yes, including rest rooms
Customers: Diverse, travelers, loyal regulars, locals,
  business, single diners and couples, celebrities
  including Steve Lawrence, Eydie Gorme, Jane
  Meadows, and Paul Newman, and politicos such as
  Mayor Richard Daley
Lunch/Dinner: Every day, noon–10:30 P.M.

Atmosphere / setting: Very authentic-looking rustic
Cape Cod setting with nautical decor. Charming and
intimate.

House specialities: The Cape Cod's famous Bookbinder red snapper soup with sherry; New England
clam chowder; bouillabaisse (with a variety of
freshwater fish and seafood); raw bar; oysters
Rockefeller; halibut papillote (fillet in parchment with
lobster, mushrooms, and red wine sauce); imported
Dover sole and turbot; New England scrod.

Other recommendations: Smoked salmon; oyster
stew; Drake stew; crabmeat a la Newburg; shrimp a la
Drake (casserole with shallots and Newburg sauce,
glazed with Parmesan). Desserts include key lime pie

and strawberry rhubarb crumble with vanilla ice cream.

Entertainment & amenities: Sitting at the bar to see the initials carved by celebrities who've dined here over the years. Longtime manager Patrick Bredin will gladly help interpret them.

Summary & comments: This seaworthy legend has been sailing full tilt since 1933, and at "60-something" is the city's oldest seafood restaurant. Before Shaw's Crab House, Nick's Fishmarket, and several other excellent seafood restaurants opened, the Cape Cod Room was synonymous with Chicago seafood dining. Located on the main floor of one of the city's finest hotels, it has long been a premier place for imported Dover sole and turbot, broiled New England scrod, bouillabaisse, and the famous Bookbinder red snapper soup. The raw bar continues to be a reliable source for oysters or clams on the shell and a great socializing spot for single travelers. Categorized by type of seafood as well as seafood salads, vegetables, and desserts, the menu also has a section, "From Our Broiler," offering four items from the land—steaks and lamb chops are a few alternatives to the array of items from the waters. There are the old classic lobster preparations (e.g., lobster Thermidor and a la Newburg) as well as the best—simply broiled or steamed. Other period pieces are shrimp de Jonghe, oysters Rockefeller, and clams casino.

Honors/Awards: *Holiday* Award for 35 years; Fine Dining Hall of Fame by *Nations Restaurant News.*

Carlos'

French	★★★★¹/₂	Moderate/Expensive

429 Temple Avenue, Highland Park
(708) 432-0770
Zone 11   Northern Suburbs

Quality	Value
96	C

Reservations: Recommended, especially for
  weekends
When to go: Sunday and Monday
Entree range: $24.50–27.50
Payment: All major credit cards
Service rating: ★★★★¹/₂
Friendliness rating: ★★★★★
Parking: Free valet
Bar: None
Wine selection: 40-plus-page list; bottles for $20–
  1,700; 12 selections by the glass, $6–12; helpful
  wine steward will assist in matching wines to the
  food and preferences
Dress: Jacket required, tie optional
Disabled access: No, but easy entrance; accessible
  rest rooms
Customers: North Shore local, business, couples,
  family, eclectic clientele
Dinner: Summer: Sunday, Monday, Wednesday,
  and Thursday, 5–8:30 P.M. (last seating); Friday
  and Saturday, seatings 5–6:30 P.M. and 8:45–
  9:30 P.M.; Tuesday, closed. During other seasons,
  dinner starts at 5:30 P.M. and the kitchen closes
  earlier in the evening, but patrons can stay as late
  as they want.

Atmosphere / setting: Elegant, stylized fine-dining
ambiance: wood-paneled walls, mirrors, and attractive
art deco, etched glass; many brass accents; quiet and
intimate with some banquettes; seats 55–60 diners;
facilities for private parties.

House specialities: Galette of house-smoked salmon
with crème fraiche, ossetra caviar, and bouquet of baby
greens (a cold appetizer); grilled duck breast and leg
confit, braised savoy cabbage, and duck juice; roasted
veal loin and basmati rice; shrimp risotto in rosemary-
scented cèpe juice.

Other recommendations: Roasted sea scallops with
artichokes, braised salsify, Gorgonzola, and aged
balsamic vinegar (appetizer); roasted hazelnut-crusted

yellow fin tuna with white truffle–whipped potatoes in green onion broth; game offerings, such as New Zealand antelope with black olive reduction; degustation menu with regularly changing items (often showcasing game), $70 or $90 with wine; vegetarian degustation also available on advance request. Artistic pastries are as delicious as they look (e.g., colorful fruit tarts and ginger mousse).

Summary & comments: This North Shore French dining establishment has been owned by Carlos and Deborah Nieto for more than 13 years. Several previous top-flight chefs have flown off to operate their own places, including Roland Liccioni (now running Le Francais) and Gabriel Viti (now operating Gabriel's nearby). Current chef Don Yamauchi (Japanese-Filipino-American) adds Italian and Mexican influences and some from his Asian heritage to fine French cuisine, and his food has taken on a multi-cultural dimension. His light sauces are largely reductions of onion, garlic, mushroom, and vegetables, with seafood and meat juices scented with herbs. The ratio of staff members to diners on a busy night is about one to three; there are many people "behind the scene" contributing to the dinner event. Guests are given complimentary hors d'oeuvres to start and sweets at the end. Carlos' continues to be one of the best fine-dining restaurants in the Chicago area.

Honors / Awards: Chef Don Yamauchi was selected as one of the "top 10 chefs" by *Food & Wine* and won the James Beard Award for "up and coming chefs in the Midwest"; Grand Award from *Wine Spectator.*

Carlucci

Italian ★★★★½ Moderate

2215 North Halsted Street
(312) 281-1220
Zone 1 North Side

Quality	Value
95	**C**

Reservations: Recommended
When to go: Dinner; early or late less crowded
Entree range: $12–22
Payment: All major credit cards
Service rating: ★★★★½
Friendliness rating: ★★★★½
Parking: Free valet
Bar: Full service
Wine selection: Italian
Dress: Casual
Disabled access: Yes
Customers: Business, couples
Dinner: Monday–Thursday, 5:30–10:30 P.M.;
Friday, 5:30–11:30 P.M.; Saturday, 5–11:30 P.M.;
Sunday, 5–10 P.M.

Atmosphere / setting: Beautiful entryway, side room, and large main dining room; smaller adjacent dining room filled with colorful paintings. Bar/lounge area opens onto lovely outdoor garden with a fountain and a whimsical clothesline filled with garments, for a touch of the real Italy.

House specialities: Carpaccio montenaro (thin-sliced beef with Parmesan cheese, crimini mushrooms, and white truffle oil); fazoletti di verdure (ravioli with leek, zucchini, carrots, prawn, and balsamic vinegar dressing).

Other recommendations: Antipasto of the day is usually an assortment of grilled vegetables, cold meats, cheeses, olives, and more.

Entertainment & amenities: Live jazz pianist on Friday and Saturday nights.

Summary & comments: One of the best Italian regional restaurants in the city, continuing to improve over the years. Well run by the Carlucci family and partners. Attention to detail here means staff classes in Italian pronunciation, so servers sound intelligent when discussing the food and wines. The menu is comprehensive and well balanced, as is the wine list.

Carlucci

Tuscan Italian   ★★★¹/₂   **Moderate**

6111 North River Road, Rosemont
(708) 518-0990
Zone 2   North Central/O'Hare

Quality	Value
88	C

Reservations: Recommended
When to go: Any time
Entree range: $11.95–24.95
Payment: All major credit cards
Service rating: ★★★★
Friendliness rating: ★★★★
Parking: Free valet and lot
Bar: Full service
Wine selection: Extensive Italian; selected for the
  rustic food; several by the glass; fairly priced
Dress: well-dressed, business preferable
Disabled access: Yes
Customers: Business, travelers, couples especially in
  the evenings
Lunch: Monday–Friday, 11 A.M.–2.30 P.M.
Dinner: Monday–Thursday, 5–10 P.M.; Friday and
  Saturday, 5–11 P.M.; Sunday, 4:30–9 P.M.

Atmosphere / setting: Open kitchen with rotisserie;
handsome bar area; frescoes and tiles.

House specialities: Roasted quail; roasted pork loin;
wood-fired pizzas; black olive pasta with sea scallops;
chianti-poached pears.

Other recommendations: Antipasto; Tuscan seafood
soup.

Summary & comments: This, the second of the
Carlucci restaurants, has served excellent Tuscan
cuisine since it opened several years ago. The space is
beautifully designed with a lovely bar area, exquisite
doorways, and a welcoming open kitchen with a
rotisserie in the main dining room. There's lots of
bustle, especially on weekends, and showmanship with
grappa carts displaying the liquor infused with fruits.
Well managed by the Carlucci family and partners,
who train their staff well, including in the art of proper
Italian wine and dish pronunciation. The menu here is
not as expansive as that of the Halsted location.

Catch 35

Seafood   ★★★★   **Moderate/Expensive**

**35 West Wacker Drive,
   Leo Burnett Building**
(312) 346-3500
Zone 4   The Loop

Quality	Value
93	**C**

Reservations: Recommended
When to go: Early weekdays, 5:15–6:30 P.M.
Entree range: $12.95–31.95, with most items around
  $16
Payment: All major credit cards
Service rating: ★★★★
Friendliness rating: ★★★★½
Parking: Valet, $5
Bar: Full service
Wine selection: Extensive, mostly Californian with a
  few French; several nice choices by the glass
Dress: Chic casual or business; no dress code
Disabled access: Yes
Customers: Diverse, many from nearby ad agencies,
  local, tourist, suburban
Lunch: Monday–Friday, 11 A.M.–1:45 P.M. (after
  1:45 bar remains open through dinner)
Dinner: Monday–Thursday, 5:15–10 P.M.; Friday
  and Saturday, 5:15–11 P.M.; Sunday, 5–9 P.M.

Atmosphere / setting: Spectacular granite lobby
entryway of the Leo Burnett Building. Revolving
piano bar lounge area with a display of enlarged,
award-winning ads. Stunning step interior with marble
walls and white tablecloths; colorful, elegant setting.
Seats 200 at various niches and levels.

House specialities: Menu changes daily. Typical
items are grilled grouper with olive oil, garlic, and
Thai basil; grilled swordfish with cracked peppercorns
and light cognac-avocado salsa. Appetizers include
Catch's crab cake (not fried) with remoulade sauce;
Szechuan scallops with vegetables; Martha's Vineyard
salad with blue cheese, pine nuts, tomato, and
raspberry-honey dressing.

Other recommendations: From the wok section: stir-
fried crab claws, shrimp, and scallops with a hint of
tomato sauce; nice variety of oysters on the half shell;
homemade desserts, all displayed, including chocolate

Kahlua mousse (semisweet chocolate and Kahlua
liqueur blended in a velvety mousse, served in a
caramel basket); pecan tart; white-chocolate cheesecake; classic key lime pie with a graham cracker crust;
homemade cannoli.

Entertainment & amenities: Piano player and a
variety of vocalists perform evenings.

Summary & comments: Nicely prepared, showy
food, some with Thai influences reflecting the chef's
background. Daily menu lists categories (e.g.,
appetizers, soups, salads, pasta), and main-course
seafood is grouped by preparation methods (baked,
grilled, wok, pan-seared). Nothing is fried. Popular
with the advertising agency crowd, this is an impressive restaurant for entertaining clients.

Honors / Awards: Silver Platter Award.

Charlie Trotter's

New American ★★★★★ **Very Expensive**

---

816 West Armitage Avenue
(312) 248-6228
Zone 1   North Side

Quality	Value
98	**C**

Reservations: Required

When to go: Wednesdays seem to be the least crowded

Entree range: Tasting menu, $65–85

Payment: VISA, MC, AMEX, CB, DC

Service rating: ★★★★½

Friendliness rating: ★★★★½

Parking: Valet

Bar: Full service

Wine selection: Extensive, award-winning, international list with 1,000 different wines including French, Californian, and Italian. Rich in Burgundies and Bordeaux, $40–1,000 per bottle. Choices by the glass, $9–16, change daily with the menu. Sommelier will assist customers with ordering

Dress: Business; jackets requested, not required

Disabled access: Yes

Customers: Local, tourist, business

Dinner: Tuesday–Thursday, 6 P.M.–?; Friday and Saturday, 5:15 P.M.–? (until management decides according to business)

Atmosphere / setting: Upscale, understated elegance in a renovated townhouse built in the 1880s. Quietly elegant contemporary dining rooms on two floors. Burgundy carpeting, cream wall covering, white linen tablecloths, china and crystal setting.

House specialities: Menu changes daily. Examples are mustard spaetzle, caramelized salsify, roasted salsify, roasted vegetable broth; porcini risotto with wild mushroom and saffron sauces; marinated hamachi with Russian ossetra caviar crème fraiche. Many items flavored with chef's infused oils. Warm butternut squash tart with blackstrap molasses sorbet and caramelized oranges.

Other recommendations: Mosaic of lobster and foie gras with ginger coulis; multi-layered tomato terrine; lamb saddle with artichokes; smoked pheasant breast; eggplant tartlets and thyme oil.

Summary & comments: Chef/owner Charlie Trotter is extremely gifted (he's been termed a culinary genius) in creating dishes in a new realm with sometimes disparate ingredients and eclectic foreign influences. Classic dish foundations are often given an element of surprise and become unexpected pleasures. Trotter's cooking is difficult to define since it has long had French underpinnings, uses 95% American ingredients, and is influenced by numerous foreign cuisines. It began more as experimental contemporary French and recently turned in the direction of contemporary American. It is usually wonderful. The fixed degustation menu limits the diners' choices, however, and is not everyone's favored way of dining. There's no a la carte, but call ahead to request any special food for dietary restrictions. Available for special parties.

Honors / Awards: James Beard Best Chef Award, James Beard Best Wine List Award, AAA Diamond Award; *Wine Spectator* Grand Award, 1993.

Chez 'D

Mediterranean ★★★ **Inexpensive/Moderate**

	Quality	Value
746 West Webster Avenue	**82**	**B**

746 West Webster Avenue
(312) 348-0333
Zone 1   North Side

Reservations: Recommended weekends
When to go: Quieter on weeknights; more specials on Friday and Saturday; Sunday brunch
Entree range: $8.75–12.95; Sunday brunch buffet, $7.95
Payment: Major credit cards
Service rating: ★★★¹/₂
Friendliness rating: ★★★★
Parking: Valet, street
Bar: Full service
Wine selection: Reasonably-priced American, French, Italian; several good choices by the glass, average $3
Dress: Moderately casual
Disabled access: Yes
Customers: Local, mixed
Brunch: Sunday, noon–4 P.M.
Open: Tuesday–Thursday, 11 A.M.–9 P.M.; Friday and Saturday, 11 A.M.–11 P.M.; Sunday, 9 A.M.– 4 P.M.

Atmosphere / setting: Charming European-style store front cafe. Interior is cozy with two front-alcove tables and shelves of books for customers to read while waiting. Lovely pastel tablecloths with contrasting napkins colorfully accent booths and tables. A large Degas wall mural and smaller Renoir paintings add to the homey charm of this 36-seat place. Sidewalk cafe with umbrella tables and flowers in summer.

House specialities: Appetizer crêpes stuffed with seafood, curried bechamel, or chicken with mush-rooms; unique potato torte (sautéed tubers layered with onions, ham, and grated cheese); la salad variee (grilled, marinated vegetables); pasta tricolor entree (with tomatoes, spinach, artichoke hearts, and asiago); catch of day is frequently salmon—the version in wine sauce with pink peppercorns is excellent.

Other recommendations: Apple liver pâté; baked goat cheese with tomato-basil sauce; hot or cold creamy leek-potato soup; chicken strudel; vegetarian chili; pollo de pesto (grilled chicken breast, linguini, and creamy pesto); freshly baked assorted French pastries such as fruit tart or refreshing lemon squares.

Summary & comments: Named for Eastern European owner Dragana Simon, this intimate cafe is the result of her dream of opening her own place because she was a good cook. Chez 'D opened in 1993 on the site of the former Tastebuds restaurant/takeout where she was a partner. The Mediterranean mode here expands to include her Hungarian chicken paprikash, offered as a special. Her cooking represents French and Italian cuisines more than any of the other Mediterranean countries' cuisines. The menu is basically simple (although some dishes need descriptions, e.g., Mediterranean pasta), the cooking is fresh and healthy overall, and the food is presented tastefully. A real find for the cuisines of the sun.

Chicago Chop House

Steak ★★★★ **Moderate**

---

60 West Ontario Street
(312) 787-7100
Zone 3   Near North

Quality	Value
94	**C**

Reservations: Recommended
When to go: Before 7 P.M. or after 10 P.M.; lunch is less busy
Entree range: $15–29
Payment: All major credit cards
Service rating: ★★★★
Friendliness rating: ★★★★½
Parking: Valet, $4 lunch, $5 dinner
Bar: Full service
Wine selection: International, extensive (has own warehouse)
Dress: Semicasual
Disabled access: No, but managers are willing to help those who need it
Customers: Business, VIPs, lots of celebrities
Lunch/Dinner: Monday–Friday, 11:30 A.M.–11 P.M.
Dinner: Saturday, 5–11:30 P.M.; Sunday, 5–11 P.M.

Atmosphere / setting: Century-old brownstone with three floors of dining rooms and more than 1,400 historical Chicago pictures. Every city map is on the wall—not even City Hall has that!

House specialities: Dry-aged, charred, U.S. prime rib; Chop House broiled New York strip steak, either 16- or 24-ounce; T-bone steak, 24-ounce; namesake potato pancake.

Other recommendations: Spring lamb chops; roast loin of pork chops; broiled Lake Superior whitefish with lemon butter; Russ's American fries; sautéed spinach.

Entertainment & amenities: Pianist on Monday–Friday, 5–11 P.M.; Saturday and Sunday, 6–11 P.M.

Summary & comments: One of Chicago's best restaurants for quality steaks and chops, founded by the late well-known restaurateur, Henry Norton. It has a loyal following, especially with certain celebrities. A place to see VIPs. Menu is traditional steak house–

style, featuring steaks and chops, a couple of chicken items, several seafood preparations, a handful of appetizers (all seafood), and some sides. It's kept simple and properly prepared.

Honors / Awards: *Knife and Fork* Award '92–'94 for America's Top Ten Steak Houses. In '94 voted Number Two steak house in the United States.

Chowpatti Vegetarian Restaurant

Indian/Vegetarian ★★★ **Inexpensive**

	Quality	Value
1035 South Arlington Heights Road, Arlington Heights	**80**	**B**

(708) 640-9554

Zone 10 Northwest Suburbs

Reservations: Not accepted
When to go: 2:30–5:30 P.M.
Entree range: $7–15
Payment: All major credit cards for checks over $10
Service rating: ★★★
Friendliness rating: ★★★★
Parking: Free lot
Bar: Juice bar with 20–25 fruit juice combinations; non-alcoholic beer
Wine selection: None
Dress: Casual
Disabled access: Yes
Customers: International, out-of-towners, couples, families
Lunch/Dinner: Tuesday, Wednesday, Thursday, and Sunday, 11:30 A.M.–9 P.M.; Friday and Saturday, 11:30 A.M.–10 P.M.; Monday, closed.

Atmosphere/setting: Upscale casual, spring-looking, quiet.

House specialities: Special bhel puri with dahl; basic bhel puri with whipped homemade yogurt and finely chopped cucumber and tomatoes; samosa with dahl: samosa topped with whipped homemade yogurt, sweet chutney sauce, onions, and coriander; masala dosa (dosa filled with lightly sesasoned onions, potatoes, tomatoes, coriander, cashews, and raisins); aloo mutter (potato chunks and pea curry).

Other recommendations: Special sev batata puri with dahl (loaded Indian nachos); grilled club pav bhaji (grilled sandwich with layers of meatless stew and cheese); aloo paratha (paratha stuffed with mildly spiced potatoes); veg biryani (basamati rice cooked with green beans, carrots, green peas, cashew nuts, and mild herbs and spices). Kulfis (homemade Indian ice cream): malai (plain), mango, kesar-pista (saffron pistachio), and chiku (exotic fruit).

Summary & comments: Over 400 items on the menu; building recently remodeled with a state-of-the-art air-filtration system and lead-free dishes. Meals are low in calories, fat, and cholesterol. Family owned and run for ten years. Very health-concerned and quality-oriented owner, and it shows in the results. This place has a following.

Honors / Awards: Voted best vegetarian restaurant in *North Shore* magazine.

Coco Pazzo

Italian ★★★½ **Moderate**

---

300 West Hubbard Street
(312) 836-0900
Zone 4   The Loop

Quality	Value
89	C

Reservations: Highly recommended, especially on weekends
When to go: During the week
Entree range: $12.50–26
Payment: All major credit cards except Discover
Service rating: ★★★★
Friendliness rating: ★★★★
Parking: City garages nearby, valet in the evenings
Bar: Full service, including grappa selection
Wine selection: 85 Italian selections, some French champagne, some sparkling wines from California; prices from $20–100 per bottle
Dress: Casual to upscale, no jackets required
Disabled access: Yes
Customers: Mostly local, professional, couples, business (especially at lunch)
Lunch: Monday–Friday, 11:30 A.M.–2:30 P.M.
Dinner: Monday–Saturday, 5:30–10:30 P.M.; Sunday, 5:30–10 P.M.; late-night supper menu available Monday–Saturday, 10:30–11:30 P.M.

Atmosphere / setting: Open kitchen with wood-burning oven and rotisserie produces fine interior. Rustic decor: brick walls and wooden floors, beams, and chairs; regional wood bin; track lighting; blue velvet drapes; columns. Cozy with white linen-covered tables spaced for privacy; elegant bar.

House specialities: Rotisserie special of the day (e.g., lamb); tagliata alla fiorentina (grilled rib-eye steak); baked vegetables and roasted butterflied trout; fettuccini with sautéed lobster, mushrooms, white wine, and garlic; sea bass braised with tomato, black olives, capers, garlic, and white wine over spinach. Signature dessert is cioccolato fondente con gelato cappuccino—flourless chocolate cake with a warm mousse center, chocolate sauce, and cappuccino ice cream.

Other recommendations: Risotto del Giorno (chef's special carnaroli rice of the day, from his native

Bergamo, Italy); coscia di agnello al giarrosto (leg of lamb seasoned with fresh herbs, slowly cooked on the rotisserie, thinly sliced, and served with potatoes); osso bucco (veal shank); vegetali al forno (assorted thinly-sliced seasonal vegetables with extra virgin olive oil, baked in a wood-burning oven).

Summary & comments: The young star executive chef, Christano Bassani, prepares creative, hearty Tuscan-style dishes; specialties change every day. The pastry chef bakes bread and wonderful simple, flavorful desserts such as torta di limone, and puff pastry with fresh berries and light pastry cream. This restaurant is restaurateur Pino Luongo's only Chicago entry of his successful group of New York–based dining establishments.

Honors / Awards: *Mobil Travel Guide* Award.

The Corner Bakery

Bakery Cafe   ★★★   Inexpensive/Moderate

---

516 North Clark Street
(312) 644-8100
Zone 4   The Loop

Quality	Value
82	**C**

Route 83 at 22nd Street, Oak Brook Center, Oak Brook
(708) 368-0505
Zone 8   Southern Suburbs

Reservations: Not accepted
When to go: Any time; busiest at peak breakfast and lunch hours
Entree range: Loaves, $1.50–5; sandwiches and soups, $1.95–5.25
Payment: All credit cards with $15 minimum
Service rating: ★★★
Friendliness rating: ★★★½
Parking: Street (Clark Street); mall lot (Oak Brook)
Bar: None
Wine selection: None
Dress: Casual
Disabled access: Yes; call first
Customers: Varied, professionals who stop before and after work and come in for lunch
Open: *Clark Street:* Monday–Thursday, 7 A.M.–10 P.M.; Friday, 7 A.M.–11 P.M.; Saturday, 8 A.M.–11 P.M.; Sunday, 8 A.M.–9 P.M. *Oak Brook Center:* Monday–Friday, 8 A.M.–10 P.M.; Saturday, 8 A.M.–11 P.M.; Sunday, 8 A.M.–9 P.M.

Atmosphere / setting: Clark Street location: small, cozy shop with several tables near windows; hearth bakery; great aromas. Other locations are slightly different, but the basic concept is the same.

House specialities: Baguettes; country loaves; specialty breads such as olive, chocolate-cherry, multi-grains, and ryes. Lunch items: focaccia and various sandwiches.

Other recommendations: Raisin-nut bread; kugelhopf (seasonal); cheese bread; variety of muffins; cookies; cappuccino.

Summary & comments: This Lettuce Entertain You Enterprises bakery produces some of the finest hearth-cooked, European-style breads and rolls anywhere;

therefore, their sandwiches are excellent. An assortment of 10–15 freshly baked loaves are available daily. The number of locations is growing: bakeries are now in the Water Tower Place and Union Station, and adjacent to other Maggiano's Little Italy restaurants. The success of this place proves that people have been starving for great bread beyond the packaged varieties. The staff of life is very alive here.

Costa D'Oro

French/Italian   ★★★★   **Moderate/Expensive**

1160 North Dearborn Street
(312) 943-6880
Zone 3   Near North

Quality	Value
93	**C**

Reservations: Recommended
When to go: Any time
Entree range: $18–28
Payment: VISA, MC, AMEX, CB, DC
Service rating: ★★★★½
Friendliness rating: ★★★★
Parking: Valet
Bar: Full service
Wine selection: Extensive French, Italian, and
   American selections that enhance the menu;
   sommelier will recommend wise choices
Dress: Upscale
Disabled access: Yes
Customers: Diverse, local, tourist
Dinner: Monday–Thursday, 5:30–10:30 P.M.;
   Friday and Saturday, 5:30–11:30 P.M.

Atmosphere / setting: Linen tablecloths, silver, and
crystal in a relaxed, sophisticated setting. Contemporary look: cozy alcove near bay window is set off by
large sleek bar, which everyone passes to get to other
dining rooms on different levels, each decorated with
colorful murals; 50-seat sidewalk cafe.

House specialities: Fresh pastas (available in half
portions): conchiglie with Parma prosciutto, peas, red
peppers, and cream sauce; mezzaluna ravioli, ricotta,
mascarpone, and pecorino cheese, with an earthy
hazelnut butter sauce; Maine lobster cooked in garlic
broth and served shelled with tomato relish; sautéed
fillet of salmon napped with a fish bordelaise, with
morel mushrooms and asparagus gratin; roasted rack
of lamb with mustard crust and rosemary au jus.

Other recommendations: Smoked sturgeon and
Granny Smith apple salad with frisee and mustard oil;
Alaskan crabmeat with papaya and mint compote.
Desserts, including crêpes with tart, fresh plums and a
counterpoint of vanilla sugar and champagne sauce;
"double pot de crème with gold" combines dark and
white chocolate cream with a sugar glaze.

Summary & comments: Named for Chicago's famous Gold Coast, this chic restaurant with an Italian name has a chef who has blended his distinctive French/Italian culinary style with American touches. Steven Chiappetti's training is in both French and Italian classical cuisines, and his cooking reflects that. His heritage is French and Italian, as well. Some creations are a fusion of the cuisines, and all his presentations are modern. The menu is peppered with Italian and French words, and its offerings include indigenous American ingredients, but sauces and techniques reveal a French pedigree. Be seduced by the pastries—they're some of the best. Take home a sweet memory in the form of homemade assorted chocolates, sold in boxes.

The Cottage

New American/French ★★★★ **Moderate**

525 Torrence Avenue, Calumet City
(708) 891-3900
Zone 8   Southern Suburbs

Quality	Value
92	**B**

Reservations: Recommended weekends
When to go: Less crowded weekdays or at lunchtime
Entree range: $13.95–19.95
Payment: All major credit cards accepted
Service rating: ★★★★¹/₂
Friendliness rating: ★★★★
Parking: Owns 2 adjacent lots
Bar: Full service
Wine selection: Wide-ranging, well-balanced list
with 102 items priced mostly from $13–22
Dress: Chic casual; dressier on weekend evenings
Disabled access: Yes
Customers: Business and couples, especially for
special occasions; people drive here from far away
Lunch: Tuesday–Friday, 11:30 A.M.–2 P.M.
Dinner: Tuesday–Friday, 6–10 P.M.; Saturday,
5–10 P.M.; Sunday, 4–8 P.M.

Atmosphere / setting: An intimate, romantic
European country cottage with a large stone fireplace,
fresh flowers, burnished silver flatware, and other
charming touches; library; two cozy mini-rooms.

House specialities: Striped open ravioli of marinated
rock shrimp, seared vegetables, mango, and red pepper
coulis; pork schnitzel; roasted rack of lamb with curry
and port-wine sauces.

Other recommendations: Appetizer: tea-smoked
duck confit spring roll, pickled ginger, and tomato jam;
pan-seared sea scallops, cilantro and black-bean relish,
and orange and saffron oil; fresh fish specials. Desserts
are not to be missed.

Summary & comments: This charming place, built
in the style of a French country inn, has long been
considered the best restaurant on the South Side and
one of the best in the Chicago area. Although the
owner was hiring a new chef at press time, his
reputation for maintaining high quality ensures that an
excellent style of cooking will remain. There are plans
for an outdoor cafe in spring of 1995.

Cuisines

Italian/French ★★★★ Inexpensive/Moderate

Stouffer Riviere Hotel,
  One West Wacker Drive

Quality	Value
91	B

(312) 372-4459
Zone 4   The Loop

Reservations: Requested and suggested
When to go: Weekdays
Entree range: $8.95–18.95; one item at $28.95
Payment: VISA, MC, AMEX, D, DC, CB, JCB
Service rating: ★★★★½
Friendliness rating: ★★★★★
Parking: Valet
Bar: Full service
Wine selection: Extensive and a best value, at just
  $10 per bottle over wholesale cost. The only place
  around known to mark up wines so little. Over 220
  bottles with focus on French, Italian, and Califor-
  nian; many nice vertical cabernet sauvignon tasting
  possibilities; 8-page list and 1-page wines-by-the-
  glass list. Helpful ratings and designations (e.g.,
  "best buy") from *Wine Spectator* and symbols from
  Connoisseurs Guide
Dress: Tastefully casual (no shorts or T-shirts);
  dressier on Friday and Saturday evenings
Disabled access: Yes
Customers: Tourist, hotel guests, local, theatergoers
Lunch: Monday–Friday, 11:30 A.M.–2 P.M.
Dinner: Every day, 5:30–10 P.M.

Atmosphere / setting: Plush, romantic, elegant;
comfortable banquettes; wood and marble; open
kitchen with wood-burning oven.

House specialities: Starters of thinly sliced roasted
veal with tuna caper sauce and beef carpaccio; lobster
bisque; osso bucco (braised veal shanks, pan juices,
and saffron risotto); shellfish risotto with saffron (soft
consistency—paella-like); grilled swordfish (ordered
with accompaniments from red snapper—ragout of
artichokes, leeks, tomato, and muscat wine).

Other recommendations: Robust, grilled small pizza
with dried tomato, sausage, and mozzarella; appetizer
of crabmeat and shiitake mushrooms in phyllo;
oregano- and potato-encrusted lamb chops; three-layer
chocolate torte; papaya compote; ethereal tiramisu.

Summary & comments: Start with the nine-page wine list here, then look at the one-page menu for dishes to match your bottle selection. The menu leans toward Italian with many French and some American choices. There's a Mediterranean influence, and overall the cooking has bold flavors from herbs, sun-dried items, and olives. There's an element of surprise (e.g., a salad of field greens with quail eggs and prosciutto cracklings) and a comfort zone with standards like minestrone and tortellini in beef broth. Most pastas and risottos are offered in appetizer and larger portions. The risotto here is cooked to a softer consistency than usual. Only one item sampled could have been better: a grilled veal flank special was chewy, although flavorful; it was accompanied by a host of items, including an apricot chutney and fresh rosemary. The value here is excellent, considering the quality of food, wine, and hospitality.

Honors / Awards: *Wine Spectator* Award of Excellence, 1992 and 1993

Cy's Crab House

Seafood/Persian   ★★★   **Inexpensive**

3819 North Ashland Avenue
(312) 883-8900
Zone 1   North Side

Quality	Value
84	**B**

Reservations: Recommended for 5 or more
When to go: Monday through Thursday
Entree range: $5.95–16.95 and market price
Payment: VISA, MC, AMEX
Service rating: ★★★½
Friendliness rating: ★★★★½
Parking: Own 2 adjacent lots
Bar: Full service
Wine selection: American; several by the glass,
   $3–4.50
Dress: Casual
Disabled access: Yes, including rest rooms
Customers: Local, diverse, business, couples,
   families
Lunch/Dinner: Monday–Thursday, 11:30 A.M.–
   11 P.M.; Friday–Sunday, 11:30 A.M.–midnight

Atmosphere / setting: Simple comtemporary decor;
semiformal, spacious, two-level dining room; outdoor/
indoor cafe.

House specialities: Prawns stuffed with crabmeat;
Cy's crabcake; joojeh kebab (charcoal-broiled,
marinated chicken with dilled rice).

Other recommendations: Mussels steamed with
garlic; oysters on the half shell; blackened catfish with
Persian rice; key lime pie; turtle cheesecake.

Entertainment & amenities: Eating all the oysters
you can for $2.95 at the raw bar from 4–6:30 P.M.

Summary & comments: Daily ordering ensures that
about ten different fish are offered in addition to the
shellfish during the week; occasionally the restaurant
runs out of a particular fish item—a good sign of
turnover. Besides this four-year-old restaurant, owner
Cy Sadaka owns King Crab Tavern & Seafood Grill,
(312) 280-8990. One page of Cy's menu features
Persian specialties, including vegetarian dishes and
many kebabs—some with mahi mahi, shrimp, and
scallops; combination platters include "crabs and
slabs" (barbecue baby back ribs and snow crab legs).

Da Nicola Ristorante

Italian ★★★ **Inexpensive/Moderate**

3114 North Lincoln Avenue

Quality	Value
84	B

(312) 935-8000
Zone 1   North Side

Reservations: Recommended on weekends
When to go: Any time
Entree range: Lunch, $4.95–12.95; dinner, $8.95–22.95
Payment: All major credit cards
Service rating: ★★★★
Friendliness rating: ★★★★¹/₂
Parking: Lot
Bar: Full service
Wine selection: About 50 selections; mostly Italian with a few Californian and French, $15–125 (Dom Perignon champagne); 1 page lists Italian wines by region, and 2 on that list were great for the price; several available by the glass
Dress: Moderately casual, jackets not required
Disabled access: Yes
Customers: Mixed, business, yuppie, family
Lunch: Monday, Wednesday–Friday, 11 A.M.–3 P.M.
Dinner: Monday, Wednesday, and Thursday, 5–11 P.M.; Friday and Saturday, 5–11:30 P.M.; Sunday, 4–11 P.M.; Tuesday, closed.

Atmosphere / setting: Romantic and intimate with an Italian feel; tile roof alcove decor, stucco and stone, beamed ceilings.

House specialities: Ravioli porcini (homemade, filled with porcini mushrooms in a sauce of cream and barolo wine); rotini napoletani (pasta layered with sautéed spinach, bocconcini di mozzarella, sautéed beef, prosciutto, and Parmigiano Reggiano, and rolled, sliced, and topped with fresh plum-tomato sauce); salmone portofino (salmon fillet sautéed with balsamic vinegar, honey, pine nuts, and green onions); scampi alla Miguel; stuffed artichoke; tomato, red onion, and fresh Gorgonzola cheese salad.

Other recommendations: Vitello Caprese (medallions of veal, lightly sautéed, served in a plum-tomato sauce, and topped with fresh basil and melted

bocconcini di mozzarella); vitello Rossini (veal
medallions sautéed in tomato cream sauce with green
peppercorns); linguini with littleneck clams served in
your choice of red or white sauce; bruschetta (toasted
rounds of Italian bread brushed with olive oil and
topped with sliced plum tomato, basil, and mozzarella); tiramisu served unusually in a tall footed
glass—light and brandy-flavored—not so sweet;
tortoni; granita lemon ice.

Summary & comments: Charming neighborhood
restaurant offers a substantial menu with a good
variety of daily specials, including antipasto, pasta, and
main courses, which come with a choice of soup or
salad and a side of pasta or vegetable. The couple who
own it work hard to make it as good as possible, from
getting local farm tomatoes to fine-tuning the wine list
so it complements the menu; wife makes the desserts.
Very accommodating—they will split pastas and other
dishes on request.

Del Rio

Italian   ★★★   **Inexpensive/Moderate**

228 Green Bay Road, Highwood
(708) 432-4608
Zone 11   Northern Suburbs

Quality	Value
83	B

Reservations: Recommended for 6 or more
When to go: 5–6 P.M.
Entree range: $10.95–19.95
Payment: All major credit cards
Service rating: ★★★½
Friendliness rating: ★★★★
Parking: Lot
Bar: Full service
Wine selection: Extensive, international; one of the largest selections in the Midwest
Dress: Moderately casual to dressy
Disabled access: Yes
Customers: Diverse
Dinner: Sunday–Thursday, 5–10 P.M.; Friday and Saturday, 5–11 P.M.

Atmosphere / setting: Home-style "family restaurant look," linen tablecloths.

House specialities: Veal Del Rio and other veal dishes; homemade bread and pastas (e.g., ravioli al forno); low-fat healthy chicken items; custard grussini.

Other recommendations: Steak; fresh fish (e.g., salmon modenese).

Entertainment & amenities: Reviewing the grand wine list.

Summary & comments: This is one of the oldest Italian family-owned restaurants in Highwood—about 71 years old. Family pride in overseeing the operation keeps it running smoothly. Cooking is solid, with the predictable standards, and you can be blown away by the wines.

The Dining Room

New French ★★★★½ **Moderate/Expensive**

The Ritz Carlton Hotel,
  160 East Pearson Street
(312) 266-1000, ext. 4223
Zone 3   Near North

Quality	Value
95	**C**

Reservations: Strongly recommended, especially for
  weekends and holidays; call one week ahead for
  Sunday and holidays, and midweek for weekends

When to go: Weekends are busiest; business depends
  on conventions in the hotel and Chicago events

Entree range: $24–30

Payment: VISA, MC, AMEX, DC, CB

Service rating: ★★★★★

Friendliness rating: ★★★★★

Parking: 3 hours free with validation at restaurant;
  car parked by valet at hotel entrance

Bar: Full service, 2 bars in hotel

Wine selection: Extensive 50-page list with about 300
  selections representing over 470 vintages; more than
  20,000 bottles in temperature-controlled cellars;
  from $30–1,800 per bottle; mostly French Burgundy
  and Bordeaux with a fair number of American wines

Dress: Jacket required, tie optional; brunch, casual—
  no cutoffs or tank tops

Disabled access: Yes, entrance and rest room

Customers: Many business, hotel guests, and local;
  not touristy; families and couples, honeymooners
  and anniversary celebrators

Brunch: Sunday, 2 seatings for buffet brunch at
  10:30 A.M. and 1 P.M.

Dinner: Monday–Thursday, 6–11 P.M.; Friday and
  Saturday, 5:30–11 P.M.; Sunday, 6–10 P.M.

Atmosphere / setting: Luxurious Edwardian-style
two-level room with carved French pine, beveled
mirrors, crystal, and Louis XV chairs at tables in the
central area. Quiet, cozy niches; large tables for
families; intimate banquettes in raised tier for couples.
Sunday brunch served on outdoor terrace.

House specialities: Duck liver terrine with warm figs
and port-wine sauce, toasted brioche (appetizer);
*Chilled terrine of artichokes, baby spinach, and oven-
dried tomatoes, and French green bean salad; *Grilled
veal chop with tempura lemon rings, portobello

mushroom, baby carrots, and roasted potatoes; (*=low in fat, sodium, calories, and cholesterol); four to five items change daily; always five meat entrees and five seasonal fish; verbal special of the day.

Other recommendations: Muscovy duck with marinated purple pearl onions and truffle-baby corn salad; Maine lobster and lobster cake with summer vegetables and sautéed Texas shrimp; three-course vegetarian menu available; set pre-theater menu between 6–7 P.M.; degustation menu, $48.

Entertainment & amenities: Pianist (classical, contemporary, and requests) during dining hours.

Summary & comments: Voted by readers of several magazines to be the best hotel dining room in Chicago, and every visit here proves why. Top-flight, progressive French cuisine, opulent atmosphere, and professionally friendly—never intimidating—service. This is a stellar dining experience at one of the finest hotels anywhere. Sarah Stegner became the chef of the Dining Room in January 1991. Her cooking is predominantly light, incorporating low-fat alternative cuisine dishes and featuring an abundance of vegetables, herbs, and strong flavors, while stressing simplicity in presentation.

Honors/Awards: Chef Sarah Stegner won New York's James Beard Award for upcoming chefs; restaurant and hotel won 5 stars and 4 diamonds; wine list received the *Wine Spectator* Grand Award for 12 years in succession.

Dixie Que

Barbecue ★★★¹/₂ **Inexpensive**

**2001 West Fullerton Parkway
   at Damen Avenue**
(312) 252-5600
Zone 1   North Side

Quality	Value
87	B

Reservations: Recommended, especially weekends
When to go: Any time; weekends busier
Entree range: $7.95–13.95
Payment: VISA, MC, AMEX
Service rating: ★★★★
Friendliness rating: ★★★★
Parking: Two lots
Bar: Full service, including good beers such as Dixie
   Blackened VooDoo
Wine selection: Limited; by glass or bottle
Dress: Casual
Disabled access: Yes
Customers: Yuppies, truck drivers, locals, couples,
   business
Brunch: Sunday, 10:30 A.M.–3 P.M.
Lunch/Dinner: Monday–Thursday, 11 A.M.–11
   P.M.; Friday and Saturday, 11 A.M.–midnight;
   Sunday, 10:30 A.M.–11 P.M.

Atmosphere / setting: Designed after a southern
barbecue roadhouse. From the tiny "Large Bar" to the
Memphis Blues artwork, the "Elvis wall of fame," and
the authentic appearance, this place transports you to
the South.

House specialities: Original Caesar salad and
southern Caesar, with chicken, red pepper, and pecans;
chicken specialties (e.g., Kentucky bourbon half
chicken, kickin' good bourbon barbecue, fries, and
apple raisin beans; Southwest chicken breast with chili
salsa, vegetables, and cilantro); catfish basket (fried
and cornmeal battered with spicy Creole sauce); ribs
(St. Louis cut) and new Cajun ribs; Dixie fish menu
(e.g., cilantro-buttered trout, green chili salsa, and rice;
grilled tequila-lime shrimp).

Other recommendations: Chili pepper wings; sweet
potato fritters; smoked Georgia hot bird (turkey, slaw,
peach dressing, and bun); Jackson hickory-smoked

ham with Jezebel sauce; sandwiches, including veggie-que with light dressing; Dr. Pepper cake; frozen drinks.

Summary & comments: This cleverly packaged southern barbecue roadhouse is the brainchild of owner Mel Markon, who carefully researched similar places in Memphis. A seasoned restaurateur, Markon has created a whimsical barbecue roadhouse replica complete with delicious, creative Dixie-style food. The sauces are addictive, and after you taste just several items, the varied menu entices you to return and so does the setting. Go with several companions so you can sample more.

Don Juan

Mexican　　★★★　　**Inexpensive/Moderate**

6730 North Northwest Highway
(312) 775-6438
Zone 1　　North Side

Quality	Value
84	**C**

Reservations: Recommended for 5 or more; not
accepted on Friday and Saturday
When to go: Monday–Thursday; Sunday is good for
families
Entree range: $6.95–13.25 on menu; up to $21 on
special menu
Payment: All major credit cards
Service rating: ★★★
Friendliness rating: ★★★★
Parking: Free lot or street
Bar: Full service; all Mexican beers
Wine selection: Spanish, Chilean, and some Mexican
wines
Dress: Very casual, shorts to ties
Disabled access: Yes
Customers: Families, couples, twenty-somethings,
mostly local
Lunch/Dinner: Monday–Thursday, 11 A.M.–
10 P.M.; Friday and Saturday, 11 A.M.–11 P.M.;
Sunday, noon–9 P.M.

Atmosphere / setting: Mexican feeling in split-level
dining room.

House specialities: Seafood dishes on daily special
menu (e.g., fillet of red snapper seared crisp, spicy
cucumber and red onion salad with reduced citrus
juices and chile pequín); game such as grilled venison
chop, barley risotto with wild mushrooms, and dried
blueberry pasilla sauce. From the regular menu,
traditional items such as classic steak tacos, burrito
Don Juan, and enchiladas suizas.

Other recommendations: Nachos de marisco, with
crabmeat, shrimp, and melted cheese; stuffed jalapeños
with shrimp, crabmeat, and melted cheese; duck
tamales; fajitas with chicken, steak, pork, or shrimp—a
combo or vegetarian. Homemade desserts include
traditional flan, good sorbets and ice creams, and
plum-almond tart.

Entertainment & amenities: Variety of entertainment (except in the summer) including flamenco guitar and harpist.

Summary & comments: Named for the legendary promiscuous lover, Don Juan's has a flirtatious menu appeal with a creative departure from the carbon copy Mexican fare. Allow yourself to be seduced by the chef's most creative specials, which probably showcase his talents best. On busy nights, the restaurant's noise level can be annoying.

Honors / Awards: *Chicago* magazine—"best fajita."

Don Roth's in Wheeling

American ★★★ **Moderate**

---

61 North Milwaukee Avenue (north of Dundee Road), Wheeling

Quality	Value
84	C

(708) 537-5800

Zone 10   Northwest Suburbs

Reservations: Recommended
When to go: Any time
Entree range: $15.75–24.95
Payment: VISA, MC, AMEX, D, DC, CB
Service rating: ★★★
Friendliness rating: ★★★★
Parking: Lot
Bar: Full service
Wine selection: Limited—mostly American and French
Dress: Casual but in good taste
Disabled access: Yes
Customers: Families, northwest suburban locals, business
Lunch: Monday–Friday, 11:30 A.M.–2:30 P.M.
Dinner: Monday–Thursday, 5:30–9:30 P.M.; Friday, 5–10:30 P.M.; Saturday, 5–11 P.M.; Sunday, 4–8:30 P.M.

Atmosphere / setting: Memorabilia especially from the 1920s, 30s, and 40s, when owner Don Roth's father Otto started (in 1920) and ran the famed former Blackhawk Restaurant downtown. It was a big-band supper club where WGN Radio broadcasted live on Saturday nights. Original menus (filet mignon was $1), contracts of performers, and a collection of big band instruments are displayed. Lovely outdoor garden.

House specialities: Roast prime ribs of beef (three cuts); Boston scrod (as prepared at Anthony's Pier 4 and Jimmy's Harbor Side, Boston); the legendary Spinning Salad Bowl and special dressing with blue cheese, egg, and shrimp (incuded with entree).

Other recommendations: Sirloin strip steak; specials such as broiled Lake Superior whitefish with home-made tartar sauce, and chicken Blackhawk (dedicated to the downtown flagship) roasted with herbs, spicy peppers, and a hint of garlic.

Entertainment & amenities: No live entertainment, but tapes of original WGN broadcasts from the Blackhawk.

Summary & comments: Owner Don Roth is a veritable encyclopedia of history from the big-band supper club era, and has wisely displayed his memorabilia collection—a trip down memory lane. He credits Lawry's The Prime Rib for getting his first roast beef cart in 1952, and together with prime rib and his famous Spinning Salad Bowl (dressing now sold), he transformed his restaurant from the costly big-band entertainment to entertaining customers tableside, where "food is the show." The older generation especially enjoys browsing at this Wheeling location. The menu is simple, the cooking good, and the service consistently accommodating.

Honors / Awards: Don Roth, a highly recognized restaurateur, has been the recipient of many awards over the years, including the IFMA Gold Plate Award in 1978.

Don's Fishmarket and Tavern

Seafood ★★★★ **Inexpensive/Moderate**

	Quality	Value
9335 Skokie Boulevard, Skokie	**93**	**B**

9335 Skokie Boulevard, Skokie
(708) 677-3424
Zone 11   Northern Suburbs

Reservations: Accepted
When to go: Any time
Entree range: Fishmarket, $11.95–22; tavern, $6–12
Payment: VISA, MC, DC, CB
Service rating: ★★★½
Friendliness rating: ★★★★
Parking: Lot
Bar: Full service, extensive beer list
Wine selection: Award-winning California wines; nice glass selections; fairly priced; tavern more limited, but good varietal list by glass and bottle
Dress: Casual, both places
Disabled access: Yes, both places
Customers: Diverse, both places; some moviegoers (theaters across the road); local North Shore and city; travelers
Lunch: *Fishmarket:* Monday–Friday, 11:30 A.M.–2:30 P.M. *Tavern:* Monday–Saturday, 11:30 A.M.–4 P.M.
Dinner: *Fishmarket:* Monday–Thursday, 5–10 P.M.; Friday and Saturday, 5–11 P.M.; Sunday, 4–9 P.M. *Tavern:* Monday–Saturday, 5–10 P.M.; Sunday, 4–9 P.M.

Atmosphere / setting: The Fishmarket has a casual ambiance with a cozy home atmosphere and slight nautical decor. The Tavern is cozy, dimly lit, and rustic.

House specialities: Fishmarket: baby octopus marinated with olive oil, lemon, and spices, and mesquite grilled with sautéed spinach and tomato; fresh Caribbean red snapper, mesquite grilled and topped with sun-dried tomato and pesto beurre blanc; Don's platter (combo of grilled swordfish, pan-blackened catfish, and broiled Lake Superior whitefish over spinach). Tavern: New England clam chowder; peel-n-eat shrimp; Snug Harbor mussels (steamed in garlic, butter, and sherry broth); blackened tuna salad; lobster pasta (with linguini); eggplant Parmigiano.

Other recommendations: Fishmarket: fresh Florida diver scallops, sautéed with garlic and Frangelico. Tavern: fish and chips, ocean perch, tempura shrimp, jambalaya, fajitas.

Summary & comments: Don's Fishmarket has been a dependable, comfortable North Shore seafood restaurant over the years. Daily menus list origins of the freshline seafood and the day's features. The chef offers a mix of low-fat preparations with vinaigrettes, as well as some with butter and cream sauces. Always seasonal seafood promotions, such as soft-shell crabs or lobster. The Tavern features special bargain deals at specific times on certain days (e.g., shrimp and oysters, 40 cents each, Tuesday, 2–1 1 P.M.).

Eccentric

American   ★★¹⁄₂   **Moderate**

---

159 West Erie Street
(312) 787-8390
Zone 3   Near North

Quality	Value
79	**C**

Reservations: Recommended
When to go: Early in the week; avoid peak lunchtime
Entree range: Lunch, $7.95–12.95; dinner, $9.95–21.95
Payment: VISA, MC, AMEX, DC
Service rating: ★★★★
Friendliness rating: ★★★★
Parking: Valet, $5
Bar: Yes
Wine selection: 47 selections: largely American with a smattering of French, Italian, and German; smartly organized by style and body with suggestions for type of foods; since whites and reds are grouped together by category, the red wines are printed in red ink; good selection by glass
Dress: Casual, dressy, eccentric
Disabled access: Yes
Customers: Locals, business, tourists
Lunch: Monday–Friday, 11:30 A.M.–2 P.M.
Dinner: Monday–Thursday, 5:30–10 P.M.; Friday and Saturday, 5–11 P.M.; Sunday, 5–10 P.M.

Atmosphere / setting: Expansive, grand, star-spangled dining rooms filled with whimsical art; one entry wall is a changing art gallery. Comfortable booths and tables. Usually bustling with a mix of people, including Oprah Winfrey fans, business types, and eccentrics.

House specialities: Venison meatloaf, white cheddar mashed potatoes, caramelized onion-beer sauce; rice-crusted tuna, orange oil, and crisp noodle-vegetable salad. Lunch: Thai chicken curry and lemon noodles. Sides: Oprah's famous potatoes (whipped with horseradish); collard greens. Chocolate espresso crème brûlée.

Other recommendations: Lunch: orange garlic chicken salad; grilled salmon with tomato, herb, and olive relish. Dinner: grilled swordfish; fennel-prosciutto salad; blue cheese polenta; peach and berry cobbler.

193

Summary & comments: T.V. talk-show queen
Oprah Winfrey and Lettuce Entertain You Enterprises
joined in partnership on this place. She's a mashed
potato lover, so her recipe is on the menu. There were
several versions, including "skinny," depending on
where her weight was. She often hyped the roast turkey
and potatoes on her popular show. This place has
shown inconsistency, but in the summer of 1993, Jody
Denton became executive chef to change that. Now it's
on track with his boldly flavored American cuisine
representing a diversity of cultures and seasons. This is
a great place for a before-dinner cocktail on weekdays,
4:30–7 P.M., during the complimentary buffet in the
bar.

El Dinamico Dallas

Caribbean	★★½	Inexpensive

1545 West Howard Street
(312) 465-3320
Zone 1   North Side

Quality	Value
79	**B**

Reservations: Accepted but not necessary
When to go: Any time
Entree range: $6.50–16
Payment: Major credit cards
Service rating: ★★½
Friendliness rating: ★★★★
Parking: Street
Bar: BYOB; wine by the glass, $1.50
Wine selection: BYOB
Dress: Casual
Disabled access: Yes
Customers: Local, ethnic, students
Open: Monday, Wednesday–Thursday, noon–
10 P.M.; Friday and Saturday, noon–11 P.M.;
Sunday, 5–10 P.M.; Tuesday, closed.

Atmosphere / setting: Homey, colorful, plant-filled
store front reminiscent of the Caribbean.

House specialities: Spicy jerk pork or chicken;
curried chicken; chilindron de chivo (goat meat stewed
in beer and wine with green olives, capers, and
onions); lambi (conch in Creole tomato-wine sauce);
homemade desserts; homemade tropical juices.

Other recommendations: Curried goat; black bean
soup; Armonize tamales; fried plantains and congri
(rice and beans).

Summary & comments: This long-lived Caribbean
cafe offers a slice of the island culture as well as well-
prepared Jamaican, Cuban, and Haitian dishes that
reflect the owners' heritage. The service is friendly and
relaxed, and the menu is just as laid-back; some items
need translations and descriptions, so you must ask.
Homemade bread comes with dinner, and banana
bread can be ordered as dessert. Bring your own
wine—a Gewurztraminer holds up to this slightly hot
fare—or try their delightful array of tropical juices,
such as papaya, orange banana, or passion fruit. They
also make shakes from mamey, guanabana, tamarino,
and mango. Catering is available.

El Tinajon

Guatemalan ★★★ **Inexpensive**

	Quality	Value
4638 North Western Avenue	**82**	**B**

4638 North Western Avenue
(312) 878-5862
Zone 1   North Side

Reservations: Recommended
When to go: Any time
Entree range: $4.95–16
Payment: Major credit cards
Service rating: ★★★
Friendliness rating: ★★★★
Parking: Street; 2 city lots across the street
Bar: Full service, including Guatemalan rum and beer
Wine selection: Limited to house wine: Chablis, blush, Burgundy
Dress: Casual
Disabled access: No
Customers: Mixed
Lunch/Dinner: Sunday, Monday, Wednesday, and Thursday. 11 A.M.–9 P.M.; Friday and Saturday, 11 A.M.–11 P.M.; Tuesday, closed. Call for winter hours.

Atmosphere/setting: Attractive, sparkling store front decorated with Guatemalan artifacts on brick wall. Tile floor and ceiling fans add a touch of Guatemala. Candles on glass tabletops over embroidered cloths, and lots of flowers and plants create an intimate atmosphere, enhanced by taped native music.

House specialities: Tamal Guatemalteco (corn tamale) with tomato sauce and cheese; pepian Antigueno (Indian chicken stew with vegetables and rice); jocon Cobanero (a traditional dish from the north—chicken pieces simmered in a green sauce made with several green herbs and vegetables); longanizas o chorizos (pork sausages with black beans, rice, and broiled tomato chutney).

Other recommendations: Quesadillas; pollo Zacapaneco (chicken simmered in tomato-wine sauce with melted cheese); red snapper cooked in its own juices with condiments and wine; shrimp in garlic butter, served with avocado. Desserts: flan; the torreja (a very sweet, fried bread pudding) is an acquired taste.

Entertainment & amenities: Guatemalan organist and marimba musician occasionally.

Summary & comments: The only Guatemalan restaurant in Illinois, now into its second decade. Owner visits her homeland twice a year to get spices and other items not available here. Guatemalan cuisine is lighter and less spicy than Mexican, and here it is authentic. Although Guatemala and Mexico are neighbors, the cuisines have many distinct differences. Most items on the menu come with rice and/or black beans and a salad garnish. Several vegetarian dishes are available.

El Tipico

Mexican ★★¹/₂ **Inexpensive**

1836 West Foster Avenue
(312) 878-0839
Zone 1   North Side

Quality	Value
79	**B**

3341 Dempster Avenue, Skokie
(708) 676-4070
Zone 11   Northern Suburbs

Reservations: Recommended for weekends
When to go: Weekdays
Entree range: $5–12
Payment: All major credit cards
Service rating: ★★★
Friendliness rating: ★★★★
Parking: Yes
Bar: Full service; Mexican beers and margaritas
Wine selection: Limited; mostly American
Dress: Casual
Disabled access: Yes
Customers: Mixed, young professionals, families, business
Lunch/Dinner: Sunday–Thursday, 11 A.M.–midnight; Friday and Saturday, 11 A.M.–2 A.M.

Atmosphere / setting: Intimate, charming, colorful (red tablecloths) with some authentic artifacts; quiet overall. Non-smoking dining rooms at each location. Outdoor garden.

House specialities: Appetizer combo: shrimp fajitas (also chicken and beef), steak tacos, pollo en mole, burrito ranchero; steak a la pequeña. Huge portions.

Other recommendations: Traditional Mexican dishes (e.g., enchiladas); good flan.

Entertainment & amenities: Occasional weekend trio.

Summary & comments: Very comfortable and pleasant neighborhood restaurant serving good south-of-the-border fare and huge portions. Attractive setting and caring management.

Emilio's Meson Sabika
Tapas Bar Restaurant

Spanish/Tapas ★★★ **Moderate**

1025 Aurora Avenue, Naperville
(708) 983-3000
Zone 8   Southern Suburbs

Quality	Value
82	**C**

Reservations: Accepted Monday–Thursday through
9:30 P.M.; Friday–Saturday through 6 P.M.; after
6 P.M., limited to 6 or more
When to go: Weekdays
Entree range: $9.95–13.95; tapas, $2–12
Payment: Major credit cards
Service rating: ★★★
Friendliness rating: ★★★
Parking: Lot
Bar: Full service
Wine selection: Largely Spanish; good selection,
including sherries and sangria
Dress: Casual to formal
Disabled access: Yes
Customers: Diverse
Lunch/Dinner: Monday–Thursday, 11:30 A.M.–
10 P.M.; Friday, 11:30 A.M.–11 P.M.
Dinner: Saturday, 5–11 P.M.; Sunday, 4–10 P.M.

Atmosphere / setting: The restaurant is in the elegant
1847 Willoway Manor mansion. Six dining rooms are
named after Spanish cities, wine regions, geographic
areas, or foods in Spanish cuisine. Murals, hand-
painted Spanish ceramics, mosaics, and lace curtains
offer a distinct authentic flair.

House specialities: Patatas con alioli (cold potato
salad with garlic mayonnaise); sautéed escargot baked
on croutons with alioli; paella a la Valenciana; flan de
coco al caramelo; caramelized bread pudding.

Other recommendations: Thin roast veal slices; sun-
dried tomatoes and green olives with raspberry
vinaigrette; grilled shrimp; citrus rice pudding.

Entertainment & amenities: Flamenco guitarist and
dancer every Friday evening.

Summary & comments: The menu here is similar to
Emilio's first tapas bar in Hillside. Food and service
may not always be as finely tuned here, but this larger
mansion setting is unique, and the special event
dinners and wine tastings are educational.

Emilio's Tapas Bar Restaurant

Spanish/Tapas   ★★★★   **Moderate**

4100 West Roosevelt Road, Hillside
(708) 547-7177
Zone 9   Western Suburbs

Quality	Value
91	**C**

Reservations: Accepted Monday–Thursday and
 Saturday
When to go: Weekdays
Entree range: $13–14; tapas, $2–12
Payment: Major credit cards
Service rating: ★★★½
Friendliness rating: ★★★★
Parking: Lot
Bar: Full service
Wine selection: Mostly Spanish, including sherries
 and sangria; good range of types and price,
 beginning at $15 a bottle; a few Californian
Dress: Casual
Disabled access: Yes
Customers: Diverse
Lunch/Dinner: Monday–Thursday, 11:30 A.M.–
 10 P.M.; Friday, 11:30 A.M.–midnight.
Dinner: Saturday, 5–11 P.M.; Sunday, 4–9 P.M.

Atmosphere / setting: Colorful ceramic decor; very
Spanish.

House specialities: Grilled oysters rolled in cracked
peppers; cazuela de pollo in garlic sauce; paella de
mariscos (seafood).

Other recommendations: Cazuela de pulpo (marinated octopus with peppers and sherry vinaigrette,
Spanish ham, tomato bread, and Manchego cheese).

Entertainment & amenities: Flamenco on occasion.

Summary & comments: Known as the King of
Tapas, Emilio Gervilla brought the Spanish tapas
concept to Chicago more than a decade ago. He opened
Emilio's Tapas Bar Restaurant in 1988, the first of his
own restaurants. Since then he's expanded to several
more, mostly in the western suburbs, and the latest,
Emilio's Tapas, on the mid-North Side of the city.
Emilio is from Granada, knows his cuisine well, and is
a hands-on restaurateur. This suburban place is
definitely worth the half-hour drive from downtown
for an authentic, delicious trip to Spain.

Emperor's Choice

Chinese   ★★★¹/₂   **Inexpensive/Moderate**

2238 South Wentworth Avenue,
Chinatown

Quality	Value
88	B

(312) 225-8800
Zone 5   South Loop

Reservations: Recommended on weekends
When to go: Any time
Entree range: Lunch, $5.95–9.95; dinner, $6.95–
   19.95
Payment: VISA, MC, AMEX, D
Service rating: ★★★★
Friendliness rating: ★★★★
Parking: Validated parking in Chinatown lot
Bar: Full service
Wine selection: Limited; several by glass
Dress: Casual
Disabled access: Yes
Customers: Family, local, tourist
Lunch: Monday–Friday, 11:45 A.M.–3 P.M.
Lunch/Dinner: Monday–Saturday, 11:45 A.M.–
   1 A.M.; Sunday, 11:45–midnight. Kitchen closes
   a half hour before dining room

Atmosphere / setting: Intimate store front with
tablecloths and walls decorated with framed prints of
the most famous emperors of the ten dynasties. The
focal point of this cozy restaurant is a robe worn by a
Ching dynasty emperor.

House specialities: Seafood dishes such as Maine
lobster baked with ginger and onion; pea pod sprouts
with crabmeat sauce; Empress's beef (marinated
tenderloin); sole two ways.

Other recommendations: Scallop and shrimp with
walnuts; shrimp and chicken in bird's nest; pot stickers; Emperor's egg rolls; Peking duck (one-day notice).

Summary & comments: One of the best restaurants
in Chinatown and one of the most creative for seafood
dishes. Quality ingredients, careful cooking, and
attentive service have made this place popular for
years, and it continues to get high reviews from critics.
The food is served on beautiful china in a regal
fashion, and happily, the prices are not royal. This is
one of the best values for excellent Chinese cuisine.

Entre Nous

French ★★★½ **Moderate/Expensive**

Fairmont Hotel, 200 North Columbus Drive

Quality	Value
88	C

(312) 565-7997
Zone 4   The Loop

Reservations: Highly recommended
When to go: Early evenings
Entree range: Lunch, $9.95–16.50; dinner, $18–27
Payment: All major credit cards
Service rating: ★★★★½
Friendliness rating: ★★★★★
Parking: Hotel garage, validated
Bar: Full service
Wine selection: Award-winning, extensive, international, world-class collection; lovely wine library in the dining room
Dress: Moderately upscale
Disabled access: Yes
Customers: Mostly local, a few tourist
Lunch: Monday–Friday, 11:30 A.M.–2:30 P.M.
Dinner: Monday–Saturday, 5:30–10:30 P.M.

Atmosphere / setting: Elegant, plush, and sophisticated. Large table with flowers and display of some dishes is the central focus of dining room, and one wall is a wine library.

House specialities: Lunch specials change weekly. Caesar salad (with sourdough croutons and aged Parmesan). Lunch entrees: seared paillard of salmon (with gazpacho salad and leek vinaigrette); woodland mushrooms in puff pastry (over mesclun greens, pecans, and a grapeseed oil vinaigrette). Dinner appetizer: pan-fried Chesapeake crab cakes (with sautéed arugula and lobster sauce). Dinner entrees: pot-au-feu of grouper and prawns with root vegetables and basil; roast rack of Sonoma lamb with mustard-herb crust and rosemary lentils. Weekly table d'hôte 4-course dinner menu, $23.

Other recommendations: Lobster bisque; applewood smoked chicken breast with caraway cabbage and fire-roasted chestnuts. Dessert tray holds several light, layered pastries; almond cheesecake; chocolate raspberry torte.

Entertainment & amenities: Jazz in the Metropole; ask about dinner-jazz package in Entre Nous; $39, three-course dinner and ticket to the Metropole show.

Summary & comments: Entre Nous (between us) is an intimate French phrase and charming name for this romantic hotel dining room. The creative cuisine has many innovative touches (the marrow melted over herbed tenderloin, for example). The service is gracious and accommodating and, overall, dining here is distinctive.

Honors / Awards: Wine collection has received the Award of Excellence from the *Wine Spectator* for two consecutive years. Entre Nous won 4 stars from *Mobil Travel Guide*.

Everest

---

440 South LaSalle Street (One Financial Place, 40th Floor)
(312) 663-8920
Zone 4   The Loop

Quality	Value
98	**C**

Reservations: Required
When to go: Varies; call before you go
Entree range: A la carte, $26.50–32.50; pre-theater menu, $39; evening tasting menu, $69
Payment: All major credit cards
Service rating: ★★★★★
Friendliness rating: ★★★★½
Parking: Complimentary valet in building garage
Bar: Full service
Wine selection: Extensive award-winning list with 650 international wines, mostly French, Alsatian, and American; $30+ per bottle; 10–12 selections by the glass
Dress: Jacket and tie suggested
Disabled access: Wheelchair accessible; call ahead for special accommodations
Customers: Upscale, business, couples
Dinner: Tuesday–Thursday, 5:30–8:30 P.M.; Friday and Saturday, 5:30–10 P.M.; Sunday and Monday, closed.

Atmosphere / setting: Softly lit, romantic, simple elegance; flowers and candlelight; 75-seat dining room separated into an atrium level for a private atmosphere and a spectacular western view of Chicago; tuxedo-clad waiters. Six private dining rooms for parties of eight or more, open daily for breakfast, lunch, and dinner (reservations must be made in advance for these rooms).

House specialities: Smoked salmon served with warm oatmeal blinis (cold appetizer); creamless navy bean soup and confit of rabbit; terrine of pheasant, partridge, and squab marbled with wild herbs and vegetables; Maine lobster roasted with Alsace Gewurtztraminer and ginger.

Other recommendations: Ballotine of wild Atlantic salmon and marinated cabbage, Alsace-style; double lamb consommé, mini–goat cheese ravioli; saddle of

Millbrook venison, wild huckleberries, Alsace
Wassertriwella; ballotine of skate stuffed with
mushrooms and wrapped around non-sour Alsatian
sauerkraut in a light Riesling juniper berry sauce. Pre-
theater dinner menu with seatings at 5:30 P.M., $39;
degustation menu, $69 per person.

Entertainment & amenities: The spectacular
western view of Chicago.

Summary & comments: Mount Everest was climbed
first by Sir Edmond Hillary, and Chef Jean Joho has
succeeded in making his Everest the pinnacle of
French gastronomy in Chicago—in fact it's one of the
country's premier restaurants. In partnership with
Lettuce Entertain You Enterprises, Joho is a protégé of
Paul Haeberlin of the acclaimed L'Auberge de L'Ill in
Alsace, France. He began training at 13 as an appren-
tice. His education continued in French, Italian, and
Swiss kitchens, and at age 23, he became sous chef of a
Michelin 2-star restaurant with the command of a staff
of 35. His French cuisine is masterful, with much use
of his beloved Alsatian homeland's ingredients; each
dish is a work of art to behold. Dining here is truly tops
for food, service, and view of the city.

Honors / Awards: Four-star reviews from the
Chicago Tribune, the *Chicago Sun-Times, Chicago*
magazine; featured in *Playboy* and *Esquire;* winner of
Ivy Award and *Gault Millau* honors; chef/owner Jean
Joho won the James Beard Award for Best Chef in
Midwest and *Food and Wine* magazine's Top Chef of
the Year Award; he's been inducted into Nation's
Restaurant News' Fine Dining Hall of Fame and
received the *Wine Spectator* Award of Excellence,
1992.

Filippo's

Italian   ★★★   **Inexpensive/Moderate**

2211 North Clybourn Avenue
(312) 528-2211
Zone 1   North Side

Quality	Value
82	**C**

Reservations: Recommended
When to go: Any time
Entree range: $6.95–16.95
Payment: VISA, AMEX, MC
Service rating: ★★★½
Friendliness rating: ★★★★
Parking: Street, theater lot; might have a valet soon
Bar: Full service, including grappa selection
Wine selection: Italian, 30-plus types; $16–55 a
   bottle; several by the glass
Dress: Casual to dressy
Disabled access: Yes
Customers: Yuppie, business, dates, family
Lunch: Planning to serve lunch soon
Dinner: Monday–Thursday, 5–11 P.M.; Friday and
   Saturday, 5 P.M.–midnight; Sunday, 5–10 P.M.

Atmosphere / setting: Intimate storefront with gold-hued walls and old-world Italian touches, such as pictures of cherubs and an antique copper cappuccino machine. Tables are covered with mix-and-match tablecloths handmade by one owner's mother.

House specialities: Homemade ravioli annarella (ricotta and spinach in cream sauce with Parmigiano); daily fish (swordfish steak with Mediterranean sauce of lemon, olive oil, basil, rosemary, and garlic); veal scallopini in sage sauce with mushroom and mozzarella. Desserts: flourless chocolate espresso cake, chocolate hazelnut torte, zuccotto.

Other recommendations: Calamari fritti; antipasto vegetariano (assorted grilled veggies); fettuccini Giorgione (light tomato sauce, sautéed chicken breast, broccoli, and blue cheese).

Summary & comments: The owners have great pride in their new place. The atmosphere is warm and inviting—customers are personally greeted at each table. The menu includes the chef's refined interpretations of dishes his mother cooked for everyday meals.

foodlife

American   ★★¹/₂   **Inexpensive**

835 North Michigan Avenue, Water Tower Place

Quality	Value
79	**B**

(312) 335-3663
Zone 3   Near North

Reservations: Not accepted
When to go: Any time, but to avoid busiest times, steer away from peak lunchtime and rush hour business
Entree range: $4.50–8
Payment: All major credit cards
Service rating: ★★¹/₂
Friendliness rating: ★★★★
Parking: Water Tower underground garage
Bar: Wine, beer, sangria only
Wine selection: Wine in glasses, sangria
Dress: Casual
Disabled access: Yes
Customers: Professionals, shoppers, tourists, families, couples
Open: *Juice, espresso, and Corner Bakery:* Monday–Saturday, 7:45 A.M.–10 P.M.; Sunday, 7:45 A.M.–9 P.M. *All other kiosks:* Monday–Saturday, 11 A.M.–10 P.M.; Sunday, 11 A.M.–9 P.M.

Atmosphere / setting: Attractive food court that resembles an outdoor cafe with trees. Environment-friendly atmosphere. Credo is "Be kind; eat true; it's now." Large variety of food stations; all food is displayed in an appealing manner.

House specialities: Thirteen food stations: juice bar, grains, burgers, Mexican, greens, pizza, pasta, hot stuffs (stuffed potatoes), rotisserie chicken, stir-fry heaven, desserts, sacred grounds (espresso, candy, cakes, cookies), and Corner Bakery. Mediterranean rice dishes; grilled, marinated.vegetables; "enlightened" Caesar; vegetarian pizza with multi-grain crust; pot stickers; rotisserie chicken; homemade pies and cookies.

Other recommendations: Cold and hot bean salads; health burgers; salsa bar; stir-frys with Pan-Asian influences; yogurt-fruit shakes and power drinks.

Summary & comments: This food court concept drew great press upon opening in 1993. It is one of the most innovative food concepts, by Rich Melman of Lettuce Entertain You Enterprises. He explains, " We have a social life, a business life, a family life, and a love life. Now there is an environment dedicated to your food life. It's about choices." Whatever your craving, you can eat healthfully, indulge, or compromise a bit in between. The freshest ingredients, without preservatives are used. Customers are given a sensor card to use at each station. The card tracks the meal cost, is given to the cashier before you exit, and the total cost is tallied. Convenient and fast. It's largely self-service, but the staff at each kiosk assists. A new adjacent foodlife market offers freshly prepared foods for carryout. Call (312) 335-3663.

Francesco's Hole in the Wall

Italian   ★★★   **Inexpensive/Moderate**

254 Skokie Boulevard, Northbrook
(708) 272-0155
Zone 11   Northern Suburbs

Quality	Value
83	**B**

Reservations: Not accepted
When to go: Early, just after 5 P.M.
Entree range: Average is $10
Payment: Cash only
Service rating: ★★★¹/₂
Friendliness rating: ★★★★
Parking: Lot
Bar: Limited; liquor can be provided on request
Wine selection: Fairly wide selection; all Italian;
  several by the glass
Dress: Casual
Disabled access: No
Customers: Diverse, from locals to limos
Lunch: Monday, Wednesday–Friday, 11:30 A.M.–
  2:15 P.M.; Tuesday, closed.
Dinner: Monday, Wednesday, and Thursday, 5–
  9:15 P.M.; Saturday, 5–10:15 P.M.; Sunday,
  4–8:45 P.M.; Tuesday, closed.

Atmosphere / setting: Rural Italian; unfinished
wooden floor; blackboard menu. Non-smoking. Small
and intimate, but larger than the original.

House specialities: Chicken and veal Vesuvio;
fettuccini with shrimp, scallops, broccoli, tomato, and
asiago; porcini ravioli; osso bucco; risotto pichi-pachi
(Italian rice with sautéed spinach and tomato sauce).
The special house salad is like a tossed antipasto with
greens, pepperoni, cheese, and roasted peppers.

Other recommendations: Spidini (homemade bread
rolled around mozzarella and tomato); thin pizza;
bruschetta; lemon-roasted chicken, broccoli, and red
peppers. Unusual dessert: chocolate cannoli with
chocolate ricotta, studded with tiny chocolate chips.

Summary & comments: This small restaurant's
comical name dates to pre-expansion when a full house
meant 21! The daily menu is written on the board, but
certain specialties are frequently available. The owner
opened an Italian bistro next door, and named it just
that—Next Door, (708) 272-1491.

Froggy's French Cafe

New French ★★★ **Moderate**

---

306 Green Bay Road, Highwood
(708) 433-7080
Zone 11   Northern Suburbs

Quality	Value
84	B

Reservations: Accepted only for 6 or more
When to go: Monday–Wednesday, early and late
Entree range: $11.95–15.95
Payment: All major cards except AMEX
Service rating: ★★★★
Friendliness rating: ★★★★½
Parking: Street, lot at library
Bar: Yes
Wine selection: About 100 selections; list changes
  every 45 days; $13.95–150 a bottle; 3–4 selections
  by the glass, $4–5
Dress: Chic casual
Disabled access: Entrance, yes; rest rooms, no
Customers: Local, corporate, tourist, family, couples
Lunch: Monday–Friday, 11:30 A.M.–2 P.M.;
  Saturday and Sunday, closed.
Dinner: Monday–Thursday, 5–10 P.M.; Friday and
  Saturday, 5–11 P.M.

Atmosphere / setting: Casual, comfortable, cozy
(some tables close together); low-key and a bit old-
fashioned in decor; French art on the walls. The frog
theme is depicted in various charming ways (e.g., salt
and pepper shakers). Outdoor seating available.

House specialities: Lobster served with vanilla sauce
on a bed of leeks; cassoulet of duck or tripes; broiled
salmon in Provençal sauce; baked red snapper or
striped bass with herbs. Menu changes every 90 days.

Other recommendations: Salads (e.g., Belgian
endive salad, sweet onion confit); rack of lamb;
kidneys; desserts (e.g., lemon mousse in pastry shell).

Summary & comments: Chef Thierry Lefeuvre has
consistently produced great French food at modest
prices. He wanted to prove that French cuisine need
not include costly ingredients and wear high price tags.
He considers cost one of the challenges of cooking,
and with his keen marketing and kitchen skills, he's
proven that you don't require a king's ransom to dine
in a French restaurant.

Frontera Grill/Topolobampo

Mexican ★★★★ **Inexpensive/Moderate**

445 North Clark Street
(312) 661-1434
Zone 4   The Loop

Quality	Value
93	**C**

Reservations: Only for parties of 5–10 (Frontera
   Grill); recommended to reserve a day before
   (Topolobampo)
When to go: Tuesday, Wednesday, or Thursday;
   early or late (Frontera Grill)
Entree range: $8–17 (Frontera Grill); $14–21
   (Topolobampo)
Payment: All major credit cards (both places)
Service rating: ★★★¹/₂
Friendliness rating: ★★¹/₂
Parking: Valet, $4 (both)
Bar: Common bar for both; good tequila and Mexican
   beer list
Wine selection: Quite extensive; very international
Dress: Casual (Frontera Grill); more formal, upscale
   (Topolobampo)
Disabled access: Yes (both)
Customers: Mixed, local and traveler, business,
   couples
Lunch: *Frontera Grill:* Tuesday–Friday,
   11:30 A.M.–2:30 P.M.; *Topolobampo:* Tuesday–
   Friday, 11:30 A.M.–2 P.M.
Dinner: *Frontera Grill:* Tuesday–Thursday, 5:20–
   10 P.M.; Friday and Saturday, 5–11 P.M.
   Topolobampo: Tuesday–Thursday, 5:30–
   9:30 P.M.; Friday and Saturday, 5:30–10:30 P.M.

Atmosphere / setting: *Frontera Grill:* casual and
rustic; attractive Mexican art and touches; sidewalk
cafe. *Topolobampo:* more formal and elegant;
comfortable.

House specialities: Menu changes every two weeks.
Examples from *Frontera* include: tacos al carbón
(beef, poultry, or fish grilled over a wood fire, with
roasted pepper rajas, salsas, other accompaniments,
and homemade tortillas); wood-grilled fish and meats
such as pork tenderloin marinated in red chili-apricot
mole sauce, and black tiger shrimp in green pumpkin
seed mole with roasted chayote and zucchini. Cooking
is more refined at *Topolobampo*. Appetizer sampler

might offer crispy, smoky-flavored pork carnitas, guacamole with tomatillos, cactus salad, and more. Fish get unusual treatment, such as succulent pan-roasted sea bass with roasted garlic, sweet plantains, toasted pecans, wine-marinated prunes, and olive oil, with red chili rice. Another sampler plate might offer chicken enchiladas in green pumpkin seed mole; griddle-baked quesadilla of cheese, duck, and peppers; tostada of marinated cactus salad and black beans. Good desserts at both places, such as special ice cream and cooked plantains.

Other recommendations: *Frontera Grill:* tortilla soup; jicama salad; pollo en crema poblana. Various types of chilies are used in sauces that range from mild and earthy to hot and spicy. *Topolobampo:* sopa Azteca with chicken breast, avocado, and cheese; cod empanadas; tamale of fresh masa with pheasant; roasted capon breast stuffed with squash blossoms and wild greens.

Summary & comments: The menu offers a great variety of some rarely known dishes from regional Mexican cuisine. Owners Rick Bayless (chef) and wife Deanne (manager) lived in Mexico and co-authored a cookbook, *Authentic Mexican,* which was published about the time their Frontera Grill restaurant opened several years ago. Both the book and restaurant received good reviews. Many reports from diners and one personal experience indicate that service could be friendlier and more accommodating, especially at the entrance regarding seating.

Honors / Awards: *London Herald* and *New York Times* reviews. Recognized as the best-researched Mexican restaurant offering regional dishes.

Gabriel's Restaurant

French/Italian   ★★★★   **Moderate**

---

310 Greenbay Road, Highwood
(708) 433-0031
Zone 11   Northern Suburbs

Quality	Value
93	**C**

Reservations: Recommended
When to go: Busiest on weekends but also full during
   week
Entree range: $17–26; 4-course degustation menu,
   $29.95
Payment: All major credit cards
Service rating: ★★★★¹/₂
Friendliness rating: ★★★★¹/₂
Parking: Street and behind restaurant
Bar: Full service; also separate bar from dining area
Wine selection: 90 French, Italian, and Californian
   wines, $22–225; by the glass, $6–7
Dress: Upscale casual, from chic shorts to business
   suits
Disabled access: Yes
Customers: Varied, couples, families, business, local
Dinner: Tuesday–Saturday, 5–10 P.M.

Atmosphere / setting: European bistro with mahogany wood paneling; beautiful open kitchen with hanging copper pots, and the chef-owner and several sous chefs in white toques; well-lit, alive, and active. When bustling, it can be noisy and a "rocking place."

House specialities: Pastas, such as the flavor-intense fettuccini with artichokes, sun-dried tomatoes, and crespelle with spinach and cheese; roasted capon with prosciutto and mushrooms; grilled portobello mushrooms with roasted red peppers; fettuccini with artichokes and sun-dried tomatoes; papillote of bass with lemon and herb vinaigrette (beautifully served with the top of the paper wrap peeled off, showing the bass and potatoes with green herbs around); tender veal saltimbocca with sage sauce and a garden of colorful vegetables.

Other recommendations: Risotto (e.g., with corn, spinach, Gorgonzola); roasted saddle of rabbit with rosemary sauce. Desserts like roasted pear with mascarpone cream and warm apple tart with caramel ice cream.

Summary & comments: Gabriel Viti was executive chef at Carlos' in nearby Highland Park after working with some of the best European chefs in France, Switzerland, and Italy. In May 1993, he opened his own place and designed it to be relaxed and comfortable, offering both Italian and French cooking at moderate prices. He's avoided the luxury high-priced items, but uses his classic techniques on quality ingredients and produces some wonderful food, all served with style. Try the degustation meal, a surprise menu from the chef, which includes an appetizer, pasta, entree, and dessert for $29.95.

Galans

Ukrainian   ★★   **Inexpensive/Moderate**

2212 West Chicago Avenue
(312) 292-1000
Zone 2   North Central/O'Hare

Quality	Value
74	C

Reservations: Accepted
When to go: Any time; weekends for music
Entree range: $5.95–15.95
Payment: Major credit cards
Service rating: ★★★
Friendliness rating: ★★★
Parking: Lot
Bar: Features Russian beer and many vodkas
Wine selection: Californian and Chilean selections,
  $14–18 a bottle; sparkling, $25; several Californian,
  by the glass up to $3.50
Dress: Casual to dressy, depending on time
Disabled access: Yes
Customers: Mixed, including ethnic
Lunch/Dinner: Tuesday–Thursday, 11:30 A.M.–
  10 P.M.; Friday and Saturday, 11:30 A.M.–
  11 P.M.; Sunday, noon–9 P.M.

Atmosphere / setting: Comfortable, spacious,
attractive room; chairs on coasters.

House specialities: Galan's herring; the Kozak feast
includes borscht, salad, cabbage rolls, delicious
Ukrainian sausage, varenyky (filled dumplings),
kebabs, potato pancake, dessert (average apple
strudel), and coffee a la Galan's (with brandy and
whipped cream), $15.95.

Other recommendations: Chicken Lviv (boneless
breasts in wine sauce with rice pilaf); ground veal
patties in mushroom sauce.

Entertainment & amenities: Dancing on Friday
evening; guitar and accordian duo, Saturday evening.

Summary & comments: Seemingly the only
Ukrainian restaurant, so there's no comparison, except
with similar Slavic cuisines. The dishes are hearty and
presented nicely, but cooking is uneven—sometimes
too salty (ikra, creamy roe dip, for example), sometimes tasteless (stuffed cabbage), and the potato
pancakes might be greasy. Very friendly, nice staff and
overall a pleasant ethnic experience.

Geja's Cafe

Fondue	★★★½	Moderate

340 West Armitage Avenue
(312) 281-9101
Zone 1   North Side

Quality	Value
88	**B**

Reservations: Accepted Sunday–Thursday; on Friday and Saturday first seating at 5 P.M.

When to go: Weeknights, early in evening

Entree range: $75 dinner for 2 includes appetizer, wine, and entree

Payment: Major credit cards

Service rating: ★★★½

Friendliness rating: ★★★★

Parking: Valet, $5

Bar: Full service

Wine selection: 250 international selections; 24 by the glass

Dress: Upscale casual to formal

Disabled access: Stairs; no access

Customers: Couples, business, yuppie, all ages

Dinner: Monday–Thursday, 5–10:30 P.M.; Friday, 5 P.M.–midnight; Saturday, 5 P.M.–12:30 A.M.; Sunday, 4:30–10 P.M.

Atmosphere / setting: Voted "most romantic restaurant" many times by *Chicago* magazine.

House specialities: Classic cheese fondue; seafood, chicken, steak, and combo fondues; chocolate fondue served with fruit and cake.

Other recommendations: Sausage and cheese platter with salad.

Entertainment & amenities: Nightly flamenco or classical guitarist.

Summary & comments: Walk down a few steps into a romantic oasis in Lincoln Park and enter a sensual culinary experience. Fondue is a communal way of dining, and it's alive and thriving at Geja's, celebrating its 30th year in 1995. Order a la carte or the complete dinners. For a taste of Switzerland, try the classic cheese fondue made with Gruyère and kirschwasser, served with bread and crisp apple wedges for dipping. Flaming chocolate fondue is flambéed with orange liqueur and served with fruit and pound cake for dipping.

Gibson's Steakhouse

Steak   ★★★★½   **Moderate/Very Exp.**

1028 North Rush Street
(312) 266-8999
Zone 3   Near North

Quality	Value
94	**C**

Reservations: Recommended
When to go: Crowded most evenings
Entree range: $11–48; colossal surf and turf, $85
Payment: All major credit cards
Service rating: ★★★★½
Friendliness rating: ★★★★
Parking: Valet
Bar: Full service; the signature drink is the Gibson (large martini)
Wine selection: International; mostly Californian and French
Dress: Business, dressy—tuxedos are not unusual
Disabled access: Yes
Customers: Diverse, masculine group spanning various backgrounds; mostly locals ages 20–60; lots of "local celebs" including Harry Caray, and international celebs such as Frank Sinatra
Dinner: Monday–Saturday, 5:15 P.M.–midnight; Sunday, 4:15 P.M.–midnight; bar remains open every day, 3 P.M.–1:30 A.M.

Atmosphere / setting: 1940s clubby wooden art deco; looks old (but not worn) with antiques and dated photos; comfortable.

House specialities: Steaks are prime aged. Bone-in sirloin (also known as Kansas City strip); Chicago cut (huge rib-eye steak with fat trimmed); snow and stone crab claws appetizer.

Other recommendations: Lobster tail; planked whitefish; chargrilled swordfish; 1 1/4-lb. baked potatoes; carrot cake.

Entertainment & amenities: Live piano every evening; lively bar.

Summary & comments: Recognized by steak afficionados as one of the city's top places for prime cuts, with prices to match. All the quality steakhouses are expensive, so this one is competitive with the herd. Food is elegantly served by polite waiters in attractive, comfortable surroundings.

Golden Ox

German/American   ★★★★   **Moderate**

1578 North Clybourn Avenue
(312) 664-0780
Zone 1   North Side

Quality	Value
90	**C**

Reservations: Appreciated but not necessary
When to go: 11 A.M.–2 P.M., 5–9 P.M.
Entree range: $11.50–25
Payment: All major credit cards
Service rating: ★★★
Friendliness rating: ★★★¹/₂
Parking: Free valet
Bar: Full service
Wine selection: Substantial international list; French, Spanish, German, domestics
Dress: Casual to formal
Disabled access: Yes
Customers: Diverse, local, travelers, couples, business, family
Lunch/Dinner: Monday–Saturday, 11 A.M.– 11 P.M.; Sunday, 3–9 P.M.

Atmosphere / setting: Magnificent and very comfortable. Intricate decoration with shiny brown shellacked walls, paintings, murals depicting classics (the Ziegfield and Brunhilde story), cuckoo clocks, ornate beer steins. Looks like an ancient castle or museum. Carpeted; red ceiling with black beams; fireplace; brown leather chairs; gold tablecloths with white covers; dirndl-clad waitresses.

House specialities: Bavarian-style bratwurst; smoked Thuringer; potato pancakes; Wiener schnitzel; sauerbrauten; paprika rahm schnitzel; crisp half roasted duckling; fresh seafood (e.g., imported Dover sole, broiled walleyed pike). Entrees are served with choice of spaetzle, potato, or butter noodles.

Other recommendations: Hasenpfeffer (in season— imported rabbit, marinated and stewed); sausage plate; fresh chopped chicken liver; oyster a la Golden Ox; kalte kartoffel (cold potato) suppe; tortes.

Entertainment & amenities: Zither player on Saturday evenings; strolling musician on Friday evenings. Browsing through the spectacularly decorated rooms.

Summary & comments: Pricier than most German restaurants, but Golden Ox has a fuller traditional German menu—well-prepared—and an exquisite atmosphere. It is the best German restaurant I know of. Quality has been maintained over the years, but service can be slow and occasionally uninformed in the wine area. Overall, friendly and accommodating.

Honors / Awards: *Food Industry News* award for Best German Restaurant.

Gordon

New American ★★★★ **Moderate**

500 North Clark Street
(312) 467-9780
Zone 4   The Loop

Quality	Value
93	**C**

Reservations: Recommended
When to go: Major destination dining—corporate and special occasions
Entree range: $19–26
Payment: All major credit cards
Service rating: ★★★★
Friendliness rating: ★★★★
Parking: Valet
Bar: Full service; specializes in single malt scotches
Wine selection: In depth American and French; many nice choices by the glass and half bottle
Dress: Jackets requested; business attire; tends to be dressier in evenings
Disabled access: Yes
Customers: Corporate executives and business, movie and TV personalities, social; couples, especially weekend evenings
Dinner: Sunday–Thursday, 5:30–9:30 P.M.; Friday and Saturday, 5:30 P.M.–midnight

Atmosphere / setting: Attractive bar entry; divided dining space includes one elevated section. Eclectic and ornate; slightly surreal contemporary art with colorful, amusing avant garde murals. Large vases of flowers.

House specialities: Signature appetizer: artichoke fritters with béarnaise sauce; warm angelhair salad of nine organic greens, marinated tomatoes, chiffonade arugula, olives, and balsamic vinaigrette; grilled rack of lamb, crispy Gorgonzola polenta, and red wine–olive sauce; roast or pan-fried sturgeon, mushroom risotto, haricots verts, corn, and truffle oil. Desserts: warm flourless chocolate cake (a soufflé) with chocolate sauce and homemade vanilla ice cream is one of the best chocolate desserts anywhere; raspberry and chocolate crème brûlée is constructed so the custard is atop a chocolate ganache layer with a raspberry garnish.

Other recommendations: Gordon salmon gravlax, crispy vegetable salad, watercress, and orange vinaigrette; roasted lobster (off the shell) and spiced Chinese cabbage with curry-kaffir lime sauce scented with garlic; jalapeño-ginger–crusted salmon with peanut-glazed soba noodles and fermented black beans (nine flavors on the plate). One daily special: grilled swordfish, olive pesto, potato puree, roast shallot, and tomato salsa.

Entertainment & amenities: Live mellow jazz (usually a trio) and dancing on Friday and Saturday nights.

Summary & comments: When Gordon Sinclair started this business more than a decade ago, the neighborhood was still scruffy and derelict. It has since blossomed into a thriving restaurant, antique shop, and gallery district. His flamboyant style, ability to maintain high standards despite rotating chefs (almost one per year), and occasional promotional events make this a rather eccentric place of quality with distinctive character. The menu includes quotes such as, "Sex is good, but not as good as fresh sweet corn"—Garrison Keillor. Complimentary appetizers are served, such as marinated shrimp in puff pastry. Entrees are available in half portions, which doubles your sampling pleasure. Gordon enjoys working on his farm; certain days, his lettuces, tomatoes, and other produce appear on the menu. Restaurateur John Fleming recently became his partner, and together they opened Gordon's Cafe in the space of the former Cricket's in the fall of 1994. The cooking of the latest chef, Mark Dorian, was some of the finest in Gordon's history, and he is scheduled to move on to the cafe.

Honors / Awards: *Mobil* 4 Star; *Wine Spectator* Award of Excellence.

The Greenery

American   ★★★½   **Moderate/Expensive**

---

117 North Avenue, Barrington
(708) 381-9000
Zone 10   Northwest Suburbs

Quality	Value
88	C

Reservations: Recommended
When to go: Any time
Entree range: $16–24
Payment: All major credit cards
Service rating: ★★★★
Friendliness rating: ★★★★★
Parking: Street
Bar: Full service, including award-winning beer list
Wine selection: Extensive, award-winning all-American list
Dress: Casual but elegant
Disabled access: Has 3 front stairs, but staff will help those in wheelchairs
Customers: Diverse
Dinner: Monday–Thursday, 5:30–9 P.M.; Friday and Saturday, 5:30–10 P.M.

Atmosphere / setting: Casually elegant. Housed in a wing of an 1850 schoolhouse; five distinctive rooms, decorated with plants, pastel prints, and colorful valances. White linen-covered tables, fresh flowers.

House specialities: Seasonal menu; jumbo gulf shrimp and sausage grilled and served with a Creole mustard sauce; sauté of wild mushrooms; Maryland blue crab cakes and three-citrus sauce; homemade dessert of apple pie with caramel and peanuts.

Other recommendations: Grilled Missouri pheasant, leeks, roasted red peppers, and jalapeños; roasted South Carolina quail stuffed with caramelized garlic, mashed potatoes; hickory-grilled breast of turkey with sage mustard marinade; southern Florida spicy chicken and sweet potato salad; homemade banana cream pie.

Entertainment & amenities: Jazz music.

Summary & comments: The menu here takes the diner on a regional tour of America, with many state foods featured, such as Wisconsin goat cheese and Missouri pheasant. There's a sprinkling of Creole and other touches from New Orleans, where owners

Catherine and Chef David Koelling worked before coming here. David's cooking is delightfully simple and derives most of its flavor from herbs, infused oils, condiments (such as mustard), and imported items such as sherry, wasabi, and soy. It's healthful, with very few butter sauces, and it's patriotic with foreign accents, correctly representing our country's people. The added pleasure of dining at the Greenery is the charming, historical building and peaceful setting in a residental suburban neighborhood. It's worth a drive from the city—unless there's a snowstorm.

Honors / Awards: *Wine Spectator* Award of Excellence since 1988; 3 stars by the *Chicago Tribune;* 4 stars by *North Shore* magazine.

Gypsy's Cove

Spanish/Tapas ★★★ **Inexpensive/Moderate**

3203 North Clark Street
(312) 281-6698
Zone 1   North Side

Quality	Value
83	**B**

Reservations: Recommended
When to go: Weekdays
Entree range: $7.95–12.95; tapas, $1.95–5.95
Payment: Major credit cards except DC
Service rating: ★★★
Friendliness rating: ★★★½
Parking: Valet
Bar: Full service, including margaritas
Wine selection: Mostly Spanish and Chilean; nice selection; sangria
Dress: Casual
Disabled access: Yes, including rest rooms
Customers: Mostly yuppie, mixed
Lunch/Dinner: Saturday, 11:30 A.M.–11 P.M.
Dinner: Monday–Friday, 4:30–10:30 P.M.; Sunday, 5–10:30 P.M.

Atmosphere / setting: Sophisticated yet informal with unique tile tabletops, carpets on wall, vivid paintings from Spain and Peru, and a bottle collection.

House specialities: Gambas al horno (soufflé-like shrimp and goat cheese); tortilla gitana (double-decker potato omelette); specials such as shrimp or thinly cut steak en las rocas (lightly broiled and flipped onto hot rock salt to continue cooking); plain flan and various flavors, including lemon, orange, and brandy.

Other recommendations: Several types of octopus, such as pulpo a la diabla (bedded in spicy annatto-seed sauce); patata bravas (potatoes with hot sauce); tortilla gitana (potato omelette); ceviche (fish marinated in lime juice); or shrimp with avocado and pink sauce.

Entertainment & amenities: Romantic Spanish and Latin American music on weekend nights.

Summary & comments: One of the newest tapas cafes, owned by a couple. Ossie Arciniega, the chef, is of Basque heritge and has lived in Peru. The cuisine reflects his background. His wife is fluent in Spanish and runs the dining room. The place has charm, and the cooking is creative and very full flavored.

Hans' Bavarian Lodge

German/American ★★★ **Inexpensive**

---

931 North Milwaukee Avenue, Wheeling

Quality	Value
80	B

(708) 537-4141

Zone 10   Northwest Suburbs

Reservations: Recommended
When to go: Weekdays
Entree range: Lunch, $6.25–9.25; dinner, $10.25–15.50
Payment: All major credit cards
Service rating: ★★★
Friendliness rating: ★★★$\frac{1}{2}$
Parking: Lot
Bar: Full service
Wine selection: Limited German, Californian; available by the glass (from $2.75) or bottle (from $9.50)
Dress: Casual
Disabled access: Yes, including rest rooms
Customers: Local; busloads come from other areas for Oktoberfest celebration
Lunch/Dinner: Tuesday–Thursday, 11:30 A.M.–11 P.M.; Friday and Saturday, noon–9 P.M.; Sunday, noon–4 P.M.

Atmosphere / setting: Large, old-world dark, quaint with stained-glass windows.

House specialities: Sausage sampler; sauerbrauten; beef roulade; veal creations (e.g., Wiener schnitzel; natur schnitzel Berghoff).

Other recommendations: German pot roast; roast duck; chicken schnitzel; chicken Cordon Bleu; combinations; American items (e.g., crab cakes and stuffed mushrooms).

Entertainment & amenities: Friday, zither and piano player; Saturday and Sunday, strolling accordianist.

Summary & comments: This suburban restaurant is owned by a member of the Berghoff family and is hugely successful. They sure know how to throw a big Oktoberfest party that continues for weeks, all under heated tents with many bands.

Honors / Awards: Rated Number One German Restaurant by *North Shore* magazine.

Harry Caray's

American/Italian ★★★½ **Moderate/Expensive**

---

33 West Kinzie Avenue
(312) 465-9269
Zone 4   The Loop

Quality	Value
86	**C**

Reservations: Lunch, recommended; dinner, recommended for 8 or more

When to go: Any time

Entree range: $8.95–39.95; pastas average $9.95; steaks average $28.95

Payment: Major credit cards

Service rating: ★★★★

Friendliness rating: ★★★★

Parking: Valet

Bar: Full service; bar is 60-feet, 6-inches long, which is the same distance from the home plate to the pitcher's mound

Wine selection: Extensive Italian and American; several by the glass

Dress: Casual

Disabled access: Yes, including rest rooms

Customers: Diverse, local, business, baseball fans, couples

Lunch: Monday–Friday, 11:30 A.M.–4 P.M. Appetizers and sandwiches served in the bar daily

Dinner: Monday–Thursday, 5–10:30 P.M.; Friday and Saturday, 5 P.M.–midnight; Sunday, 4–10 P.M.

Atmosphere / setting: Located in a historic red brick building. Pictures, memorabilia of the famous sportscaster; active bar/lounge; comfortable—usually busy—dining room. Private rooms upstairs.

House specialities: Grilled steak; fried calamari; chicken Vesuvio with terrific potatoes.

Other recommendations: Cheese ravioli with sea scallops; grilled fresh fish (marinated tuna, lightly crumbed, seasoned with rosemary, shines); trio of double lamb chops oreganato.

Entertainment & amenities: Browsing through the Harry Caray memorabilia and seeing the sportscaster when he makes an appearance.

Summary & comments: You can't miss the Chicago restaurant because Harry Caray's favorite exclamation, "Holy Cow!", is emblazoned on an outside wall. Named for the Cubs announcer, Harry Caray's is a splendid dining experience from the masterful opening pitch all the way through. Unlike many celebrity sports-figure places, this one takes the restaurant business seriously. Cubs announcer Harry Caray loves Italian fare, so it's on the menu, from salads to pastas and chicken Vesuvio (really a Chicago invention—not Italian). All the fish is fresh and grilled or otherwise cooked to perfection. Fresh herbs season much of the food. Desserts include a great carrot cake and small ice cream profiteroles with hot fudge and crème anglaise. Weekend lunch-goers might try the sandwich cart. The country cousin in Wheeling has separate management and some menu differences, but otherwise is very similar. Good Italian desserts and wines. The star makes appearances at both locations.

Harry Caray's (Wheeling)

American/Italian ★★★¹/₂   **Moderate**

---

933 North Milwaukee Avenue, Wheeling

Quality	Value
85	**C**

(708) 537-CUBS
Zone 10   Northwest Suburbs

Reservations: Recommended
When to go: Less busy 5–7 P.M. or after 9 P.M.
Entree range: $8.95–28.95
Payment: Major credit cards
Service rating: ★★★★
Friendliness rating: ★★★★
Parking: Nearby lot; complimentary parking Monday–Saturday
Bar: Full service
Wine selection: Italian and American; several by the glass
Dress: Casual to dressy
Disabled access: Yes
Customers: Diverse, local, business, baseball fans, family
Lunch: Monday–Friday, 11 A.M.–4 P.M.
Dinner: Monday–Thursday, 4–10 P.M.; Friday and Saturday, 4–11 P.M.; Sunday, 4–9 P.M.

Atmosphere / setting: Cubs memorabilia; fun, loud at times; comfortable dining room; one room is non-smoking. Lovely outdoor deck.

House specialities: Chicken Vesuvio; sirloin steak; various pastas and salads.

Other recommendations: Special seafood lasagna; fresh fish.

Summary & comments: This second Harry Caray's, named for the Cubs announcer, might have separate management and some differences in the menu and atmosphere, but it is a kindred spirit to its city cousin. It closes a bit earlier. The well-known veteran sportscaster makes appearances here, too.

Hatsuhana

Japanese	★★½	Inexpensive/Moderate

160 East Ontario Street
(312) 280-8287
Zone 3   Near North

Quality	Value
76	C

Reservations: Recommended
When to go: Before 7 P.M.
Entree range: $11–18; Hatsuhana special, complete dinner, $30
Payment: All major credit cards except DC
Service rating: ★★★
Friendliness rating: ★★★
Parking: Public lot nearby
Bar: Full service, including Japanese beer
Wine selection: Mostly Japanese; nice selection of cold saké, some hot; very limited Californian selection
Dress: Casual, business
Disabled access: Yes, including rest rooms
Customers: Local, mostly American
Lunch: Monday–Friday, 11:45 A.M.–2 P.M.
Dinner: Monday–Friday, 5:30–10 P.M.; Saturday, 5–10 P.M.

Atmosphere / setting: Similar to a Japanese sushi bar with tables off to the side. Often busy at lunch and certain dinner times.

House specialities: American combination sushi and chef's choice sushi. This is the best reason for coming here.

Other recommendations: Tempura and teriyaki dinners, which include soup, rice, and dessert. Some items available a la carte.

Entertainment & amenities: Sitting at the sushi bar to watch the chefs' skilled hands quickly cut fish fillets into sashimi. Order as you eat for more interaction and fun.

Summary & comments: Long-standing Gold Coast place with a following as well as some newcomers and tourists. Pricey compared to neighborhood sushi houses, but quality and variety are usually very good. Sushi bar items are the highlight; some Japanese dishes are inconsistent, as is the service.

Heaven on Seven

Cajun/Creole	★★★½	Inexpensive

111 North Wabash Avenue
(312) 263-6443
Zone 4   The Loop

Quality	Value
86	**B**

Reservations: Not accepted
When to go: Breakfast, 7 A.M.; lunch, 11:30 A.M.;
    before the lines or after lunchtime
Entree range: $3.50–9.95
Payment: Cash only
Service rating: ★★★½
Friendliness rating: ★★★★
Parking: Garage
Bar: None
Wine selection: None
Dress: Casual
Disabled access: Yes
Customers: Diverse, business, professional, shoppers
Breakfast/Lunch: Monday–Friday, 7 A.M.–5 P.M.;
    Saturday, 7:30 A.M.–3 P.M.
Dinner: Every third Friday of the month, 5–9 P.M.,
    and Fat Tuesday. Live New Orleans jazz band.

Atmosphere/setting: Upbeat; brown tables, each
with several bottles of hot sauce. Wooden floor, red
plantation plants, big hot-sauce collection, New
Orleans art.

House specialities: Southern fried chicken salad;
soft-shell poboys; pasta shrimp angry, pasta shrimp
voodoo; crayfish tamales; jambalaya; Louisiana soul.

Other recommendations: Crab cakes; chicken-fried
steak; rabbit with mushroom étouffée.

Summary & comments: Funky place on the seventh
floor of the Garland building in the Loop, which began
as the Garland Restaurant and Coffee Shop. The
Bannos family-owned place still serves regular
breakfast, but has made its reputation on the great
Creole and Cajun fare, every bit as delicious as in
Louisiana. Long lines at lunch move quickly. Those
who love food with a burn will have a field day trying
the various hot sauces on the table. After a meal here,
you'll think you've gone to Cajun heaven.

Honors/Awards: Recommended by various local
publications and *Newsweek* and *National Geographic*.

The Helmand

Afghani   ★★★½   **Inexpensive**

3201 North Halsted Street
(312) 935-2447
Zone 1   North Side

Quality	Value
80	**B**

Reservations: Recommended on Friday and Saturday
When to go: Weekdays
Entree range: $7.95–9.95; specials, $8.95–14.95
Payment: Major credit cards
Service rating: ★★★½
Friendliness rating: ★★★★
Parking: Garages nearby
Bar: Full service
Wine selection: Limited; mostly American; international; inexpensive overall; available by the bottle and by the glass
Dress: Casual
Disabled access: Rest rooms
Customers: Local, mostly upscale
Dinner: Monday–Thursday, 5–10:30 P.M.; Friday and Saturday, 5–11 P.M.; Sunday, 4–9 p.m.

Atmosphere / setting: Elegant, high-ceilinged room with chandeliers, Afghani rugs on brick walls, plants, and fresh flowers and candles on white tablecloths. Authentic taped music.

House specialities: Chowpan (half a rack of lamb with brown rice); chicken Lawand (boneless breast sautéed with tomatoes and mushrooms); marinated chicken kebab; cumin rice with pumpkin, yogurt, and garlic sauce; other vegetarian dishes.

Other recommendations: Aushak (Afghani ravioli appetizer with leeks, served on minted yogurt with ground beef sauce—there's also a vegetarian entree version); mantwo (onion- and beef-filled pastry shells on yogurt topped with carrots, yellow split peas, and beef sauce); and the popular kabuli (brown rice baked with chunks of lamb tenderloin, raisins, and carrots.

Summary & comments: Afghanistan is east of Iran and north of Pakistan, and its cuisine is a cross between Middle Eastern and Indian/Pakistani. This sophisticated restaurant is well established and has been consistently serving this exotic food with style in a charming atmosphere. Most entrees come with challow (cumin white rice) or pallow (Afghani brown rice) and vegetables. Sauces use yogurt, mint and other herbs, garlic, and lemon. The only hot spiciness was in one of the chutneys. Two of the four desserts, feereny (bland but velvety custard) and burfee (a dry mixture made with half each milk and cheese), combined to make a better sweet. Spiced cardamom tea is a good finale.

Hoang Mai

Vietnamese/Chinese   ★★★¹/₂   **Inexpensive**

5020 North Sheridan Road
(312) 561-3700
Zone 1   North Side

Quality	Value
89	**A**

Reservations: Accepted, but usually not necessary on
weekdays
When to go: Any time
Entree range: $3.95–8.95
Payment: VISA, MC
Service rating: ★★★
Friendliness rating: ★★★★¹/₂
Parking: Street
Bar: None
Wine selection: BYOB
Dress: Casual
Disabled access: Yes, including rest room
Customers: Local, yuppie, ethnic, family, singles
Open: Tuesday–Thursday, 10 A.M.–10 P.M.;
Friday, 10 A.M.–11 P.M.; Saturday, 9:30 A.M.–
11 P.M.; Sunday, 9:30 A.M.–10 P.M.; breakfast
items available all day

Atmosphere / setting: Attractive, clean store front
seating up to 100; simple decor with Asian wall
hangings and plants. Warm and rather intimate.

House specialities: Roast quail; fresh spring rolls;
Vietnamese crêpe (filled with shrimp-pork-vegetable
mixture); fried catfish with ginger sauce; lemongrass
shrimp; camp-fired beef; seafood in bird's nest.

Other recommendations: Hoang Mai special soup
with shrimp, pork, mushroom, and vegetables; crab
rangoon; shrimp wrapped in sugar cane with vegetables and vermicelli; eel in coconut milk curry in a clay
pot; steamed rice noodles, grilled beef, and lemongrass; exotic chicken stir-fried with vegetables and
spicy plum sauce; crispy noodle with combo topping.

Summary & comments: This restaurant is family-
owned, with the mother, Mai, as chef. Caring pervades
here from the fine, cooked-to-order food to the
attentive service. The extensive menu lists 183 items
—awesome! On several visits over the years, every
item has been delectable. Thai coffee is a nice finish.
Available for private parties.

Home Bakery

Polish/European ★★½ **Inexpensive**

2931 North Milwaukee Avenue
(312) 252-3708
Zone 2   North Central/O'Hare

Quality	Value
77	B

Reservations: Recommended
When to go: Any time
Entree range: $5–10
Payment: VISA, MC, D
Service rating: ★★½
Friendliness rating: ★★★½
Parking: Street; can be somewhat difficult
Bar: Beer, wine, vodka, cognac, and limited other drinks
Wine selection: About 10 selections; American, German, Hungarian, Polish, Austrian, Italian, and Australian; $12–15 a bottle; wine by the glass, $3
Dress: Casual; dressier on the weekend
Disabled access: Yes
Customers: International, couples, business, family, Polish, American, local, out-of-towners
Open: Monday–Saturday, 8 A.M.–9 P.M.; Sunday, 9 A.M.–9 P.M.; same menu day and evening

---

Atmosphere / setting: Space includes shop, deli, bakery, and 100-seat restaurant. Semi-romantic, medium lighting; gallery of paintings on the wall.

House specialities: Roast duck with rice, peppers, and mushrooms; Wiener schnitzel; beef stroganoff; Polish hunter's stew (bigos); Hungarian goulash; pierogi (dumplings stuffed with choice of cheese, potato, meat, blueberry, or strawberry filling).

Other recommendations: Polish plate; Swiss steak; large, crispy potato pancakes (some of the best); chicken Kiev; variety of herring; barley sausage. Soups of the day, including chicken noodle, white borscht, tomato, and potato. Polish pastries and torte.

Summary & comments: Food is simple, honest, well seasoned, and very home-style. Breakfast items include omelettes, waffles, and cereal. Lunch includes sandwiches or an a la carte special. Dinner can be a la carte or, for $1 more, complete with potato, rice or dumplings, vegetables, choice of Polish salad, soup, and dessert. You can have a full dinner for under $5.

Honda

Japanese   ★★★¹/₂   **Moderate**

540 North Wells Street
(312) 923-1010
Zone 4   The Loop

Quality	Value
88	**C**

Reservations: Accepted
When to go: Any time
Entree range: $17–22.50; sushi bar dinners, $15.50–22.50
Payment: Major credit cards
Service rating: ★★★¹/₂
Friendliness rating: ★★★★
Parking: Street
Bar: Full service
Wine selection: Californian, Japanese, saké
Dress: Business, dressier in evening
Disabled access: Yes
Customers: Local
Lunch: Monday–Friday, 11:30 A.M.–2 P.M.
Dinner: Monday–Thursday, 5:30–10 P.M.; Friday, 5:30–11 P.M.; Saturday, 5–11 P.M.; Sunday, 5–10 P.M.

Atmosphere / setting: Casual, plush Japanese decor; fine dining; sushi and kushi bar. The restaurant has two levels and tatami rooms (private Japanese rooms for groups of 10–20 people), which should be booked in advance.

House specialities: Kushi (skewered vegetables, meat, and seafood grilled and served with various condiments and dipping sauces). The only place in town with a kushi bar, where appetizers are served. Sushi (as one of sushi bar dinner selections, a la carte, or maki sushi, rolled with seaweed).

Other recommendations: Puree of winter squash soup; quail salad; kani su (cold crabmeat appetizer); hotategai yaki (sautéed scallops, asparagus, and lemon-soy butter); steamed salmon Honda-style.

Entertainment & amenities: Live piano.

Summary & comments: Large, elegant, Japanese-built fine dining establishment with overall good quality food and service. Menu has enough assortment to please a variety of tastes. Great for business entertaining and special occasions.

Hong Min Restaurant

Chinese/Dim Sum ★★★ **Inexpensive**

	Quality	Value
221 West Cermak Road, Chinatown (312) 842-5026 Zone 5 South Loop	85	B

8048 West 111th Street, Palos Hills
(708) 599-8488
Zone 8   Southern Suburbs

Reservations: Only accepted for 6 or more
When to go: Weekdays; weekends from 11 A.M.–
  3 P.M. and from 6–9 P.M. are busiest
Entree range: $5.95–19.95; one item $21
Payment: VISA, MC (Chicago); MC, AMEX (Palos
  Hills)
Service rating: ★★
Friendliness rating: ★★
Parking: 2-hour free parking at community lot on
  Cermak and Wentworth with validation (Chicago);
  60-car lot (Palos Hills)
Bar: BYOB (Chicago); full service (Palos Hills)
Wine selection: International (Chicago); mostly
  domestic (Palos Hills)
Dress: Casual
Disabled access: No (Chicago); yes (Palos Hills)
Customers: Local, ethnic, yuppie, tourists
Lunch/Dinner: *Chicago:* every day, 10 A.M.–2 A.M.;
  Palos Hills: every day, 11:30 A.M.–10 P.M.

Atmosphere / setting: Chicago: casual, store front,
booths and tables; capacity 105. Palos Hills: casual,
American, booths and tables; capacity 150.

House specialities: Seafood (e.g., fish with black
bean sauce; steamed sole; butterfly scallops); dim sum;
special hot pot dishes.

Other recommendations: Special menu with over 75
special Chinese dishes (e.g., bird's nest soup; duck of
West Lake—with barbecue pork and vegetables; kung
pao chicken—with roasted peanuts and hot sauce).

Summary & comments: Chef/owner William Tam
created a very ambitious menu, including some items
the Chinese love, such as duck feet with black
mushrooms, and some mundane chop suey and egg foo
young items. Virtually every category holds some
culinary treats.

Hubbard Street Grill

New American ★★★ Inexpensive/Moderate

---

351 West Hubbard Street
(312) 222-0770
Zone 4   The Loop

Quality	Value
81	C

Reservations: Recommended
When to go: Any time, but less busy in early
evenings, 5–5:30 P.M.; Wednesday–Saturday
evenings for live piano
Entree range: Lunch, $6.95–15.95; dinner, $7.95–
17.95
Payment: VISA, MC, AMEX, D, DC
Service rating: ★★★¹/₂
Friendliness rating: ★★★★
Parking: Valet for dinner
Bar: Full service
Wine selection: 100 American wines; up to $35;
9 by-the-glass choices, $3.95–4.95, including 3
Robert Mondavi Woodbridge selections and Iron
Horse Brut sparkling wine from Alexander Valley
Dress: Chic casual
Disabled access: Yes
Customers: Mixed locals; business, especially from
nearby Merchandise Mart and East Bank Club
(fitness center); couples
Lunch/Dinner: Monday–Thursday, 11:30 A.M.–
10 P.M.; Friday, 11:30 A.M.–11 P.M.
Dinner: Saturday, 5–11 P.M.

Atmosphere / setting: Large 140-seat loft space
decorated in muted greens and tans with colorful
mural. Open kitchen; chic and casual interior designed
by Marve Cooper.

House specialities: Appetizer: dill-cured king salmon
with Dijon mustard glaze. Entrees: mixed grill with
salmon fillet, shrimp skewer (the best of the trio), and
skirt steak (slightly dry); grilled ahi tuna steak (was
properly cooked to medium rare) with roasted peppers,
mixed greens, and zesty soy-sherry vinaigrette; grilled
gulf shrimp with angelhair pasta in spicy bouillabaisse
broth; herb-roasted half chicken in natural juices with
whole garlic and cracked pepper. All entrees come
with generous portions of side dishes. Sides to try:
roasted garlic-Romano mashed potatoes; wilted

spinach with olive oil and lemon; steamed broccoli in pine-nut butter.

Other recommendations: Boneless grilled chicken breast with goat cheese-pesto filling and beefsteak tomato; traditional Caesar salad with good egg-less dressing, but was missing croutons; superb Grillroom salad with tomatoes, mushrooms, red onions, and blue cheese; grilled calamari appetizer with flavorful tomato-citrus relish; Ketchapeno, the chef's creation— a ketchup-salsa blend (bottled and available in supermarkets), accompanies sandwiches and hand-cut french fries.

Entertainment & amenities: Pianist featured Wednesday–Saturday evenings.

Summary & comments: This sophisticated but casual modern American grill was a new venture in spring of 1994 of two alumni of Lettuce Entertain You Enterprises: executive chef David Schy (former LEYE corporate chef and executive chef of Hat Dance, where he made culinary waves by fusing Japanese and Mexican cuisines) and general manager Marty Schwartz. Schy is offering all his favorite dishes here—he desires to treat guests to what he enjoys most. Portions are large, so many appetizers can be shared. His cooking is rather hearty but light, using naturally reduced sauces and lively salsas. A couple of items were bland, such as the red chili–black bean couscous. The menu lists items by price, starting with the lowest, and seems to have something for just about any taste. Service is attentive, knowledgeable, and cordial.

Hunan Cafe

Chinese   ★★★   **Inexpensive/Moderate**

625 North Michigan Avenue
(312) 482-9898
Zone 3   Near North

Quality	Value
83	**C**

Reservations: Recommended
When to go: Any time
Entree range: $6.95–19.95
Payment: All major credit cards
Service rating: ★★★¹/₂
Friendliness rating: ★★★¹/₂
Parking: Discount parking available
Bar: Full service
Wine selection: Mostly Californian and French; some
   Chinese (e.g., plum wine); $14–26 a bottle; several
   by the glass, $4.50
Dress: Casual
Disabled access: Yes
Customers: Diverse
Lunch/Dinner: Every day, 11:30 A.M.–10:30 P.M.

Atmosphere / setting: Modern Chinese; spacious,
handsome, comfortable interior; one level below
sidewalk level.

House specialities: Dim sum available all day (e.g.,
steamed shrimp dumplings, vegetarian dumplings, pot
stickers, shrimp toast, stuffed bean-curd rolls). Stuffed
crab claws (Hunan appetizer); imperial honey ham
(with lotus seeds in sweet laurel bloom flower sauce);
empress sizzling lamb with leek; crispy chicken.

Other recommendations: Roast Peking duck
(available with no advance notice); chrysanthemum
fish sweet and sour; lobster with ginger and tomato
sauce; peacock pork; stuffed banana with red bean
paste (for two).

Summary & comments: This is one of the only
places to get dim sum downtown, and perhaps the only
Chinese restaurant serving it all day long. Make a meal
from the dim sum special menu, or start with dumplings and select one of the many unusual entrees. It's
even possible to order Peking duck at the last moment
here, unlike most other places, which request a day's
advance notice. Hot and spicy dishes are starred.

Ishtar Inn

Middle Eastern ★★★½ **Inexpensive**

615 North Wells Street
(312) 587-0721
Zone 3   Near North

Quality	Value
90	B

Reservations: Recommended for weekends
When to go: Any time
Entree range: $5.50–11.95
Payment: All major credit cards
Service rating: ★★★★
Friendliness rating: ★★★★★
Parking: 2 hours free, facilities on Erie and Wells,
  and Franklin and Ohio
Bar: Full service
Wine selection: Limited; mostly Californian, some
  Italian, $16–28 a bottle; only 3 by the glass
Dress: Casual
Disabled access: Yes, including rest rooms
Customers: 95% local, some Middle Eastern and
  travelers, business, couples
Lunch/Dinner: Monday–Thursday, 11 A.M.–
  10 P.M.; Friday and Saturday, 11 A.M.–midnight;
  Sunday, 2–10 P.M.

Atmosphere/setting: Beautiful Assyrian murals
depicting ancient Assyrian life, design circa 800 B.C.
Main dining area divided into two sections; white
tablecloths covered with paper.

House specialities: Stuffed lamb; dolmeh (stuffed
grape leaves with meat or vegetables); kibbeh (fried
cracked wheat and meat mixture); tabbouleh (cracked
wheat salad); baba ganouj (eggplant-tahini dip); Ishtar
platter: shawarma (gyros), kefta kebab, beef kebab,
and chicken.

Other recommendations: Vegetarian entrees, including a combo plate; couscous (meat or vegetarian).

Summary & comments: This downtown gem is one
of the very best Middle Eastern restaurants around for
its charming atmosphere, array of skillfully prepared
dishes, and friendly staff. The cuisine is very meat- and
vegetable-oriented—no fish. All the dishes sampled
were robustly well flavored and fresh; entrees come
with salad, rice, and pita bread. The bargain prices are
unheard of downtown—a real find!

Jackie's

French/Asian ★★★★ **Moderate/Expensive**

2478 North Lincoln Avenue
(312) 880-0003
Zone 1   North Side

Quality	Value
90	**C**

Reservations: Recommended
When to go: Weeknights
Entree range: Lunch, $7.95–14.95; dinner,
   $18.95–25
Payment: All major credit cards
Service rating: ★★★★
Friendliness rating: ★★★★
Parking: Lunch, free lot behind resturant; dinner,
   valet, $5
Bar: Full service
Wine selection: Variety of European and American;
   50–60 bottles, $20 and up; 6–7 by the glass, $5–7
Dress: Nice casual
Disabled access: Yes
Customers: Couples, young families with kids
Lunch: Tuesday–Saturday, 11:30 A.M.–1:30 P.M.;
   Sunday and Monday, closed.
Dinner: Tuesday–Thursday, 5:30–8:30 P.M.;
   Friday and Saturday, 5:30–9:30 P.M.; Sunday and
   Monday, closed.

Atmosphere / setting: Romantic, simple elegance,
comfortable, pleasant with floral paintings and fresh
flowers; seats 80.

House specialities: Tri-colored wontons (appetizer):
half of them filled with crabmeat, ginger, goat cheese,
and sun-dried tomato, and half filled with snails, goat
cheese, garlic, basil, and sun-dried tomatoes, served
with napa cabbage and shiitake mushrooms in a ginger
butter sauce; fresh fish pyramid trilogy: tower of crab
cake, fish of the day, and fresh shrimp combination,
surrounded by red chili pepper fettuccini, diced
tomato, peas, feta cheese, Greek olives, and Szechuan
pepper-butter sauce; poached salmon with linguini
noodles and beluga caviar with white wine-chive
sauce. Signature dessert: chocolate bag filled with
white chocolate mousse, strawberries, and kiwi, with
raspberry sauce.

Other recommendations: Hot seafood terrine served with lemon-butter sauce (appetizer); scallopini veal, sweet breads, and goose liver mousse with morel mushroom sauce; fresh tuna with risotto and flageolets (tuna marinated with soya and ginger, sautéed medium-rare and garnished with raspberry, snails, and blue cheese, and raspberry demi-glacé butter sauce).

Summary & comments: Owner/chef Jackie Shen infuses her French cooking with touches from her Hong Kong Chinese background, with results such as a Szechuan pepper-butter sauce for her fish pyramid. She gathers various foreign ingredients, from Polish kielbasa to Moroccan couscous, and melds them with the likes of Wyoming ranch-raised buffalo and New Zealand venison with green peppercorn sauce. She has a penchant for raspberry sauce—used in entrees as well as desserts, and she sprinkles fresh, edible flowers as garnish. Her signature "chocolate bag" dessert is a must.

Honors / Awards: DiRoNA Award.

Jerome's

American   ★★★   **Inexpensive/Moderate**

2450 North Clark Street
(312) 327-2207
Zone 1   North Side

Quality	Value
82	**C**

Reservations: Accepted
When to go: Any time
Entree range: Lunch, $5.25–9.95; dinner, $8.95–15.95. Winter Sunday buffet brunch, $12.95
Payment: VISA, MC, AMEX
Service rating: ★★★
Friendliness rating: ★★★½
Parking: 2 hours in free lot
Bar: Full service
Wine selection: American, Spanish, French, Italian
Dress: Casual
Disabled access: Yes
Customers: Lincoln Park locals, young professionals
Breakfast: Saturday, 9:30 A.M.–3 P.M.
Brunch: Sunday buffet, 9:30 A.M.–3 P.M.
Lunch/Dinner: Summer, 11:30 A.M.–11 P.M.; winter, 11:30 A.M.–10 P.M.

Atmosphere / setting: Casual fine dining in a smoke-free dining room a few steps up from the entry room. Lovely outdoor deck overlooking sidewalk and street in summer.

House specialties: Brie and pear empanada; grilled salmon with chef's butter sauce; Billy's pride rib-eye steak with peppercorns, grilled mushrooms, and onions. Lunch: Alan's vegetarian chili; curried chicken salad. Brunch: millet bread French toast.

Other recommendations: Hummus with pita; spinach salad with kiwi, orange, strawberry, cashews, chevre, and raspberry vinaigrette; marinated grilled skirt steak. Lunch: all-homemade hamburger (including the pickle); smoked turkey on millet bread with cranberry mayonnaise.

Summary & comments: Ever since Jerome Kliejunas started this restaurant (now under new management; Jerome does the catering) he's prepared fresh, pure food without preservatives and processed foods. Many old favorites remain while the menu is enlivened with new specials.

Jilly's Cafe

New American ★★★½ **Inexpensive/Moderate**

2614 Green Bay Road, Evanston
(708) 869-7636
Zone 11   Northern Suburbs

Quality	Value
85	**B**

Reservations: Recommended
When to go: Any time
Entree range: $9–15
Payment: VISA, MC, AMEX
Service rating: ★★★★
Friendliness rating: ★★★★½
Parking: Street
Bar: Wine and beer
Wine selection: International; mostly American, French, Italian, German, Australian, and Spanish, $15–72; many by the glass, $3.50–6.; some half bottles
Dress: Casual to elegant
Disabled access: Yes
Customers: Local North Shore clientele, business, couples
Brunch: Sunday, 10:30 A.M.–2 P.M.
Lunch: Tuesday–Friday, 11:30 A.M.–2 P.M.
Dinner: Tuesday–Thursday, 5–9 P.M.; Friday and Saturday, 5–10 P.M.; Sunday, 5–8 P.M.

Atmosphere / setting: Charming, intimate setting—resembles cozy French country inn with white stucco and dark wood walls, ceiling fans, French pictures, wine bottles, copper pots, white tablecloths, fresh flowers, and plants. Non-smoking restaurant.

House specialities: Escargot with Gorgonzola cream and grilled polenta; daily foccacia; fresh fish, such as oven-roasted Chilean sea bass with sesame seed crust and stir-fry angelhair pasta in ginger tomato broth. Nicely balanced small menu with pastas, seafood, fowl, game, beef, and veal, such as the creative scallopini with Maytag blue cheese, capers, potato Napoleon, and veal jus. Pastries are homemade by co-owner. Trio of desserts: strawberry crème brûlée (flavors change); ice cream and lemon sherbet with raspberry sauce; chocolate apricot cake with chocolate sauce.

Other recommendations: Special appetizer: toasted cheese ravioli with tomato sauce; vegetarian entree: eggplant Napoleon with sweet potato haystack and vegetable coulis; special lamb chops, mashed potato topped with mashed sweet potato, green beans, and minted carrots; apricot almond tart.

Summary & comments: A little gem in Evanston that's worth seeking out. The atmosphere is charming, and the service reflects the tastes of the European owner, Eric, and his wife, Diane, who is the pastry chef. Much of the wait staff is French and very attentive and friendly. They proudly show dishes being served so you can see them. Lovely presentations. Generally full-flavored, healthful cooking. Entrees come with soup or house salad and sorbet intermezzo, which once was honeydew melon and strawberry sorbet of perfect consistency. A great value, too.

Honors / Awards: *Mobil* 2 Stars.

Jimmy's Place

New French   ★★★★   **Moderate/Expensive**

3420 North Elston Avenue
(312) 539-2999
Zone 1   North Side

Quality	Value
90	**C**

Reservations: Recommended
When to go: Any time; weekends might be busier
Entree range: $28.50–32.50; best option is $45 prix fixe (choice of any appetizer, house salad, entree, and dessert)
Payment: All major credit cards except AMEX
Service rating: ★★★★¹/₂
Friendliness rating: ★★★★¹/₂
Parking: Free adjacent lot
Bar: None
Wine selection: Excellent list of 80 selections featuring mostly French and American, $20.50–125; 2 whites and 2 reds by the glass, $4.50–6.50; several half bottles
Dress: Neat attire, jacket recommended but not required
Disabled access: Yes
Customers: Couples, local, business
Dinner: Monday–Saturday, 5–9:30 P.M. (last seating)

Atmosphere / setting: Operatic theme; walls decorated with a great collection of opera memorabilia and tapes of great operas help create the mood. Two well-appointed, cozy rooms, one with windows. This was the first fine-dining restaurant in Chicago to be declared non-smoking, but now smoking is allowed on weekdays only in one room.

House specialities: Menu changes every six weeks; mixed green salad included with main courses; assorted house pâtés and terrines; "Jimmy's Place" salad (assorted baby greens in champagne vinaigrette, warm Sainte Maure goat cheese, tapenade croutons, and prosciutto); sweet breads and other organ meats such as calves' brains (e.g., sautéed medallion of veal and braised sweetbreads in Madeira sauce with red lentils and truffle oil); grilled saddle of lamb with "eggplant caviar" in sun-dried tomato cream sauce; Tosca's Kiss, a seductive turtle-type pastry with pecans, dark chocolate, and warm caramel sauce.

Other recommendations: Chef's specials, including fresh fish; appetizer of house-cured salmon in herbs with yogurt-dill sauce; Dungeness crab and cucumber salad.

Summary & comments: Owner Jimmy Rohr is the savvy, hands-on owner at this most creative restaurant in an unlikely industrial neighborhood on Elston Avenue. His love and knowledge of opera is infused throughout his place. Due to allergies, he's had to ban smoking and perfumes for periods of time. His chef Sandra Beckett continues the fine cooking of her predecessor and Rohr's partner, Kevin Shikami, but without as much Asian influence. There are many Italian touches which she creatively integrates with her light French cuisine.

Honors / Awards: 4 stars from *Mobil,* 3.5 stars in *Chicago* magazine, top rating in *Gault Millau Guide.*

Julio's Latin Cafe

Caribbean   ★★★   **Moderate**

---

95 South Rand Road, Lake Zurich
(708) 438-3484
Zone 10   Northwest Suburbs

Quality	Value
83	**C**

Reservations: Recommended
When to go: Any time
Entree range: $9.75–16.75
Payment: VISA, MC, AMEX, D, DC
Service rating: ★★★★
Friendliness rating: ★★★★
Parking: Free lot
Bar: Small bar; several types of margaritas
Wine selection: American, Chilean, Argentinean,
   Spanish, and Californian
Dress: Casual
Disabled access: Yes
Customers: Local
Lunch: Tuesday–Friday, 11:30 A.M.–3 P.M.
Dinner: Monday–Thursday, 4:30–10 P.M.; Friday
   and Saturday, 4:30–10:30 P.M.; Sunday, 4–
   8:30 P.M.

Atmosphere / setting: Casual fine dining; cozy with
South American touches.

House specialities: Pollo Caribe (skinless, boneless
chicken sautéed, garnished with shrimp, and served
with mango sauce); paella (seafood, chicken, and
sausage over Spanish saffron rice); parrillada gaucho
(grilled New York strip steak with chicken and turkey
sausage, roast bell peppers, and fried bananas).

Other recommendations: Ceviche; shrimp avocado
salad; Caribbean Cornish hen (semi-boneless with
sweet-sour tamarind sauce).

Entertainment & amenities: Live entertainment on
weekends, 7:30–10:30 P.M. Classical and jazz guitarist
from Brazil; Spanish and English singers.

Summary & comments: This intimate spot has
carved a niche for itself in the northwest suburban area.
Discriminating diners enjoy the food and the friendly
service any time, and the bonus of live jazz on
weekends doubles the pleasure. An expansion is slated
for end of 1994.

Kanval Palace

Indian	★★½	Inexpensive

2501 West Devon Avenue
(312) 761-7270
Zone 1   North Side

Quality	Value
76	**B**

Reservations: Recommended
When to go: Weekdays
Entree range: $5.50–13.95
Payment: All major credit cards
Service rating: ★★★
Friendliness rating: ★★★
Parking: Street
Bar: Full service, including Indian beer
Wine selection: Mostly Californian; house by the
  glass, carafe, or half carafe
Dress: Casual, business
Disabled access: Yes, including rest rooms
Customers: Local, some Indian
Lunch: Every day, 11:30 A.M.–3:30 P.M.
Dinner: Sunday–Thursday, 5–10 P.M.; Friday and
  Saturday, 5–11 P.M.

Atmosphere / setting: Attractive, cozy, moderately
elegant.

House specialities: Assorted appetizers including
pakora (vegetable fritters); papadum (crisp lentil
wafer); samosas (meat and vegetable patties). Chicken
tikka (boneless tandoori chicken with butter-onion
sauce); tandoori assorted grill (marinated chicken,
lamb, and fish); charga chicken (whole bird marinated,
deep fried, and garnished with dry mango powder and
cilantro); murg (chicken) and/or lamb vindaloo
(cooked with potatoes in tangy sauce).

Other recommendations: Bhuna gosht (boneless
lamb cooked with tomatoes, onion, and bell peppers in
a spicy gravy); Palace Royal biryani (basmati rice with
saffron, cooked with lamb, chicken, shrimp, and nuts);
pista kulfi (homemade ice cream).

Summary & comments: Straightforward traditional
dishes with a well-balanced menu. On one occasion the
biryani was on the dry side, with the meats appearing
to have been leftover. Tandoor-cooked food fared
better. Cooking tends to be Americanized with less
spiciness.

Katsu Japanese Restaurant

Japanese   ★★★¹/₂   **Inexpensive/Moderate**

2651 West Peterson Avenue
(312) 784-3383
Zone 1   North Side

Quality	Value
90	B

Reservations: Recommended
When to go: Early weekday evenings
Entree range: $8.50–19.50
Payment: VISA, MC, AMEX, DC, D
Service rating: ★★★★
Friendliness rating: ★★★★★
Parking: Abundant on street; city lot nearby
Bar: Full service
Wine selection: Small; Californian and Japanese; some nice selections
Dress: Casual
Disabled access: Yes
Customers: Japanese, enlightened Americans, locals, sushi lovers
Dinner: Every day, 5 P.M.–midnight

Atmosphere / setting: Simple, contemporary, Japanese decor with lantern lights. Sushi bar and dining room with booths and tables.

House specialities: Katsumaki (avocado, crab stick, cucumber, and fresh tuna); sushi; authentic Japanese ramen noodles.

Other recommendations: Tempura; combination box; beef roll; grilled squid; gomae (steamed spinach with delicate sesame sauce); maki sushi (popeye roll, spinach roll, and salmon roll); combination dinners.

Summary & comments: A charming, quiet, little Japanese jewel in an inconspicuous northwest neighborhood. Japanese businessmen who work and live in the suburbs come here weekly or more for their sushi and home-style food fix, and they entertain clients here, as well. Prices are right and encourage repeat visits. Some dishes served are only found in Japanese homes, not in restaurants. Husband-and-wife team excel in service and graciousness. Kampai! (Bottoms up!)

Honors / Awards: Highest rating by Sherman Kaplan, dining critic, WBBM (CBS) Radio.

Kenessey's Cypress

Continental/Hungarian ★★★¹/₂ **Moderate**

---

500 East Ogden Avenue, Hinsdale
(708) 323-2727
Zone 9   Western Suburbs

Quality	Value
86	**C**

Reservations: Highly recommended, especially on weekends and holidays
When to go: Any time
Entree range: Lunch, $9.95–14.95; dinner, $14.95–25.95
Payment: All major credit cards
Service rating: ★★★¹/₂
Friendliness rating: ★★★★
Parking: Free lot; Valet, $2
Bar: Full service
Wine selection: Extensive international list at very good value; large Hungarian selection
Dress: Dressy, business
Disabled access: Yes
Customers: Mostly business; couples and family, especially on weekends
Breakfast: Every day, 7–11 A.M.
Brunch: Sunday, 11 A.M.–3 P.M.
Lunch: Every day, 11:30 A.M.–3 P.M.
Dinner: Monday–Thursday, 5–10 P.M.; Friday and Saturday, 5–11 P.M.; Sunday, 4–9 P.M.

Atmosphere / setting: Comfortable, attractive, fine-dining environment.

House specialities: Hungarian bean soup with smoked sausage; bakonyi veal paprikas with spaetzle; grilled smoked salmon fillet with soy-ginger vinaigrette; filet mignon with zinfandel sauce; classic Wiener schnitzel; daily specials (e.g., fish, veal chop, beef); breads and pastries from on-premise bakery, including many Hungarian items.

Other recommendations: House-cured salmon with dill sauce; chicken diablo (with Dijon sauce); pork chop Hungarian-style; roast prime rib of beef.

Entertainment & amenities: Lounge: Wednesday–Saturday evenings, pianist and sing-along; Restaurant: Wednesday–Sunday evenings, live Gypsy music (violin and cimbalon).

Summary & comments: Kenessey's Cypress is a large complex with a formal dining room; Crabby's, a casual island-decor restaurant (Caribbean cuisine with an emphasis on seafood); a gourmet shop with a bakery; a retail wine cellar with 1,500 different international wines; and banquet facilities. Pastries are a must! Ask about wine tastings the second Tuesday of each month. The French chef, who has cooked for world leaders in various cities, prepares excellent continental dishes and Hungarian specialties—about the only place serving this cuisine in the Chicago area. The Kenessey husband-and-wife team directs the operation, and they have infused their restaurant with gracious European hospitality.

Honors / Awards: The Best of Award of Excellence from *Wine Spectator* four years in succession.

Kiki's Bistro

French Bistro   ★★★★   **Inexpensive/Moderate**

900 North Franklin Street
(312) 335-5454
Zone 3   Near North

Quality	Value
94	**C**

Reservations: Recommended for lunch and dinner
When to go: Any time
Entree range: Lunch, $8.50–12; dinner, $9.50–16.95
Payment: All major credit cards
Service rating: ★★★★
Friendliness rating: ★★★★
Parking: Free valet
Bar: Full service; bar/lounge separate from dining room
Wine selection: 20 French and 15 American (Californian) white wines; over 30 reds; wines, $17.50–50; 8 champagnes, $20–95; 12 wines by the glass, $4.50
Dress: Informal
Disabled access: Yes, entrance and rest rooms
Customers: International, celebrities (Prince Albert), business, family, couples
Lunch: Monday–Friday, 11 A.M.–2 P.M.
Dinner: Monday–Thursday, 5–10 P.M.; Friday and Saturday, 5–11 P.M.; Sunday, closed.

Atmosphere/setting: Resembles a French inn; lovely cottage-style woodwork and rustic decor; romantic and intimate. Noise level can be high with a full house.

House specialities: Sautéed breast of duck on wild rice with corn sauce and red pepper; daily fish (Atlantic salmon, grilled grouper, or halibut with braised fennel); duck pâté with pistachio; mixed wild mushroom salad; tarte de Provence (ratatouille and goat cheese in a light pastry); steak au poivre, cognac cream sauce.

Other recommendations: Onion soup gratinée; poulet roti (roast chicken marinated in olive oil, herbs de Provence, and garlic in natural jus, with mashed potatoes); steak pommes frites; pizza du jour; seared quail with red cabbage and mixed greens; crème brûlée; croustade de poire (pear in pastry with caramel sauce); crème caramel; sautéed bing cherries with goat cheese ice cream.

Summary & comments: Many of the French bistro standards—steak pommes frites, onion soup gratinée, and poulet roti—are standouts, and Chef John Hogan crosses cuisine influences occasionally with his daily specials, such as rock shrimp with curry, coconut, and coriander. Owner Georges Cousances (Kiki) is an experienced restaurateur who makes certain the place runs smoothly. Service, food, wine, and charming atmosphere combine to make this a quintessential bistro without the claustrophobic closeness of many others.

Kinzie Street Chophouse

Steak ★★★★ **Moderate**

---

400 North Wells Street, Chicago
(312) 822-0191
Zone 4   The Loop

Quality	Value
91	B

Reservations: Suggested
When to go: 4:30–6 P.M.
Entree range: $8.95–27.95
Payment: All major credit cards
Service rating: ★★★★¹/₂
Friendliness rating: ★★★★¹/₂
Parking: Valet, Wednesday–Saturday
Bar: Full service
Wine selection: Californian and French; reserve lists; ports; several selections by the glass, $4.95–5.95
Dress: Casual, more business
Disabled access: Yes
Customers: Suburban to local, professional, executive, operagoers
Lunch/Dinner: Monday–Saturday, 11 A.M.–10 P.M.

Atmosphere / setting: Dimly lit and welcoming with a masculine look: dark brown wild-grain oak paneling and oak floor; well-appointed rooms decorated with caricatures on the walls; cozy banquettes; many private tables well-spaced.

House specialities: Sesame-crusted yellowfin tuna; Australian lobster tail (mammoth!). Daily specials: blackened one-pound T-bone with grilled corn, wild mushrooms, and roasted garlic in a natural au jus.

Other recommendations: Garlic shrimp scampi; wild mushroom and goat cheese tart; carpaccio; cheddar cheese–stuffed jalapeños; black bean soup; filet mignon; blackened double-cut lamb chops; 20-oz. porterhouse; surf and turf; crispy onions; baked scallion-smashed potatoes (with pieces of skins); asparagus—cold with vinaigrette or hot with hollandaise.

Summary & comments: Excellent quality steaks and seafood in very generous portions. A fine, dependable place for a business meal. Attentive, savvy, good-humored staff with great pride in their work. Well-rehearsed waiters roll over a cart and show the plastic-wrapped raw products to assist you in ordering. Service is professional but never intimidating.

Kitty O'Shea's

Irish Pub	★★★	**Inexpensive**

Chicago Hilton and Towers,
   720 South Michigan Avenue
(312) 922-4400
Zone 5   South Loop

Quality	Value
81	**B**

Reservations: No
When to go: Evenings
Entree range: $7.25–8.95
Payment: All major credit cards
Service rating: ★★★
Friendliness rating: ★★★½
Parking: Street and free valet
Bar: Full service, including Dempsey's red ale,
   Guinness, Harp, and various Irish items
Wine selection: American
Dress: Casual
Disabled access: Yes
Customers: Local, convention
Open: Every day, 11 A.M.–1.30 A.M.

Atmosphere / setting: Dimly lit, Dublin-style pub with authentic antiques, including the beer taps.

House specialities: Potato and leek soup; Irish lamb stew; shepherd's pie; Blarney Burger Deluxe with Irish cheese and O'Sheas fries; Biddy Mulligan's fish and chips.

Other recommendations: Dublin wings; Kitty's corned beef and cabbage; Brannigan's bread pudding.

Entertainment & amenities: Monday–Saturday, 9 P.M.–1 A.M., live performances of traditional Irish folk music.

Summary & comments: You can't get more Irish than Kitty O'Shea's. Not only is much of the interior imported from Ireland, so is the old sod staff. Guinness and Harp are drawn from antique beer taps (try the layered black and tan), the food is simple pub fare, and the spirited entertainment (some big names) completes the picture. Kilkenny-born manager Eamonn Brady uses his impressive entertainment background to book the lively musical groups here. It's hand-clapping fun!

Klay Oven

Indian ★★★★ Moderate

---

414 North Orleans Street
(312) 527-3999
Zone 4   The Loop

Quality	Value
91	**B**

Reservations: Highly recommended
When to go: Weekdays less crowded; Friday and
  Saturday very busy
Entree range: $12.95–24.95
Payment: Major credit cards
Service rating: ★★★¹/₂
Friendliness rating: ★★★★¹/₂
Parking: Street and garage nearby
Bar: Full service, including Indian beer and a large
  single malt Scotch collection
Wine selection: Extensive: American, French, and
  Italian, with several nice choices by the glass; Omar
  Khayam Sparkling Wine from India is exclusive in
  Chicago here and is a nice aperitif
Dress: Moderately casual to upscale
Disabled access: Yes
Customers: International; diverse; business,
  especially at lunch
Lunch: Tuesday–Friday, 11:30 A.M.–2 P.M.
Dinner: Tuesday–Friday, 5:30–10 P.M.; Saturday
  and Sunday, 5:30–11:30 P.M.

Atmosphere / setting: Upscale casual with lots of
light wood, white tablecloths, elegantly folded
napkins, lovely screen-like wall coverings, and
beautiful art. The space is divided nicely into intimate
alcoves, many of which are perfect for private parties.

House specialities: Thali (traditional taster platter,
either vegetarian or non-vegetarian) is a great way to
sample nine items, which come with coriander and
tamarind-banana chutneys. Included on the non-
vegetarian thali are keema samosa (lamb in pastry),
murg makhani (butter chicken curry), and raita (yogurt
sauce). From the clay oven: tiger prawns marinated in
spiced yogurt; marinated mahimahi fillets.

Other recommendations: Tandoori mixed grill
(combination of boneless lamb, boneless chicken, and
prawn, each marinated differently); rack of lamb
prepared in clay oven; and ras malai, an exquisite

dessert pudding of milk, honey, and pistachio, decorated with silver leaf.

Summary & comments: Klay Oven elevates Indian cuisine to a fine dining experience, from the refined, freshly cooked food to the non-smoking environment, lovely setting, and professional service. The centuries-old clay oven (tandoor) and the Indian wok (karahi) are virtually greaseless cooking methods. The nan bread takes 30 seconds to cook while the shrimp takes only 4 seconds.

Honors / Awards: *Chicago* magazine's "Critic's Choice Top 25 Restaurants"

Kuni's

Japanese   ★★★★½   **Inexpensive/Moderate**

511 Main Street, Evanston
(708) 328-2004
Zone 1   Northern Suburbs

Quality	Value
96	**C**

Reservations: Accepted only for 6 or more
When to go: Any time
Entree range: $10–17.50 and up, depending on whether ordering a la carte; complete dinners served with soup, salad, and rice
Payment: VISA, MC, AMEX
Service rating: ★★★★
Friendliness rating: ★★★★
Parking: Street
Bar: Wine and beer, including Japanese beer
Wine selection: Small; Japanese and American
Dress: Casual
Disabled access: No
Customers: Local, students from Northwestern University, sushi devotees
Lunch: Monday, Wednesday–Saturday, 11:30 A.M.–1:45 P.M.
Dinner: Monday, Wednesday–Sunday, 5–9:45 P.M.; Tuesday, closed.

Atmosphere / setting: Simple Japanese, clean decor with blond wood. Lovely sushi bar with display of fish.

House specialities: Sushi and sashimi: some of the most pristinely fresh, top-quality, and most expertly sliced, and a great variety as well; sashimi salads: oyster, crab, and mixed (assorted fish with vegetable and seaweed in a delicate vinegar sauce).

Other recommendations: Tempura preparations, including soft-shell crab in season, served quartered to eat with chopsticks; Kuni's special, a complete dinner including tempura, sushi, or sashimi; a teriyaki dish; gomae; sunomono.

Summary & comments: By far, in a class by itself when it comes to top-flight sushi and sashimi. Owner/chef Yuji Kunii is a master sushi expert—one of the best in the United States. Celebrities and other sushi enthusiasts stop here when in the Chicago area to indulge in this favored food. Some say there are only a few other sushi bars as fine as this in the entire country!

La Bocca Della Verita

Italian	★★★	Inexpensive

4618 North Lincoln Avenue
(312) 784-6222
Zone 1   North Side

Quality	Value
84	**B**

Reservations: Suggested on Friday and Saturday
When to go: Weekdays
Entree range: Pastas, $8.95–12.95; segundis,
$11.75–19.95
Payment: VISA, MC, AMEX, D, DC
Service rating: ★★★★
Friendliness rating: ★★★★½
Parking: Street
Bar: Full service
Wine selection: Extensive; all Italian; many nice
choices by the glass
Dress: Casual
Disabled access: Yes
Customers: Diverse, local, college, all ages
Lunch: Friday, 11:30 A.M.–3:30 P.M.
Dinner: Every day, 5–11 P.M.

Atmosphere / setting: Cozy and loaded with
European charm. None of the tables and chairs match;
white tablecloths and flowers with colorful wine
bottles as vases; smoking and non-smoking dining
areas. Italian owner was industrious in decorating this
place attractively on a budget with used furniture.

House specialities: Menu changes every week.
Risotto "Bocca" with mascarpone and Gorgonzola,
roasted red bell pepper, garlic, and Parmesan; seafood
specials might be red snapper baked in salt, or sea bass
or grouper prepared simply. From the menu: Dover
sole sautéed in extra virgin olive oil and baked in white
wine, lemon, and capers with Belgian endive.

Other recommendations: Antipasto misto; shrimps
and baby artichokes, white wine, lemon, portobello
mushroom, and olive oil; insalata di Finocheno;
gnocchi, homemade potato dumplings; ravioliana
(ravioli filled with duck meat); desserts are homemade,
including tiramisu.

Summary & comments: Restaurant's name means
"the mouth of the truth," and the owner, Caesar, has
put up a whimsical mask with a moving mouth at the

doorway. This comical practice stems from the old custom of having a hole in the city hall buildings in Italy, where people can denounce infidels and other trespassers. If people weren't truthful, their hands would be "bitten" when they stuck them in that hole. Altogether, this place is delightful and homey; we had a very caring and attentive waitress.

La Boheme

New French   ★★★★   **Moderate**

---

566 Chestnut Street, Winnetka
(708) 446-4600
Zone 11   Northern Suburbs

Quality	Value
90	**C**

Reservations: Recommended
When to go: Weekdays
Entree range: Lunch, $7.50–11; dinner, $17.50–20
Payment: All major credit cards except DC
Service rating: ★★★★
Friendliness rating: ★★★★
Parking: Free lot
Bar: Full service
Wine selection: 200 international, some specially selected from Bordeaux, Burgundy, and the south of France (the chef's birthplace), $20–1,000 per bottle; 25 by the glass, $4–8
Dress: Jacket required, tie optional
Disabled access: Yes, entrance and rest room
Customers: Families, couples, local
Lunch: Tuesday–Saturday, 11:30 A.M.–2:30 P.M.; Sunday and Monday, closed; grand lunch express served on a single large platter, $9.94
Dinner: Tuesday–Saturday, 6–10 P.M.; Sunday and Monday, closed.

Atmosphere / setting: Quiet, romantic, fine-dining settings with white tablecloths. Seats 90 in the main dining room; two private rooms seat a total of 50. Non-smoking area is clearly designated. Outdoor garden/brick-walled patio with flowers and plants can seat 30.

House specialities: Appetizers: Wisconsin Peking duck rillette flavored with lemongrass; sautéed corn risotto cakes and gulf shrimp with mustard coulis; lobster bisque with a sweet sherry. Entrees: sautéed striped sea bass in a Provençale vinaigrette; grilled salmon with onions, pancetta, and pinot noir sauce; confit of duck with a honey-green peppercorn sauce; roasted rack of lamb with herb crust and spicy carrot coulis. Dessert: Evelyne crisp with fresh berries and ice cream.

Other recommendations: Lobster ravioli and vegetables with curry oil; sautéed duck foie gras; grilled veal chop with prosciutto and tomato relish;

medley of fresh vegetables and grains; warm pear-bread pudding.

Summary & comments: True foodies follow the chefs they respect. In this case, Didier Durand did a boomerang return to La Boheme after his stints at Gordon and the former Le Perroquet downtown. His cooking is reliably light and innovative with a classical background, and he's returned to his former North Shore spot. Many Francophiles are pleased he's back at La Boheme, and there's every vote of confidence with the kitchen in his hands again. He's offering a prix fixe "Spontaneous Degustation" dinner for $24.95, including appetizer, soup or salad, entree, and dessert, Tuesday–Friday. The kitchen caters to the needs and tastes of customers.

Honors / Awards: Ambassador Award.

La Paella

Spanish	★★★	Moderate

2920 North Clark Street
(312) 528-0757
Zone 1   North Side

Quality	Value
81	C

Reservations: Recommended
When to go: Weekdays or Sunday
Entree range: $13.95–17.95
Payment: VISA, MC, AMEX, DC, CB
Service rating: ★★★¹/₂
Friendliness rating: ★★★¹/₂
Parking: Garages nearby
Bar: Full service
Wine selection: All Spanish plus 2 from California; house wine is reasonable; Spanish bottles from $16.95, but most $24-plus; some Gran Reservas; sangria; listed with vintage, region, and class
Dress: Moderately casual
Disabled access: Yes, including rest rooms
Customers: American, Spanish, diverse
Dinner: Tuesday–Saturday, 5:30–10:30 P.M.; Sunday, 5–9 P.M.

Atmosphere / setting: Elegant, quiet, romantic, softly lit store front with Spanish background music.

House specialities: Paella Valenciana (national rice dish with chicken, pork, seafood, and chorizo); paella marinera (seafood); zarzuella de mariscos (lobster and seafood flambéed in brandy); merluza a la Vasca (fresh cod with shellfish cooked in an earthen casserole with white wine, cream, and peas).

Other recommendations: Gazpacho; calamares a la gallega (squid sautéed in oil with potatoes and garlic); pâté a la casa (veal and chicken); sautéed veal in sherry sauce with mushrooms and olives; naranjas Albuferas (oranges in Cointreau syrup).

Summary & comments: Established in 1978, this mid-North Side restaurant has experienced some inconsistencies. Years ago one or two dinners were disappointing, but other times the food was as good as could be found in Spain. The Tourist Office of Spain has had many private parties catered by this place, which is a fine testimonial to the kitchen's capability. La Paella has not jumped to the tapas craze; their first courses are listed as appetizers and compare with tapas prices. The menu leans toward seafood, and there are some very traditional dishes such as sautéed fish cheeks, monkfish casserole, and rabbit sautéed with wine, garlic, fresh tomato, and artichoke hearts. Some of the hearty dishes are reminiscent of those discussed by Ernest Hemingway in *For Whom the Bell Tolls*. Homemade flan, cakes, and tarts are offered.

La Strada

Italian   ★★★½   **Moderate/Expensive**

	Quality	Value
155 North Michigan Avenue at Randolph Street	87	C

(312) 565-2200
Zone 4   The Loop

Reservations: Accepted
When to go: Any time
Entree range: Lunch, $8–14; dinner, $9–28
Payment: All major credit cards
Service rating: ★★★★½
Friendliness rating: ★★★★½
Parking: Lunch, street or garage; dinner, valet
Bar: Full line of all spirits, grappas, cognacs, ports, beers, and cordials
Wine selection: Over 200 selections from Italy, France, Spain, and California; several nice choices by the glass
Dress: Business, semiformal, no shorts
Disabled access: Glass elevator
Customers: Diverse, business, professional, traveler, and celebrities (mayor, politicians)
Lunch: Monday–Friday, 11:30 A.M.–2:30 P.M.
Dinner: Monday–Thursday, 5–10 P.M.; Friday and Saturday, 5–11 P.M.

Atmosphere / setting: Crystal chandeliers, elegant tabletops, large booths and spacious tables for privacy; Renaissance frescos.

House specialities: Prime provimi veal chops (three preparations, including Peimontese-style); lobster fra diavolo (in spicy tomato sauce with clams, mussels, and linguini); angelhair pasta with porcini and domestic mushrooms, with prosciutto; appetizer: mussels posillipo (steamed in herbed tomato-wine sauce); insalata della casa (Bibb lettuce, artichoke hearts, hearts of palm, olives, and house lemon-mustard dressing).

Other recommendations: Broiled prime New Zealand lamb chops (three preparations); veal scallopini (two preparations, including one with pears, Parmesan, calvados glaze, and red grape garni); homemade fettuccini with porcini; tiramisu; Venetian bomb; zabaglione; the Chocolate Coliseum (signature creation for serious chocoholics).

Entertainment & amenities: Every night, piano bar/ cocktail lounge.

Summary & comments: This downtown Michigan Avenue restaurant always exudes a special feeling of fine dining, and it's one of the few places to find classical Italian regional cuisine with emphasis on the Northern area. The menu is quite ambitious, offering several regional preparations for one item. The food is served in sumptuously comfortable, private surroundings with attentive service that borders on lavish. It comes as no surprise that this is one of Mayor Richard Daley's favorite places, and that it has cultivated its followers over 12-plus years in business. The restaurant's adjacent casual eatery is J. Randolph's Bar & Grill, serving breakfast, lunch, and dinner; it features historical Chicago photos, sports memorabilia, and televised sporting events. Monday–Saturday, (312) 565-2203.

Honors / Awards: *Travel Holiday* for 12 years; DiRoNA founding member.

Lawry's The Prime Rib

Prime Rib   ★★★★   **Moderate**

100 East Ontario Street
(312) 787-5000
Zone 3   Near North

Quality	Value
90	**B**

Reservations: Recommended
When to go: Weekday lunch or dinner usually less crowded
Entree range: Lunch, $4.95–6.95; dinner, $18.95–25.95
Payment: All major credit cards
Service rating: ★★★★
Friendliness rating: ★★★★
Parking: Valet
Bar: Full service
Wine selection: Very good; mostly American, some French; featured wines; several by the glass
Dress: Lunch, business; dinner, smart, dressy
Disabled access: No
Customers: Business, conventioneers, families, couples
Lunch: Monday–Friday, 11:30 A.M.–2 P.M.
Dinner: Monday–Thursday, 5–11 P.M.; Friday and Saturday, 5 P.M.–midnight; Sunday, 3–10 P.M.

Atmosphere/setting: Housed in the stately century-old McCormick family mansion on the Gold Coast, with stunning winding staircases, splendid woodwork, and fireplaces. From the 1890s, when it was a setting for receptions for foreign dignitaries, the mansion changed hands several times until Richard N. Frank, CEO of Lawry's, bought and renovated it and opened the doors to become the second Lawry's in 1974. The original Lawry's The Prime Rib opened in 1938 in Beverly Hills, California.

House specialities: This is the reason for coming here: roast prime ribs of beef, available in four cuts: California (smaller), English (thinner slices), Lawry (traditional, generous), and Chicago (extra-thick with rib bone). Original spinning bowl salad; Yorkshire pudding; mashed potatoes and whipped cream horseradish come with prime rib; a la carte Lawry's baked potato is almost a meal itself—share it.

Other recommendations: Dinner fish special, such as grilled marlin with roast tomato vinaigrette or grilled ahi tuna served with ginger soy sauce; a la carte creamed spinach. Lunch: prime rib of beef; turkey, pastrami, and corned beef sandwiches; Lawry's Cobb salad; English trifle.

Summary & comments: The name says it all—prime rib is the menu here. The tradition of over 50 years is a magical formula that works because of the restaurant's commitment to the finest prime, dry-aged beef and other quality ingredients prepared to perfection. The general consensus is that Lawry's can't be beat on prime rib. Wine list includes Lawry's private selection and two featured wines. Attention to detail and service is impressive, and the elegance of the mansion setting gilds the lily. They've broadened their menu recently with fish specials, and the quick "ale and sandwich bar" offers an affordable, casual lunch in a majestic mansion—a rare treat.

Le Bouchon

French Bistro	★★½	Moderate

1958 North Damen Avenue
(312) 862-6600
Zone 1   North Side

Quality	Value
80	**B**

Reservations: Recommended
When to go: Early, 5:30–6 P.M.; weekdays less busy
Entree range: $10–13.50
Payment: All major credit cards
Service rating: ★★★
Friendliness rating: ★★
Parking: Lot
Bar: Full service
Wine selection: About 40 French selections, from
 $15.50; several by the glass
Dress: Casual to upscale
Disabled access: Entrance, a few steps; rest rooms, no
Customers: Diverse
Dinner: Monday–Thursday, 5:30–11 P.M.; Friday
 and Saturday, 5 P.M.–midnight

Atmosphere / setting: Modeled after a Parisian bistro, with tile floor, tablecloths, fresh flowers, and small tables set close together in a bustling atmosphere.

House specialities: Roast free-range chicken with garlic cloves and potato gallette; le pâté de champagne maison (e.g., velvety chicken liver mousse); Jean-Claude onion tart; sautéed frog legs with garlic.

Other recommendations: Cold pâté of salmon with dill sauce; Belgian endive and green apple salad; le steak grille maître d'hotel and pommes frites; daily specials, including fish. Raspberry chocolate terrine.

Summary & comments: Almost everything from the kitchen is skillfully prepared, but there are occasional lapses: chewy pork that was served with too little sauce, and a salad that needed more dressing. The menu includes the French bistro favorites at affordable prices, and the cooking is more Lyonnaise here, from owner/chef Jean-Claude's background. While some enjoy close quarters and a high noise level, those characteristics detract from the overall enjoyment of savoring good food. Another problem: poor separation of smoking and non-smoking sections and inadequate ventilation. Overall, there's a lack of graciousness.

Le Français

French   ★★★★★   **Expensive**

---

269 South Milwaukee Avenue, Wheeling

Quality	Value
97	**C**

(708) 541-7471

Zone 10   Northwest Suburbs

Reservations: Strongly recommended, especially on weekends

When to go: Weeknights

Entree range: Lunch, $13–15; dinner, $27–30.50; degustation, $65; 4-course early dinner (by 6 P.M.), $35

Payment: All major credit cards except DC

Service rating: ★★★★★

Friendliness rating: ★★★★¹/₂

Parking: Free valet

Bar: Full service

Wine selection: A grand "bible" with 40–50 pages; $30–5,000 a bottle; by the glass: lunch, $5.25–6; dinner, $7

Dress: Jacket required, tie preferred

Disabled access: Yes

Customers: Couples, business, those celebrating special occasions; not many young families with kids

Lunch: Tuesday–Friday, 11:30 A.M.–2 P.M.

Dinner: Tuesday–Friday, 5–9 P.M.; Saturday and Sunday, only 2 seatings at 6 and 9:15 P.M.; Monday, closed.

Atmosphere / setting: Exquisite, opulent, country-style interior; quiet, romantic, elegant, and full of flowers.

House specialities: Marinated tuna and house-smoked salmon and a fennel salad dressed with basil vinaigrette (hors d'oeuvres); trilogy of seafood with lobster cannelloni, sautéed sea scallops and soft-shell crab served with a ginger coulis; four dessert soufflés: chocolate, Grand Marnier, raspberry, and lemon; flan; white chocolate mousse; daily specials.

Other recommendations: Artichoke terrine with fresh tomato coulis (hors d'oeuvres); pâté d'escargot with wild mushrooms and confit of garlic and asparagus sauce; game and farm plate with roasted squab with green peppercorn sauce, and stuffed rabbit

loin with chanterelle mushroom cream; tiramisu;
lemon tarte; hot symphony of chocolate.

Summary & comments: Before a customer is given
the menu, the waiter brings out a complimentary
appetizer, and at the finale, a sweet. Chef Roland
Liccioni and wife, and pastry chef, Mary Beth, leased
this internationally famous temple of gastronomy from
master chef Jean and manager/wife Doris Banchet
several years ago. Liccioni's cooking is lighter with
some Asian influences, reflecting his Vietnamese
heritage, and the menu and wine list were scaled down
a bit. Some of the loyal Banchet disciples were
disappointed at the loss of the grand haute cuisine era,
but time seems to indicate that most people want to eat
lighter French fare, even if it is mostly for special
occasions. This exquisite restaurant put Wheeling on
the culinary map.

Honors / Awards: 5 diamonds from AAA; 5 stars from
Mobil Travel Guide; Wine Spectator Grand Award the
last five years; listed in the exclusive *Tradition Et
Qualité* and *Relais Et Chateaux* guides.

Le Titi de Paris

New French   ★★★★½   **Moderate/Expensive**

1015 West Dundee Road, Arlington Heights

Quality	Value
97	C

(708) 506-0222
Zone 10   Northwest Suburbs

Reservations: Strongly recommended
When to go: Weeknights
Entree range: Lunch, $9–14; dinner, $19–24; 4-course meal with tax, tip, and drinks averages $55–60 per person
Payment: All major credit cards
Service rating: ★★★★★
Friendliness rating: ★★★★½
Parking: Free lot
Bar: None
Wine selection: Over 650 mostly French and American; also some Italian and Australian, among others; bottles cost $18 and up; average is $28–35; 7 by the glass, $5
Dress: Jacket preferred
Disabled access: Yes, entrance and rest rooms
Customers: Mostly couples, some families, business during lunch, guests celebrating special occasions
Lunch: Tuesday–Friday, 11:30 A.M.–2:30 P.M.
Dinner: Tuesday–Thursday, 5:30–9:30 P.M.; Friday, 5:30–10 P.M.; Saturday, 5–10:30 P.M.

Atmosphere / setting: Gracious, romantic, comfortable elegance—filled with flowers. There is a high level of service without stuffiness.

House specialities: Sampler of hot and cold foie gras on toasted brioche and strawberry-rhubarb coulis with a hint of brandy (hors d'oeuvres); panache of grilled Pacific swordfish and sesame-crusted golden tilapia with cucumber dill sauce; Norwegian salmon with cider sauce and apples; daily specials: at least seven appetizers, three salads, soups, and five to seven entrees.

Other recommendations: Baked nut-crusted fillets of Chilean bass with French green lentils and triple mustard vinaigrette; combination of roast boneless quail Forestiere and nut-crusted veal tenderloin with basil sauce (one of the chef's hallmarks is his talent for combining different meats); monthly prix fixe vineyard/wine dinner; special Bastille Day celebration dinner.

Entertainment & amenities: Maître'd plays guitar and sings French songs during special dinners.

Summary & comments: Owner/chef Pierre Pollin is one of the finest French chefs in the area and certainly one of the most easygoing in spirit. He never screams in the kitchen, which might be why his employees stay a long time. He cooks some specialties from his native Normandy. His wife, Judith, manages the front of the house. This place has never been pretentious—just warm and inviting and willing to educate diners.

Honors / Awards: DiRoNA Award 1994

Le Vichyssois

French	★★★★¹/₂	Moderate

220 West Route 120, Lakemoor
(815) 385-8221
Zone 10   Northwest Suburbs

Quality	Value
95	**B**

Reservations: Suggested
When to go: Wednesday or Thursday evenings or
early Friday or Saturday evenings
Entree range: $13.95–27.95
Payment: VISA, MC, DC
Service rating: ★★★★¹/₂
Friendliness rating: ★★★★¹/₂
Parking: Lot
Bar: Full service
Wine selection: 100 French and American selections,
$18–132; about 15 white, red, and sparkling by the
glass, $4–8; a split of California sparkling
Dress: No jacket or tie required, moderately casual,
neat
Disabled access: Yes
Customers: Diverse, young adult to senior citizen,
couples, business
Dinner: Wednesday and Thursday, 5:30–9 P.M.
(last reservation); Friday and Saturday, 5:30–
10 P.M. (last reservation); Sunday, 4:30 P.M.–
9 P.M. (last reservation)

Atmosphere / setting: Authentic French country inn
setting: rustic, wood, copper pots, and porcelain plate
decorations. Lovely table settings showcase the classic
French food. Display of oil paintings for sale.
Comfortable and cozy.

House specialities: Seafood and desserts are the
chef's particular forte here. House salad included with
entree. Start with the namesake vichyssoise (hot or
cold, with the feminine spelling versus the masculine
restaurant name). Other soups: shiitake mushroom and
asparagus or crayfish. House pâtés: duck and quail.
Escargots and mushroom with red wine sauce; warm
salmon crêpes and salmon caviar; Dover sole; roast
duck in sherry wine-vinegar sauce; veal loin steak in
morel sauce; salmon en croûte in champagne sauce.

Other recommendations: Navarin of lamb
printanier; tournedos Bordelaise; lobster a la nage.
Table d'hôte menu (three courses: appetizer, entree,

dessert), $18.95—an excellent value. Homemade desserts, such as the sinfully rich tarte au chocolat, shine here.

Summary & comments: The first taste of chef Bernard Cretier's creations justifies the 50-mile trip northwest of Chicago. I drove 150 miles out of my way to dine at Troisgros in Roanne, France; French diners think nothing of driving more than an hour for a great meal. Cretier studied with master chef Pierre Troisgros and his late chef brother, Pierre, and later with the renowned Paul Bocuse. He worked at Maxim's both in Paris and here. Regarding wanting his own place, Cretier says, "I am free-spirited and didn't want a partner; I found this place—the price was right, the location was not. I hoped Chicagoans would make the trip." They did, and they've been making the pilgrimage since he and his partner and wife, Priscilla, opened in Lakemoor in 1976. The menu here is seasonal, and the chef's creativity comes through in the long list of daily specials. His food is never fanciful—sauces enhance, never overpower. Some customers order dessert here before an appetizer.

Honors / Awards: DiRoNA 1992 and 1993.

Little Spain

Spanish	★★★	Moderate

4801 North Milwaukee Avenue
(312) 685-0782
Zone 2   North Central/O'Hare

Quality	Value
82	**B**

Reservations: Recommended
When to go: Between 7 and 8 P.M.
Entree range: $13; tapas, $2.95–4.50
Payment: VISA, MC, AMEX
Service rating: ★★★¹/₂
Friendliness rating: ★★★¹/₂
Parking: Street
Bar: Full service
Wine selection: Limited, mostly Spanish, including
   several sherries; house wines by the glass; bottles
   from $10; sangria
Dress: Moderately casual
Disabled access: Yes, including rest rooms
Customers: Diverse
Dinner: Monday–Friday, 4–11 P.M.; Saturday,
   4 P.M.–midnight; Sunday, 2 P.M.–midnight

Atmosphere / setting: Intimate, comfortable dining
room and separate bar/lounge area, decorated with
pictures of Spanish culture.

House specialities: Tapas: mussels casserole in white
wine sauce; pulpo a la gallega (octopus with paprika
and olive oil); tortilla Española (potato-onion omelet).
Entrees: paella pequeña España (traditional rice dish
with chicken, pork, and seafood); paella de mariscos
(seafood version).

Other recommendations: Tapas: fabada Asturiana
(white bean stew with ham and chorizo); empanadillas
gallegas (stuffed mini-pies with seafood or meat);
artichokes vinaigrette. Entrees: mariscada Asturiana
(casserole of shellfish and monkfish in sherry-seafood
broth); flan.

Entertainment & amenities: Wednesday night,
"Show Flamenco" (dancer and guitartist); Friday and
Saturday evening, Spanish guitarist, vocalist, and
organist.

Summary & comments: A hidden gem in a Northwest Side neighborhood. The food is very good, the
ambience charming, and the flamenco entertainment

excellent—a great value, considering there's no cover charge. The chorizo cooked in white wine was a bit too salty (some loved it!) and the bacalao Vizcaina (salt cod casserole in garlic, pimento, and tomato sauce) was chewy and not as tender as some tried in Spain. Aside from these flaws, the experience for a large party was delightful.

Luciano's

Italian   ★★★½   **Inexpensive/Moderate**

871 North Rush Street
(312) 266-1414
Zone 3   Near North

Quality	Value
88	**B**

2676 Green Bay Road, Evanston
(708) 864-6060
Zone 11   Northern Suburbs

800 East Ogden Road, Westmont
(708) 654-9600
Zone 9   Western Suburbs

Reservations: Recommended (Chicago and Evanston); recommended for 6 or more (Westmont)
When to go: Before 7 P.M. (Chicago); before 5 P.M. (Evanston and Westmont)
Entree range: $6.95–16.95 (all 3 locations)
Payment: All major credit cards
Service rating: ★★★★
Friendliness rating: ★★★★½
Parking: Street or city lots (Chicago); lot (Evanston and Westmont)
Bar: Full service (all 3 locations)
Wine selection: Moderate, mostly Italian
Dress: Casual
Disabled access: Yes (all 3 locations)
Customers: Mostly local
Lunch/Dinner: *Chicago and Westmont:* Monday–Friday, 11:30 A.M.–10 P.M.; Saturday and Sunday, 11:30 A.M.–11:30 P.M.
Dinner: *Evanston:* Monday–Friday, 4–10 P.M.; Saturday and Sunday, 4–11:30 P.M.

Atmosphere / setting: Homestyle Italian bistro setting; rustic walls and wooden floors; very colorful vines, painting, and trims on marbled beige walls. Outdoor seating in Chicago and Westmont; desserts displayed in Evanston location, which is also smoke-free.

House specialities: Rigatoni country-style; giambotta (hearty mix of chicken, sweet sausage, onions, sweet peppers, mushrooms, and potatoes sautéed in light olive oil and white wine sauce); eggplant Parmigiana alla Luciano. Appetizers: roasted peppers; polenta con funghi; mussels alla Luciano.

Other recommendations: Farfalle alla Stefano
(porcini mushrooms, asparagus, peas, and onions in a
light tomato sauce with a touch of cream, tossed with
bowtie pasta); seafood pomodoro (in zesty marinara
sauce over linguini); desserts (many homemade).

Entertainment & amenities: *Chicago:* piano in
evenings from 7 P.M. to closing.

Summary & comments: The classic Italian cooking
here has bold, lively flavors and is presented beautifully. The chef has a good sense of marrying ingredients
properly. Menu has "Luciano Lite" offerings—lower
in calories, fat, and sodium. Hearty portions, a good
wine selection, a casual atmosphere, and friendly and
efficient service combine to make the Evanston
location so successful that it expanded within one year.
Menus and decor similar at other locations. Western
suburban location about to open at press time.

Lulu's

Pan Asian　　★★½　　**Inexpensive**

626 Davis Street, Evanston
(708) 869-4343
Zone 11　　Northern Suburbs

Quality	Value
80	**B**

Reservations: Not accepted
When to go: Afternoons
Entree range: $5.75–6.95
Payment: VISA, MC, AMEX
Service rating: ★★★
Friendliness rating: ★★½
Parking: Street, city lot
Bar: Limited selection of beer and wine
Wine selection: Limited, mostly white wines; several
　good ones by the glass
Dress: Very casual; T-shirts OK
Disabled access: Yes
Customers: Local, Northwestern University students,
　Chicago food lovers
Lunch/Dinner: Monday–Thursday, 11:30 A.M.–
　10 P.M.; Friday and Saturday, 11:30 A.M.–
　11 P.M.; Sunday, 11:30 A.M.–9 P.M.

Atmosphere / setting: Bright; open kitchen; non-smoking restaurant; wait staff in special T-shirts.

House specialities: Japanese, Chinese, and Vietnamese noodles served in styles from soups to salads to stir-frys; many vegetarian versions. From "Small Eats" section of menu: dim sum; vegetable spring rolls; gyoza filled with pork and scallions; blue mussels in spicy chili-garlic broth; crispy fried sesame ball with mochi rice around sweet bean paste. From "Big Eats" section: Japanese udon noodle soup with chicken, mushrooms, and bamboo shoots; spicy barbecue pork and thin Chinese egg noodles stir-fried.

Other recommendations: Charcoal-grilled steak salad with mixed greens and fresh vegetables; jumbo shrimp and mixed veggies with Thai panang coconut curry and rice.

Summary & comments: Chef Daniel Kelch opened this casual spot in Evanston with his wife and partner, Laura Van Dorf. The dishes are lively with flavor and served in a no-frills environment for very reasonable prices. Instant success, and the people keep returning.

Lutnia Continental Cafe

Polish   ★★★½   **Moderate**

5532 West Belmont Avenue
(312) 282-5335
Zone 2   North Central/O'Hare

Quality	Value
87	**C**

Reservations: Recommended
When to go: Any time
Entree range: $8.95–20
Payment: Major credit cards
Service rating: ★★★★
Friendliness rating: ★★★★
Parking: Lot
Bar: Full service
Wine selection: International, including Hungarian and Polish
Dress: Casual and dressy, depending on occasion
Disabled access: Yes
Customers: Local, some European, business, couples
Lunch/Dinner: Saturday and Sunday, 1–11 P.M.
Dinner: Tuesday–Friday, 5–11 P.M.

Atmosphere / setting: Elegant and romantic: candle-labras, red carpet, and musical instruments and paintings on walls; white tablecloths with fresh roses and candles; some intimate tables; white baby grand piano.

House specialities: Half roast duck flambé in orange sauce; stroganoff tenderloin flambé served in pastry shell; stuffed boneless quail with cranberry sauce. Besides flambéed dishes, there is tableside service of certain salads, such as Caesar (for two). Traditional Polish dishes all get high marks: potato pancakes, pierogi (stuffed dumplings), and bigos (hunter's stew).

Other recommendations: Mushrooms stuffed with escargots and scallops; white borscht (tart, with sour cream and sausage); mizvie (cucumber salad); spinach salad. Homemade apple cake and flambéed blintzes; Polish old-fashioned coffee with honey liqueur.

Entertainment & amenities: Live piano nightly playing romantic music, such as Chopin.

Summary & comments: Gracious Polish couple, Chris and Evana Ruban, are owners; the recipes served here are Chris's. Dinner includes an appetizer, bread, soup, and a vegetable. The food is very good, served on fine china by an attentive staff with European flair.

L'Olive

Moroccan/Mediterranean ★★★¹/₂ **Inexpensive**

3915 North Sheridan Road
(312) 472-2400
Zone 1   North Side

Quality	Value
91	**A**

Reservations: Recommended
When to go: Any time
Entree range: $9.95–14.95
Payment: VISA, MC, DC
Service rating: ★★★
Friendliness rating: ★★★★¹/₂
Parking: Street
Bar: None
Wine selection: BYOB; limited French, Spanish, and
   Italian list available at nearby shop
Dress: Casual
Disabled access: Yes, except rest room
Customers: Local, international, Moroccan, French,
   politicians
Lunch: Saturday and Sunday, 11 A.M.–10:30 P.M.
Dinner: Tuesday–Sunday, 5–10:30 P.M.

Atmosphere / setting: Intimate and homey former
diner with olive silhouettes on windows; ceiling fans,
mirrors, and a glass display case, now topped with jars
of preserved lemons and olives. Decorated with wall
border murals, colorful rugs, Moroccan tagines
(conical clay vessels), and strings of garlic. Glass tops
over tablecloths; mix-matched chairs.

House specialities: Bastilla (traditional flaky pigeon
pie), here with chicken, almonds, and orange blossom
water. Several versions of the national dish, couscous
(steamed semolina grains): vegetarian with saffron
broth; calamari; grilled chicken breast; lamb; royal
(meat, chicken, and merguez sausage) with spicy
harissa sauce. Tajines (oven-braised clay dishes),
deliciously moist with seafood, poultry, or meat.

Other recommendations: Appetizers: Moroccan
olives with roasted eggplant and bell peppers; the
special shrimp peel; fresh sardines charmoula stuffed
with cilantro, garlic, and tomato; roasted eggplant in
vinegar-oil sauce with tarragon and thyme; braised
spinach with lentils, sweet potato, and raisins; beef-
and saffron rice–stuffed grape leaves. Daily black-

board items include some seafood and perhaps grilled quails or a Moroccan trio; warm flaky apple tart with caramel sauce; proverbial Moroccan mint tea; excellent coffee.

Summary & comments: L'Olive (pronounced "low leave" in French) is aptly named, since the olive is a key Mediterranean ingredient and paramount to Morocco, the North African homeland of chef/owner Mohamed Ben Mchabcheb. He introduced Moroccan cuisine to Chicago in 1988. His French cuisine training and passion for his native cuisine show in his exquisite versions of bastilla, couscous, and the tajines. Although he does Mediterranean cuisine with his own creative touches, the menu has a definite Moroccan slant. This is the only place in the city for this cuisine beyond couscous, and it even excels some of that tried in Morocco on several visits. With the many appetizers offered in two sizes (the tapas concept), it's fun to share several "little plates" as openers. Daily specials are listed on the blackboard, providing a forum for the chef's creativity. Available for catering, private parties, and carryout. Definitely worth going out of your way for a meal here. Excellent value.

Machu Picchu

Peruvian ★★ **Inexpensive**

5427 North Clark Street
(312) 769-0455
Zone 1   North Side

Quality	Value
74	B

Reservations: Recommended on weekends and for large groups
When to go: Any time
Entree range: $6.95; for a 3-course dinner, $14.95
Payment: VISA, MC
Service rating: ★★¹/₂
Friendliness rating: ★★★¹/₂
Parking: Street
Bar: BYOB
Wine selection: BYOB
Dress: Casual
Disabled access: Yes
Customers: Diverse; neighborhood residents, some ethnic
Dinner: Tuesday–Saturday, 5:30 P.M.–? (whenever things simmer down)

Atmosphere / setting: Ethnic artifacts, including llama figurines; lovely Peruvian rugs on the walls; and posters of Machu Picchu, the famous ruins in Peru.

House specialities: Escabeche; papa rellena (stuffed potato); steak cucho (beef marinated in anticucho sauce).

Other recommendations: Shrimp soup with corn and soft dumplings; ocopa de camarones (octopus and shrimp); langosta (small spiny lobster) pâté; pork in peanut sauce; Peruvian flan.

Summary & comments: Owner Moises Asturrizaga introduced Peruvian cooking to Chicago 25 years ago at Piqueo. Today, he is cooking and managing the front of the house at his tiny restaurant, which is intimate and charming. Service can be slow at times. Overall, the appetizers are better than the main courses. For example, the duck was overcooked and chewy. The flan and Peruvian coffee are great, and you can't beat the prix fixe dinner bargain. Bring your own wine or beer.

Maggiano's Little Italy

Italian ★★★ **Moderate**

---

516 North Clark Street
(312) 644-7700
Zone 4   The Loop

Quality	Value
81	**C**

Route 83 at 22nd Street, Oak Brook Center, Oak Brook
(708) 368-0300
Zone 8   Southern Suburbs

Reservations: Accepted (Chicago); accepted only for 6 or more (Oak Brook)

When to go: Any time, but weekends busiest

Entree range: Lunch, $6.95–13.95; dinner, $8.50–26.95 (Chicago); lunch, $8–11; dinner, $12–22 (Oak Brook)

Payment: Major credit cards

Service rating: ★★★

Friendliness rating: ★★★¹/₂

Parking: Valet, $4 (Chicago); mall lot, valet available, $3.50 (Oak Brook)

Bar: Full service

Wine selection: Italian; small by-the-glass selection

Dress: Casual

Disabled access: Yes, call first

Customers: Mixed

Lunch: *Chicago:* Monday–Saturday, 11:30 A.M.–2 P.M. *Oak Brook:* Monday–Saturday, 11:15 A.M.–3 P.M.

Dinner: *Chicago:* Monday–Thursday, 5–10 P.M.; Friday, 5–11 P.M.; Saturday, 2–11 P.M.; Sunday, noon–10 P.M. *Oak Brook:* Monday–Thursday, 3–10 P.M.; Friday and Saturday, 3–11 P.M.; Sunday, noon–9 P.M.

Atmosphere / setting: Recreation of a New York City pre-war "Little Italy" dinner house.

House specialities: Grand portions of classic Italian-style pasta, chicken, veal, and steaks; country-style rigatoni; whole roast chicken with rosemary and garlic.

Other recommendations: *Chicago:* garlic shrimp with shells; apple crostada. *Oak Brook:* angel hair al'arrabbiata; escarole with white beans and sausage.

Summary & comments: The Maggiano's Little Italy concept of traditional Italian cuisine with generous portions was so successful that it expanded to several other locations, including a new one at press time in Skokie. Downtown, you enter the restaurant through the Corner Bakery, which provides the great variety of breads and some of the desserts served. The 190-seat restaurant has old-Italian charm and hearty food, and encourages sharing by offering half or small orders of many items. Family dinners are served for parties of eight or more. In the Chicago location, once the salmon oreganato was very undercooked, but everything else was perfectly prepared and robustly seasoned. Call other locations for specifics there. Menus are basically the same with the exception of several specialties. Private party facilities can handle large groups.

Mama Desta's Red Sea Ethiopian Restaurant

Ethiopian	★★★½	Inexpensive

3216 North Clark Street
(312) 935-7561
Zone 1   North Side

Quality	Value
88	**B**

Reservations: Recommended for 4 or more
When to go: Weekdays after 7 P.M.
Entree range: $6–8.50
Payment: Major credit cards
Service rating: ★★★★
Friendliness rating: ★★★★
Parking: Public lots nearby
Bar: Full service
Wine selection: Mixed; mostly African, American, and French
Dress: Casual
Disabled access: Rest rooms
Customers: Diverse, local, international, usually the 20–30-something age group
Lunch: Thursday–Sunday, 11:30 A.M.–3 P.M.
Dinner: Monday–Friday, 3–11 P.M.; Saturday and Sunday, 3 P.M.–midnight

Atmosphere / setting: Two cozy, candlelit rooms. Diners can sit at tables and in booths in one room or at mesobes (large woven baskets that serve as tables; no chairs) in another room. The decor is simple but tasteful: white tablecloths, red carnations, and candles.

House specialities: Chicken and vegetable dishes; doro wat (chicken simmered in spicy berbere sauce, including coriander, cumin, garlic, and cardamom); yemisir wat (a lentil dish, pureed until very smooth, unlike other versions which are more textured).

Other recommendations: Yebeg tibs (lamb cubes sautéed with peppers, onions, and spices). Try the Ethiopian wine, Tej. It's made of honey and is sweet, spicy, and smooth; sounds strange for a table wine, but it's actually good with the piquant food.

Summary & comments: The saucy dishes are hearty, wholesome, and colorful, and are served on a large metal platter, family-style. The tart injera bread (like a sourdough crêpe) is served in a basket. Pick up your food with a piece of torn bread. Ethiopians do not use knives and forks.

Mandalay

Burmese　　★★★　　**Inexpensive/Moderate**

2172 South Archer Avenue,
　Chinatown Square Mall

Quality	Value
83	**B**

(312) 949-0110
Zone 6　　South Central/Midway

Reservations: Accepted
When to go: Any time
Entree range: $5.95–11.95
Payment: VISA, AMEX, DC
Service rating: ★★¹/₂
Friendliness rating: ★★★★
Parking: Small amount of parking for the mall; street
Bar: Full service; some nonalcoholic beverages:
　mango and coconut juices, tamarind palm sugar
　drink, grass jelly drink
Wine selection: Very limited (7 listed: Californian,
　French, and 1 German); all by the glass or bottle;
　affordable although a couple of selections were not
　very good; California chardonnay and merlot were
　fine
Dress: Casual
Disabled access: Yes
Customers: Mixed, local, tourist, business, family
Lunch: Every day, 11 A.M.–3 P.M.
Dinner: Sunday, Monday, Wednesday, and
　Thursday, 5–9 P.M.; Friday and Saturday,
　5–10 P.M.; Tuesday, closed.

Atmosphere / setting: Spacious dining room
decorated lavishly with plants, artifacts, and paintings—most done by Ricky (painter, gardener, and
assistant manager). One winding ivy plant is as old as
the restaurant. Nice linen tablecloths; a quality look.

House specialities: Squash fritters with tamarind
sauce; unique Burmese tea salad served as a lovely
composed arrangement, tossed tableside (granola-like
crunchy texture with fried split peas, beans, garlic
slices, sesame seed, hot peppers, and pesto-like ground
tea leaves with lime juice); black pepper-squash soup
with chicken; baked coconut rice with chicken curry;
large curried Burmese prawns; grilled, fried, or
steamed fish, Burmese-style.

Other recommendations: Hot and sour seafood soup
(just mildly hot and sour); samusa appetizer pastries

filled with curry beef, onions, and potatoes (similar to Indian samosa); ginger salad (arranged ingredients tossed with carrots, peanuts, slivered coconut, and olive oil). Desserts are all made of coconut, such as jelly, cassava cake, tapioca cake, and a semolina cake.

Summary & comments: What is Burmese cuisine? Chicago has only this one restaurant featuring the food of Burma, homeland of the owner Han Win Chou. Burma's geographic neighbors are China, India, and Thailand, and its distinctive cuisine reflects all three. Its beautiful salads tend to be arrangements of ingredients—many of them crunchy. There are curries (Indian influence), sweet and hot beef (Chinese influence), and some spicy-hot dishes (Thai influence), as well as combination plates—a good value, since they come with soup, appetizers, vegetables, rice, and dessert. Tamarind, peanuts, coconut, sesame seed, chilies, and special spices are used for flavoring the seafood, poultry, meat, vegetable, and noodle and rice dishes. The kitchen uses much restraint in spicing— nothing was spicy-hot, so ask for the degree of spiciness you'd like. Service is not professional, but is very accommodating and courteous. Rudyard Kipling wrote, "On the road to Mandalay, where the flying fishes play . . ." In Chicago, from Lake Shore Drive, take Cermak (22nd Street) west into Chinatown to Archer—the road to Mandalay.

Mandar Inn

Chinese   ★★★¹/₂   **Moderate**

2249 South Wentworth Avenue, Chinatown

Quality	Value
88	C

(312) 842- 4014

Zone 5   South Loop

Reservations: Accepted; recommended for weekends
When to go: Any time
Entree range: $6.25–28
Payment: VISA, MC, AMEX, DC
Service rating: ★★★★
Friendliness rating: ★★★★★
Parking: Community Chinatown lot offers 2 hours free with restaurant validation
Bar: Full service
Wine selection: Mostly Californian, some French (including Wan Fu), Oriental, Spanish; inexpensive; 8 by the glass
Dress: Casual, some dressy
Disabled access: Yes
Customers: Locals, some family, suburbanites, tourist, mix of Chinese and Americans
Open: Sunday–Thursday, 11:30 A.M.–10 P.M.; Friday and Saturday, 11:30 A.M.–11 P.M.; Monday, closed.

Atmosphere / setting: Recently redecorated in shades of rose and maroon with comfortable green banquettes. Attractive 95-seat dining space; pretty linen napkins and artistic touches.

House specialities: Flaming appetizers (for two), including shrimp toast, egg roll, ribs, and barbecue pork; kwoh-te (pot stickers); empress chicken; Szechuan green beans (great texture and flavor); Szechuan eggplant; lobster and scallops volcano (seafood with pea pods and mushrooms in wine and oyster sauce, dramatically served on a sizzling hot platter).

Other recommendations: Orange chicken; moo shi pork; Peking duck (one day's advance notice, and compared to most other places and downtown prices, it's a bargain); beef in a nest.

Summary & comments: You can get more than Mandarin cuisine at this respected Chinatown restaurant, which has been in this location for over 11 years after moving from a previous address. Szechuan, Hunan, and Cantonese cuisine is also offered on the extensive menu. If you're dining with a group, consider the fixed-price Mandar dinners listed for parties of two to eight; the larger the group, the more dishes can be sampled. Owner Sharolyn Jay develops the recipes and oversees the operation, and her daughter assists with the front of the house. Their graciousness prevails, and customers feel very welcome.

Honors / Awards: 3 stars from *Mobil Travel Guide* for the past three years

Maple Tree Inn

Cajun/Creole ★★★½ **Inexpensive/Moderate**

10730 South Western Avenue
(312) 239-3688
Zone 8   Southern Suburbs

Quality	Value
88	C

Reservations: Not necessary except for large groups
When to go: Any time
Entree range: $10.95–22
Payment: VISA, MC, D
Service rating: ★★★
Friendliness rating: ★★★½
Parking: Street
Bar: Full service, including Southern Comfort, New Orleans punch, and Dixie Jazz Light; reasonably priced
Wine selection: International; by glass or bottle; reasonably priced
Dress: Casual
Disabled access: Yes
Customers: Mixed
Dinner: Tuesday–Saturday, 5–10 P.M.; Sunday, 4–9 P.M.; Monday, closed.

Atmosphere / setting: Lots of antiques. Restaurant is like a large New Orleans–style home. There are two bars, and a lovely outdoor patio under a maple tree.

House specialities: Swamp alligator soup; barbecued shrimp; Dixie stuffed pork chop; Cajun jambalaya with Creole sauce piquante, rice, chicken, and ham; Mississippi mud cake with chocolate mud mousse.

Other recommendations: Seafood okra gumbo; oyster assortment (Bienville, Rockefeller, deviled); New Orleans boiled dinners (crawfish, shrimp, or blue crab); crawfish A-2-Fay; Miz Ruby's shrimp Creole; bread puddin' with Rebel Yell bourbon sauce.

Summary & comments: Maple Tree Inn has been serving Cajun/Creole cuisine for many years, and owner Charlie Orr is often on hand to offer a bit of lore and to recommend house specialties. There are blackened items, a big seafood platter, lots of sides, bread boats with a choice of fillings, and po'boys, in addition to a good selection of entrees. This is the most complete restaurant of its type in the area, and one of the best restaurants on the South Side.

The Marc

New American   ★★★¹/₂   **Moderate**

311 West Superior Street
(312) 642-3810
Zone 3   Near North

Quality	Value
87	C

Reservations: Recommended
When to go: Any time
Entree range: $19–24
Payment: All major credit cards
Service rating: ★★★
Friendliness rating: ★★★
Parking: Valet, $5
Bar: Full service
Wine selection: Fairly extensive international list; mostly American with Italian, French, and some unusual selections (e.g., New Zealand); reserve list
Dress: Well-dressed chic/casual, dressy, business
Disabled access: No
Customers: Lawyers, executives, city officials, gallery shoppers; couples, especially evenings
Lunch: Monday–Saturday, 11 A.M.–3 P.M.
Dinner: Monday–Friday 5 P.M.–midnight; Saturday, 5 P.M.–1 A.M.

Atmosphere/setting: Big loft-like space with beams and wall-to-wall flower arrangements. Relaxed brick and wood atmosphere. Japanese art on the walls.

House specialities: Andrew's egg faberge; salmon cured with fine teas and spices; Napoleon of striped bass; prix-fixe five-course tasting menu; roast rack of lamb with black sesame seed crust; warm flourless chocolate cake with homemade ice cream.

Other recommendations: Wild mushroom cappuccino with crisp brie cigar; goat cheese fondue with warm fingerling potato salad; pan-roasted sturgeon with apple potato cake; trio of crème brûlées.

Entertainment & amenities: Live jazz piano nightly.

Summary & comments: Chef/owner Andrew Mark Rothschild's style of cooking tends to be rather involved and showy; however, it's based on solid culinary techniques and a knack for combining compatible ingredients and textures. The space is comfortable with live music for relaxed listening. Since it's in the gallery district, there are artsy walk-ins now and then.

Mei-Shung Chinese Restaurant

Chinese/Taiwanese   ★★★¹/₂   **Inexpensive**

5511 North Broadway
(312) 728-5778
Zone 1   North Side

Quality	Value
87	B

Reservations: Suggested on weekend evenings
When to go: Any time; weekdays less busy
Entree range: Lunch, $6.95–10.95; dinner, $6.95–13.95
Payment: VISA, MC, AMEX, DC
Service rating: ★★★★
Friendliness rating: ★★★★★
Parking: Street and church lot
Bar: BYOB
Wine selection: BYOB
Dress: Casual
Disabled access: Yes
Customers: Diverse, local, ethnic
Lunch: Tuesday–Friday, 11:30 A.M.–3 P.M.;
    Saturday and Sunday, noon–3 P.M.
Dinner: Tuesday–Thursday, 3–10 P.M.; Friday and
    Saturday, 3–11 P.M.; Sunday, 3–9:30 P.M.

Atmosphere / setting: Elegantly decorated store front;
lovely plants and flowers add warmth and color.
Comfortable white tablecloth atmosphere.

House specialities: Taiwanese menu: Mei-Shung
scallops; prawn with spiced salt; pineapple with
shrimp; steamed bean curd roll (ugly but very good);
delicious chicken shreds salad is nicely served; sliced
chicken with sweet basil. Regular menu: pot stickers
(fried dumplings with ground meat and vegetables,
served with soy-ginger sauce); "three in a nest"
(chicken, shrimp, and scallops with vegetables in
bird's nest); "two color shrimp." Complimentary
chocolate fortune cookies and jasmine tea.

Other recommendations: Taiwanese menu: dry-
cooked string beans; red-cooked beef noodles;
stir-fried crab. Regular menu: moo shi pork; Mongo-
lian chicken; pressed duck; Peking duck (order 24
hours in advance—one of the best prices for this
specialty at $19.95).

Summary & comments: A Chinese jewel on the
mid-North Side, Mei-Shung has an ambitious menu

serving mostly Mandarin, but also Hunan, Szechuan, and Cantonese cuisine, and an entire Taiwanese menu as well. Everything tasted on several occasions has been expertly prepared and nicely served. Many creative items not seen elsewhere. Staff and couple who own the restaurant are delightful.

Honors / Awards: Voted one of the 15 best restaurants in Chicago by *Chicago* magazine.

Melange American Eatery

New American ★★★★ **Inexpensive/Moderate**

---

305 Happ Road, Northfield
(708) 501-5070
Zone 11   Northern Suburbs

Quality	Value
91	**C**

Reservations. Accepted

When to go: Best to avoid crowds; busiest on Saturday afternoons and nights

Entree range: Lunch, $6–9; dinner, $9–15

Payment: VISA, MC, AMEX, DC, CB

Service rating: ★★★¹/₂

Friendliness rating: ★★★¹/₂

Parking: Free, adjacent lot

Bar: Full service

Wine selection: American list, approximately 150 selections, affordably priced

Dress: Casual, sophisticated

Disabled access: Yes

Customers: Locals, downtown yuppies, business

Lunch: Monday–Friday, 11:30 A.M.–2:30 P.M.

Dinner: Monday–Thursday, 5–9:30 P.M.; Friday and Saturday, 5–10:30 P.M.; Sunday, 5–8:30 P.M.

Atmosphere / setting: Bright, airy Southwestern motif; front dining room is light, cheery, and reminiscent of an outdoor cafe. Bar area has hardwood sandblasted to resemble driftwood; visible wine cellar. Each handpainted table is a separate work of art. The booths are upholstered with antique kilims of Middle Eastern design. A fireplace with a copper canopy separates the bar and dining area; a stone wall divides the dining room from the kitchen, adding to the rustic feel. Energetic California colors in the wall art. Sidewalk cafe is walled in by evergreens.

House specialities: Pecan-breaded oysters, unusual with vanilla, cucumber, tomato, and cream; house pâté plate (chicken liver mousse and country duck pâtés are excellent); Thai chicken pizza with peanut sauce; roast rice paper–wrapped salmon and melange of vegetables including asparagus and sugar snap peas. Grilled: salmon; boneless rack of lamb with ribs; range chicken. Mushroom chips, mushroom salad, and exotic mushroom sauce.

Other recommendations: Tortilla soup with avocado, cilantro, and cheddar; crispy duck breast salad; warm goat cheese salad; and for the brave, Southwest pizza (covered with chilies).

Summary & comments: Melange ("a mixture"), is a perfect name for this restaurant, since it represents the variety of influences in chef/owner David Jarvis's style of cooking. His training with some of the finest chefs, including Jean Banchet at Le Français and Wolfgang Puck as consulting chef of Hotel Bel Air, had great impact on his career. His American cooking is creative, with bold flavors (oil infusions, relishes, vinaigrettes) and a flair for surprises. It's influenced by French and Italian techniques and uses fresh American products, and the presentation is distinctly southern Californian. He and his partner, wife Cindy, want to educate people about the proper balance in food and what's good for them. House salad comes with each entree. Minor flaws: the white wine was poured too full in small glasses and was overly cold; service was accommodating but lacked finesse. Overall, however, this is one of the best restaurants in the North Shore.

Honors / Awards: Chef David Jarvis has received the Ambassador Fine Dining Award, is a two-time James Beard Foundation Award winner, and won the Chicago Fish House Seafood Challenge and the Grand Masters Chef of America contest.

Mia Francesca

Italian   ★★★   **Inexpensive/Moderate**

3311 North Clark Street
(312) 281-3310
Zone 1   North Side

Quality	Value
82	**B**

Reservations: First come, first serve basis
When to go: 5–5:15 P.M. or after 9 P.M.
Entree range: $7–14
Payment: VISA, MC
Service rating: ★★★
Friendliness rating: ★★★
Parking: Valet
Bar: Full service
Wine selection: Fairly extensive; all Italian
Dress: Casual, chic
Disabled access: Yes, including rest rooms
Customers: Yuppie, young local couples, groups
Dinner: Monday–Thursday, 5–10 P.M.; Friday and
    Saturday, 5–11 P.M.

Atmosphere / setting: Simple white-wall interior with wooden floor and benches along the walls; black and white photos, ceiling fans, and paper-covered white tablecloths. The room is well lit and noisy, the opposite of romantic. Outdoor garden.

House specialities: Pollo a la Romano; mussels and spicy pomodoro. Menu changes daily.

Other recommendations: Lusty al dente pastas such as spicy penne alla verdure (sautéed wild mushrooms, cherry tomatoes, vegetables, and garlic); fish dishes such as salmon and calamari (the two sautéed with roasted peppers, capers, lemon, and garlic); robust thin-crust pizzas are made in individual servings.

Summary & comments: Very popular with young professionals, who enjoy noisy, crowded places. Although not for everyone, this place serves excellent food with full flavors, and the prices are reasonable for the quality. Many endure the other negatives for that, including tables set too close and serving platters too large for the tables. Owners just opened a similar trattoria, La Sorel la di Francesca, in Naperville.

Honors / Awards: Voted Best Italian Restaurant by the *Chicago Sun-Times*.

Michael Jordan's Restaurant

American   ★★★¹/₂   **Inexpensive/Moderate**

500 North LaSalle Street
(312) 644-DUNK
Zone 3   Near North

Quality	Value
85	**C**

Reservations: Accepted for lunch only
When to go: Less crowded from 1–3 P.M. and
    5–7 P.M.
Entree range: Lunch, $6.95–22.50; dinner, $7.50–24
Payment: All major credit cards accepted
Service rating: ★★★
Friendliness rating: ★★★★
Parking: Valet or self-park across the street
Bar: Full service with separate food menu
Wine selection: Three dozen selections, mostly
    Californian, plus 14 by the glass
Dress: Casual, sporty, dressy
Disabled access: Yes
Customers: Office execs and staff at lunch; sports
    fans, dates, and families at dinner
Lunch: Every day, 11:30 A.M.–3 P.M.
Dinner: Every day, 5–11 P.M.

Atmosphere / setting: Three-level site incuding first-
floor sports bar with video wall for state-of-the-art
sports coverage; a second-floor dining room with
sports art and glass-enclosed private dining room for
Jordan; and banquet facilities on the top floor. Sporty,
casual, and comfortable.

House specialities: Maryland lump crab cakes;
Caesar salad with garlic-herbed croutons; fresh fish
such as the crispy and colorful cornmeal-fried catfish
with chipotle pepper butter and pico de gallo, and the
soy-ginger glazed salmon; wood-grilled steaks and
chops.

Other recommendations: New England clam
chowder; rotisserie chicken; Juanita's macaroni and
cheese (although bland); Cabrini greens field salad
with balsamic dressing; hickory-smoked ribs; bowtie
pasta with grilled chicken, prosciutto, mushrooms, and
pesto cream sauce.

Entertainment & amenities: Browsing through the
restaurant and sports bar to see memorabilia and

photos of the star and other athletes. Sporting goods souvenir shop on first floor.

Summary & comments: Michael Jordan's restaurant opened to much fanfare when the Chicago Bulls were a hot team, in the spring of 1993 and they were about to go into the NBA playoffs. The star wanted his namesake restaurant to be sporty and comfortable—a place to relax. Some of his favorite foods, such as his pre-game meal of steak and potato, and recipes from his wife, Juanita, are on the menu. Outdoor cafe opened in June 1994, serving bar menu items. Bar name changed in September 1994 to Fast Break Cafe. The place is frequented by Bulls and fans, and can be crowded at times. Food has improved on the last of three visits.

Honors / Awards: *Fitness Magazine* 3-star rating

The Mity Nice Grill

American   ★★★¹/₂   **Inexpensive/Moderate**

---

835 North Michigan Avenue, Water Tower Place, Mezzanine

Quality	Value
86	C

(312) 335-4745
Zone 3   Near North

Reservations: Accepted
When to go: Any time
Entree range: Lunch, $7.95–11; dinner, $8.95–18
Payment: All major credit cards
Service rating: ★★★¹/₂
Friendliness rating: ★★★★¹/₂
Parking: Water Tower underground garage
Bar: Full service
Wine selection: Good selection; several by the glass
Dress: Business
Disabled access: Yes
Customers: Professionals, business, couples, families, shoppers, tourists
Lunch/Dinner: Monday–Thursday, 11 A.M.–10 P.M.; Friday and Saturday, 11 A.M.–11 P.M.; Sunday, noon–9 P.M.

Atmosphere / setting: Casual, neighborhood-style spot downtown. Classic bar for people-watching; comfortable 180-seat restaurant, simply decorated. A 1940s-style decor with a 1990s grill.

House specialities: Grilled flatbreads; turkey steak; crispy calamari; French onion soup; Oriental chicken salad; great homemade crumble-topped apple pie.

Other recommendations: "Minute chicken"; Copper River salmon (in season).

Summary & comments: Rich Melman, founder of Lettuce Entertain You Enterprises, says, "Today, more than ever, we need to be nice to each other. That's why I decided to call it "Mity Nice Grill." It's a great concept for a restaurant in our increasingly stressful world. The staff is mity nice here, and so is the food.

Mirabell Restaurant

German/American ★★★ Inexpensive/Moderate

3454 West Addison Avenue
(312) 463-1962
Zone 2   North Central/O'Hare

Quality	Value
82	**C**

Reservations: Recommended for Friday and Saturday
When to go: Weekdays
Entree range: Lunch, $5.95–8.95; dinner, $9.95–17.95
Payment: All major credit cards
Service rating: ★★★
Friendliness rating: ★★★★
Parking: K-Mart lot across the street is free for Mirabell customers
Bar: Full service, including domestic; German and other imported beers
Wine selection: Fairly extensive; mostly German, several available by the glass; about 7 American, 6 by the glass; 1 French champagne; several Austrian wines; affordable
Dress: Casual
Disabled access: Yes, including rest rooms
Customers: Local and suburban
Lunch: Monday–Saturday, 11:30 A.M.–3 P.M.
Dinner: Monday–Thursday, 5–10 P.M.; Friday and Saturday, 5–10 P.M.

Atmosphere / setting: German motif, charming, friendly. Pretty indoor garden. Also, a beautiful display of Hummel figurines.

House specialities: Original Wiener schnitzel and several variations; Kalbsteak Mirabell (sautéed veal over fresh spinach with ham and Swiss cheese); wiener roastbrauten (New York sirloin steak pan-fried with mushroom sauce); old world classics (e.g., sauerbrauten; Bavarian-style braised beef in Burgundy, red cabbage, and dumplings). Most entrees come with spaetzle or noodles and some vegetable.

Other recommendations: Veal (e.g., fricassee); steaks (e.g., pepperbeef, New York sirloin tips); Hungarian chicken paprikash; seafood platter (breaded shrimp, perch, and oysters, with fries and slaw); goulash soup; Hungarian goulash.

Entertainment & amenities: Only on special holidays, such as Oktoberfest

Summary & comments: This establishment, tucked away in a near northwest side neighborhood, has an old-world exterior with a garden that is very welcoming. Anita and Werner Heil, the couple who own it, are attentive and caring, and their pride in their work shows. They've put together a large selection of ethnic specialties as well as several American selections. Prices here are in between the bargain Berghoff and the top-shelf Golden Ox.

Honors / Awards: The only German restaurant listed in the *Ochsner Pocket Guide to Finest Restaurants in the World.*

Miska's

Polish	★★¹/₂	Inexpensive

6690 Northwest Highway
(312) 792-1718
Zone 2   North Central/O'Hare

Quality	Value
77	B

Reservations: Recommended
When to go: Between 5–6 P.M. it's less busy, but any
   time is fine
Entree range: $6.50–12
Payment: Major credit cards
Service rating: ★★¹/₂
Friendliness rating: ★★★¹/₂
Parking: Street
Bar: Full service
Wine selection: Limited; Polish and domestic,
   including house wines
Dress: Casual
Disabled access: Yes
Customers: Mostly local, some Polish-American
Lunch/Dinner: Tuesday–Thursday, 11 A.M.–
   9 P.M.; Friday, 11 A.M.–10 P.M.; Saturday, 2–
   10 P.M.; Sunday, noon–9 P.M.

Atmosphere / setting: Very homey, cozy interior with
curtains on the windows and Polish wood carvings and
paintings on the walls; booths and tables.

House specialities: Polish plate with pierogi (stuffed
dumplings), kielbasa (Polish sausage), and Miska's
special beef goulash; golabki (stuffed cabbage roll)
and potato pancake; nalesniki (cheese blintzes).

Other recommendations: Mushroom soup; roast
duck; pork cutlet; and pork chops. Pierogis come with
different fillings: cabbage with sausage; cheese; pork;
apple; Czarnina (sweet-tart duck's blood soup with
prunes), not for the squeamish.

Summary & comments: For straightforward, hearty
Polish fare with some continental specialties, this place
offers a good product for the price. Entrees are
generous and come with potato or dumpling and a
vegetable. The Polish owner and some of the staff do
not always understand everything spoken in English;
however, their very helpful and friendly attitude
remedy any language barrier.

Montparnasse

New French ★★★¹/₂ **Moderate/Expensive**

200 East 5th Avenue, Naperville
(708) 961-8203
Zone 8   Southern Suburbs

Quality	Value
89	**C**

Reservations: Recommended for lunch and dinner
When to go: Weeknights
Entree range: Lunch, $7–10; dinner, $22–28
Payment: All major credit cards
Service rating: ★★★★¹/₂
Friendliness rating: ★★★★¹/₂
Parking: Free lot
Bar: None
Wine selection: 250 French and California selections,
    $18–100 a bottle; 8 by the glass, $3.50–7
Dress: Jacket required, tie preferred
Disabled access: Yes, entrance and rest rooms
Customers: Mixed, couples, business, local
Lunch: Monday–Friday, 11:30 A.M.–2 P.M.
Dinner: Monday–Saturday, 6–9:30 P.M.; Sunday,
    closed.

Atmosphere / setting: Not the usual fine-dining
French restaurant look. The interesting two-level space
is a rehabilitated factory boiler room with brick walls;
quiet, soft lighting and casual elegance.

House specialities: Crab cakes with herb mustard
sauce; grilled quail salad with avocado, goat cheese,
croutons, and a smoked bacon vinaigrette; sautéed
John Dory with preserved lemon and basil butter;
grilled breast of Canadian pheasant with chanterelles,
pancetta, and white truffle oil; warm macaronade of
chocolate with crème fraîche and raspberries; mango
and cashew tart.

Other recommendations: Appetizers: cassoulet of
shrimp, corn, chanterelles, and bacon; ramequin
d'escargots chablisienne. Entrees: rack of lamb with
herbs carved tableside; grilled noisette of venison on
foie gras, cabbage, potato galette, and wild huckleberry
sauce. Charlotte of peaches, hazelnuts, and raspberries.

Summary & comments: Two alums of Le Français
combine their talents here: owner Jean-Paul Eskenazi
and his chef, Suzy Crofton. The creative, contemporary French cooking has received praise and garnered a

steady clientele since opening several years ago.
Crofton offers substantial daily specials, including five
appetizers and six entrees. Eskenazi, a former captain
at Le Français under Jean Banchet, used his expansive
knowledge to plan Montparnasse, and he organized a
terrific wine list with good variety. This growing
Naperville suburban area needed a fine-dining
establishment. No surprise that it's been a great
success, but it would be in most locations.

Honors / Awards: DiRoNA Award 1993.

Morton Steak House

Steak   ★★★★   **Expensive**

1050 North State Street
(312) 266-4820
Zone 3   Near North

Quality	Value
93	**C**

One Westbrook Corporate Center, 22nd Street and Wolf Road, Westchester
708) 562-7000
Zone 8   Southern Suburbs

9525 West Bryn Mawr Avenue, Rosemont
(708) 678-5155
Zone 2   North Central/O'Hare

Reservations: Suggested
When to go: Any time
Entree range: $16–30
Payment: All major credit cards
Service rating: ★★★★¹/₂
Friendliness rating: ★★★★¹/₂
Parking: Free (Rosemont); call other places for details
Bar: Full service
Wine selection: Extensive; several selections by the glass
Dress: Jacket preferred, tie optional
Disabled access: Yes, for suburban locations
Customers: Diverse, local, business, couples, travelers; downtown location also gets celebrities
Lunch: *Westchester:* Monday–Friday, 11:30 A.M.–2:30 P.M.
Dinner: Monday–Saturday, 5:30–11 P.M.; Sunday, 5–11 P.M.

Atmosphere / setting: Comfortable, well appointed. Suburban places quieter and more intimate; downtown bigger and more crowded.

House specialities: 24-oz. porterhouse steak, also available as a 3-lb. double; live whole Maine lobsters; black bean soup; asparagus with hollandaise.

Other recommendations: Sicilian veal chop; triple lamb chops; fresh oysters to start.

Entertainment & amenities: Watching the "show and tell " performance by the waiters with the display cart of huge cuts of steaks, chops, live lobsters, and other raw ingredients.

Summary & comments: Many steak connoisseurs stake their claim in Morton's as their favorite place for porterhouse or certain other cuts. The management is a stickler for quality, and the kitchen prepares the meat properly to order. Clockwork service makes everything move along at a great pace. Needs are anticipated by the professional servers. The downtown place is the most bustling and noisiest of the four locations. Besides the three listed here, a fourth is in Highland Park (708) 432-3484. The three suburban siblings with similar menus cover the territory fairly well.

My Place For?

Seafood   ★★★¹/₂   **Inexpensive/Moderate**

7545 North Clark Street
(312) 262-5767
Zone 1   North Side

Quality	Value
89	**B**

Reservations: Accepted
When to go: Weekdays
Entree range: $9.95–17.95
Payment: All major credit cards
Service rating: ★★★¹/₂
Friendliness rating: ★★★★¹/₂
Parking: Ample free lots nearby
Bar: Full service
Wine selection: Primarily American with some selections from Italy, Greece, and France; inexpensive to moderately priced
Dress: Casual, no jacket required
Disabled access: Yes
Customers: Neighborhood resident regulars (both young and old), jazz enthusiasts and seafood lovers from various locations, business, couples
Dinner: Monday, 4:30–9:30 P.M.; Tuesday–Thursday, 4:30–11 P.M.; Friday and Saturday, 4:30 P.M.–midnight; Sunday, 3:30–9:30 P.M.

Atmosphere/setting: Recently redecorated, the decor is a bright, contemporary environment with a nautical theme—resembles a boat interior with portholes. Bright blue and red mates' chairs; white paper over linen tablecloths, topped with blue napkins.

House specialities: Wood-grilled seafood such as marlin with roasted peppers and capers vinaigrette; features such as Thai shrimp curry with peanut-crust banana, steamed veggies, and rice pilaf; chef's platter (wood-grilled opah, marlin, and salmon with red and green pepper sauce). From the regular menu: "My Place For?" shrimp de Jonghe (appetizer or entree); whole red snapper, Grecian-style. Copper-topped raw bar. Monday night Door County fish boil (early bird discount Monday–Saturday).

Other recommendations: Wood-grilled octopus with vine-ripened tomato, red onion, and capers vinaigrette; angelhair pasta with wood-grilled scallops and shrimp; blackened catfish; roast rack of lamb. Homemade key lime pie, strawberry shortcake, and chocolate flourless cake.

Entertainment & amenities: Live jazz in lounge: Tuesday, 7:30–9:30 P.M.; Wednesday and Thursday, 8 P.M.–midnight; Friday and Saturday, 8:30 P.M.–12:30 A.M.; Sunday, 7:30–9:30 P.M.

Summary & comments: Managing partner Steve Dorizas and his brother Danis recently changed their popular North Side restaurant by redecorating and hiring a new chef, Mike Kurotobi, who has added more healthful dishes, some with an Oriental influence. The Grecian-style entrees reflecting the owners' heritage were updated. Some of the standards remain while the chef is testing the waters with his creative specials, which are delicious and definitely worth considering. His presentations are beautiful. This place offers a pleasant dining experience at a very good value.

Mykonos

Greek · ★★★★ **Inexpensive/Moderate**

8660 Golf Road, Niles
(708) 296-6777
Zone 11 Northern Suburbs

Quality	Value
92	**B**

Reservations: Recommened for 4 or more
When to go: Weekdays; avoid weekend evenings
Entree range: $6–15
Payment: Major credit cards except Diner's Club
Service rating: ★★★★¹/₂
Friendliness rating: ★★★★¹/₂
Parking: Valet in own lot
Bar: Full service
Wine selection: Mostly Greek, with about 16
    selections; several ordinary California choices
Dress: Casual
Disabled access: Yes, including rest rooms
Customers: Diverse, Greek-American
Lunch/Dinner: Sunday–Thursday, 11 A.M.–
    11 P.M.; Friday and Saturday, 11 A.M.–midnight

Atmosphere / setting: Decorated in blue and white with the interior resembling a cafe on the picturesque "white" island it's named for. The outdoor cafe may not be on the Aegean Sea, but the garden setting is charming and feels like a Greek island nonetheless.

House specialities: Broiled Florida red snapper, Greek-style with lemon juice and oregano (filleted by server on request); shrimp saganaki ala Mykonos (baked with tomato sauce and feta); tender spring lamb with artichokes in egg-lemon sauce; individual giouvetsi (baked lamb with pasta and cheese); chicken breast ala Dimitri (sautéed in white wine, lemon, and spices); avgolemono soup; baby octopus vinaigrette.

Other recommendations: Homemade loukaniko (Greek sausage with orange peel); broiled lamb chops; homemade gyros with yogurt sauce; light, custardy galaktoboureko dessert.

Summary & comments: This suburban restaurant is far more serene than the lively spots in Greektown, and the cooking is distinctive. Owner/chef Dimitri has a penchant for seafood, which is exemplified in his appealing preparations of fresh fish and his never-fail treatment for tender baby octopus.

N. N. Smokehouse

Barbecue/Filipino ★★★ **Inexpensive**

1465–1467 West Irving Park Road
(312) TNT-4700
Zone 1   North Side

Quality	Value
82	B

Reservations: Not accepted
When to go: Any time; busy during mealtimes
Entree range: $4.75–13.95
Payment: Major credit cards
Service rating: ★★★½
Friendliness rating: ★★★★½
Parking: Street, lot in back
Bar: None at press time; plans for future
Wine selection: None
Dress: Casual
Disabled access: Yes
Customers: Young professionals, suburbanites
Lunch/Dinner: Monday–Saturday, 11:30 A.M.–
    11 P.M.; Sunday, 11 A.M.–9 P.M.

Atmosphere / setting: Comfortable place with hand-painted mural. Blond wood tables, cafe chairs, and benches in seating area to one side of the carryout counter. Blues background music and black and white photos of blues musicians.

House specialities: Tender barbecue-smoked ribs; pulled Memphis pork; barbecue half chicken dinner; house platter from the smoker (beef brisket, ribs, pulled pork, and turkey with baked potato slices, slaw, beans, and rolls); pancit noodles (Filipino).

Other recommendations: Spicy seafood jambalaya; Famous Mediterranean Salad (grilled breast of chicken on romaine with feta, chopped tomatoes, and Dijon dressing); Mississippi catfish sandwich (steaks), steak fries, slaw, and cocktail sauce; Mother Mildred's homemade, velvety sweet potato pie; pecan pie.

Summary & comments: The barbecue sauce is a 100-plus-year-old recipe, according to owner Larry Tucker, who runs this bustling restaurant and a great catering business along with his brother. His Dad lived in the Philippines—thus the Filipino touches. He's expanding next door by press time. He will have a new kitchen and a liquor license then. Area VIPs frequent this place for their barbecue fix.

Nick's Fishmarket

Seafood   ★★★★½   **Moderate/Expensive**

One First National Plaza, Monroe Street at Dearborn Street

Quality	Value
95	**D**

(312) 621-0200
Zone 4   The Loop

10275 West Higgins Road, O'Hare International Center, Rosemont
(708) 298-8200
Zone 2   North Central/O'Hare

Reservations: Recommended
When to go: Weekdays
Entree range: $14–46.50 (California abalone and Maine lobster top the price scale)
Payment: All major credit cards
Service rating: ★★★★½
Friendliness rating: ★★★★½
Parking: Lot (Rosemont)
Bar: Full service
Wine selection: International; French, Italian, domestic, $20–200 a bottle; several fine choices by the glass; pricey
Dress: Jacket suggested, not required; collared shirt or sweater required
Disabled access: Yes
Customers: Largely business, professional, couples
Lunch: *Downtown:* Monday–Friday, 11:30 A.M.–3 P.M.
Dinner: *Downtown:* Monday–Thursday, 5:30–11 P.M.; Friday and Saturday, 5:30–midnight. *Rosemont:* Sunday–Thursday, 6–10 P.M.; Friday and Saturday, 6–11 P.M.

Atmosphere / setting: Lovely aquariums and plush, comfortable club-like setting; tuxedoed waiters. Three specific white-tablecloth dining rooms in each place; downtown private room seats 22; Rosemont private room seats 35.

House specialities: Grilled or sautéed Hawaiian or other fresh fish; classic house salad (a la carte) topped with tiny shrimp; black and blue ahi is served ultra rare and cold.

Other recommendations: Lobster bisque; Atlantic swordfish with soy mustard; Maine lobster; teriyaki fish preparations; steaks; chops; pastas.

Entertainment & amenities: Live music at both places; call for specifics.

Summary & comments: Top-quality seafood place with pristinely fresh catches, many from Hawaiian waters. Owner Nick Nicholas owns several restaurants in Hawaii, and he brings seafood in fresh to Chicago. He has a savvy staff with a penchant for serving seafood properly. Service is proficient and gracious, geared to expense-account business clientele. Steer toward simple preparations, since some of the more complex treatments don't enhance the delicate fresh seafood.

Oceanique

French/American	★★★¹⁄₂	**Moderate**	

505 Main Street, Evanston
(708) 864-3435
Zone 11   Northern Suburbs

Quality	Value
88	**C**

Reservations: Recommended for weekdays, required for Saturday

When to go: Avoid weekends, 6:30–8:30 P.M.

Entree range: Pasta, $12.95; fish, $16.75–21.50; meat entrees, $21–23; lobster, $27.95

Payment: All major credit cards

Service rating: ★★★¹⁄₂

Friendliness rating: ★★★★

Parking: Metered street

Bar: Full service

Wine selection: Award-winning wine and reserve wine lists; Californian, French, Australian, and Spanish; 70 white and red; 25 reserve bottles; 8 by the glass, $4.75–5.75; bottles, $18–50; reserve bottles, $60–325

Dress: Dressy casual, no jacket or tie required

Disabled access: Yes, entrance and rest room

Customers: North Shore locals, couples, professors from Northwestern University

Dinner: Monday–Thursday, 5:30–9:30 P.M.; Friday and Saturday, 5:30–10 P.M.; Sunday, closed.

Atmosphere / setting: Spanish-style building. Quaint French decor, tile floor from the 1900s, French curtains, white tablecloths, bentwood chairs; 25 tables; two separate dining rooms: one bright room, one dark and cozy.

House specialities: Roasted beet salad served warm with grilled scallop and tarragon; bouillabaisse Oceanique with salmon, bass, shrimp, squid, mussels, clams, and aioli; farfalle pasta tossed with grilled eggplant, summer squash, mushrooms, tomatoes, basil, garlic, and cream; skate sauté with bread crumbs, asparagus, and a lemon-lime caper sauce; Rouget from France and shrimp grilled with chanterelle mushrooms and a poblano pepper sauce; daily prepared pastries, ice cream, sorbets (try apricot, melon, or Michigan strawberry sorbet); gâteau Saint-Honore; lemon tart.

Other recommendations: Chilled Maine lobster and warm grilled scallops with avocado and lemon-tarragon dressing; Lake Superior whitefish sauté with caramelized red onions and a port-Beaujolais sauce; roast Australian rack of lamb with three mushrooms, Japanese eggplant, goat cheese, and tarragon juice with lemon; pan-roasted sirloin of beef with roasted shallots, chanterelle mushrooms, and a Madeira black pepper sauce.

Summary & comments: The name says it for this chef-owned restaurant—French seafood. Local ingredients are used, and there are many Italian, Spanish, and Asian influences in the cooking. New rest rooms and air-conditioning system; 99% smoke-free; smokers must make reservations and specify that they're smokers. Groscz is a Jean Benchet disciple and demonstrates his training and talent here.

Honors / Awards: *Wine Spectator* award.

The Old Carolina Crab House

Seafood ★★★★ **Inexpensive/Moderate**

	Quality	Value
455 East Illinois Street (East end of North Pier Complex)	**92**	**B**

(312) 321-8400

Zone 4   The Loop

Reservations: Recommended

When to go: Early in the week

Entree range: $8.95–29.95; Sunday brunch, $19.95, $7.95 for children 12 and under

Payment: All major credit cards

Service rating: ★★★½

Friendliness rating: ★★★★½

Parking: Validated in North Pier lots

Bar: Full service

Wine selection: Mostly Californian; several by the glass

Dress: Casual

Disabled access: Yes

Customers: Diverse, local, tourist, family

Brunch: Sunday southern brunch buffet, 11 A.M.–2:30 P.M.

Lunch/Dinner: Monday–Thursday, 11:30 A.M.–10 P.M.; Friday and Saturday, 11:30 A.M.–11 P.M.; Sunday, 11 A.M.–10 P.M. (summer hours). Close about an hour earlier in winter (usually mid-October to early May)

Atmosphere / setting: Main dining room is long with windows overlooking the Chicago River; rustic feel with hardwood floors and wooden tables; glass porched area; inner room is cozy. Spacious entryway is decorated with numerous amusing hangings and artifacts. A treasure chest holds gold-covered chocolate coins for kids.

House specialities: Crab cakes; fresh stone crab claws in season (October 15–May 1); fresh soft-shell crabs in season (March 15–October 15); grilled tuna, swordfish, or shrimp; Alaskan king crab legs.

Other recommendations: Steamed clams or mussels in buttery garlic clam broth; Dorothy's clam chowder (white); fried catfish; Old Carolina salad with shrimp, crab, blackeyed peas, and toasted pecans; Carolina grilled shore dinner (fish, seafood, and vegetables);

Friday night old-fashioned crab boil; homemade pies, peach cobbler, and key lime pie with graham-cracker crust; Carteret County School apple brown Betty.

Summary & comments: The only Chicago seafood restaurant on the water, and the dining room walled with windows gives a lovely view of the Chicago River and the lit promenade below. Certainly, the fish on the tables here don't come from the river. The menu has a selection of crabs and lobster, fried fish and shellfish (cooked in good-for-you canola oil); a trio of shore dinners; three shrimp choices; and a long list of appetizers and several salads, which are fun to share. Also included are sandwiches, grilled lunch items, three "land ho" meats, a "minnows' menu" (children under 11), and desserts. Most entrees come with hush puppies, slaw, au gratin potatoes, and the vegetable of the day—a good value. Preparations are simple and down-home southern-style. A fun place for kids.

Oo-La-La!

French/Italian ★★ **Inexpensive/Moderate**

3335 North Halsted Street
(312) 935-7708
Zone 1   North Side

Quality	Value
74	C

Reservations: Recommended for large parties
When to go: Wednesday night
Entree range: $8.95–15.95
Payment: VISA, MC, AMEX
Service rating: ★★
Friendliness rating: ★★★½
Parking: Valet, Wednesday–Saturday nights
Bar: Full service
Wine selection: Limited; half Italian, half French, with some Californian selections to be added at press time; several by the glass; overall insubstantial list; a few good wines, but some are overpriced
Dress: Casual
Disabled access: No
Customers: Hip, neighborhood, nightclub crowd, casual
Brunch: Sunday, 10 A.M.–3 P.M.; reservations required for 6 or more
Dinner: Sunday–Saturday, 5:30–11 P.M.

Atmosphere / setting: Bistro atmosphere; casual with some tables close together; small back section is non-smoking; attractive outdoor patio.

House specialities: Poulet paillard (sautéed chicken breast with lemon, shallots, spinach, and roast tomatoes); vegetariano (assorted veggies with polenta and roast tomatoes); braised lamb shank on roasted red pepper risotto; biftec bistro (tenderloin and mushrooms with Madeira sauce); grilled, boneless, marinated chicken with garlic and rosemary; carpaccio (paper-thin beef tenderloin with Parmesan cubes, not shaves).

Other recommendations: Pastas are nicely done (available in half orders), such as fusilli con pollo (chicken and spinach in tomato-brandy cream sauce); caprese mozzarella (salad of tomato, mozzarella, basil, and pepper vinaigrette); calamari grilled with black olive relish and lime; Caesar salad; tomato pumpkin ravioli; chocolate macadamia-nut brownie with raspberry sauce; very light tiramisu.

Entertainment & amenities: Wednesday night live DJ for "Oo-La-Lounge," acid jazz music.

Summary & comments: Oo-La-La! has had a following since it opened, and it offers some very good, simple, modestly priced French and Italian food (a fused menu, not fusion cooking). With its name, you expect it to be fun and it often can be, but there is room for improvement, which may come shortly as a result of a newly hired consultant. Service is inconsistent (some tables got an empty folder instead of a wine list), and there was an overall lack of staff training. Waiters were sent home when it appeared one early rainy evening that business would be slow, but the place filled by 7:30 P.M., and then service was slow. Our waiter was helpful and friendly, however. At press time, new chef Jill Rosenthall was promoted to executive chef of the corporation, Big Time Productions, and she'll supervise the kitchen here, as well as a newer place, Vinyl. Her husband, David Rosenthall, was appointed chef of Oo-La-La! She believes in conducting tastings and service reviews with her staff, so expectations are high for greater efficiency. Daily specials tend to be good (e.g., fish, pasta). Rosenthall likes preparing desserts. The kitchen makes jam, yogurt, and crème fraiche. Sunday brunch has some hearty selections, from traditional frittatas to the creative banana-stuffed French toast.

The Organic Tomato

Natural	★★★	Inexpensive

22 West Maple Street
(312) 664-7783
Zone 3   Near North

Quality	Value
83	**B**

Reservations: Not accepted
When to go: Any time
Entree range: $2.75–7.95
Payment: All major credit cards
Service rating: ★★¹⁄₂
Friendliness rating: ★★★★
Parking: Reduced prices for street parking available
Bar: No alcohol; juice bar
Wine selection: None
Dress: Casual
Disabled access: Yes
Customers: Locals from Gold Coast, tourists, health-conscious celebrities
Lunch/Dinner: Monday–Saturday, 8 A.M.–9 P.M.; Sunday, 10 A.M.–8 P.M.

Atmosphere / setting: Indoor dining area is cafe-like, within the shop; upbeat; clear tablecloths decorated with sea shells; sidewalk cafe.

House specialities: Spinach tomato tortellini; the Tomato's vegetarian chili (including red and green beans, broccoli, zucchini, and more, cooked in a chili-seasoned tomato base); organically grown couscous with garden vegetables; Thai pasta; grilled Amish chicken breast; curry mango chicken salad; smoothies (a blend of fresh fruit, apple juice, and ice with no added sugar or syrup).

Other recommendations: Garden calzone (not on menu—a crisp pastry filled with chopped, seasoned vegetables); tangy sun-dried tomato spread; ultimate oatmeal cookie (large, dense, chewy oatmeal cookie with wheat germ, organic nuts, oats, and raisins); low-fat muffins and scones.

Summary & comments: The delightful Organic Tomato, which shows great integrity, is among the newer quality cafes in the natural food genre. Owned by Denyse O'Grady, who left the real-estate business because of her strong commitment to healthful foods, this Gold Coast business is a health-food store, cafe, bakery, deli, and juice bar complex, similar to competitive places in the field. Some items (such as teas, coffees, granolas, seeds, nuts, and grains) are sold bulk. A good number of vegetarian products are available here—almost all of the 20 daily fresh salads—and all foods tend to be low in fat and sodium. The bakery operation is expanding and currently offers a small variety of breads, cakes, and more muffins and cookies. This place has a loyal clientele, and it's clearly understood why.

The Original A-1

Southwestern ★★★ **Inexpensive**

---

401 East Illinois Street (2nd floor of North Pier Complex)
(312) 644-0300
Zone 4   The Loop

Quality	Value
83	**B**

Reservations: Accepted
When to go: Any time
Entree range: $6.95–15.95
Payment: Major credit cards
Service rating: ★★★
Friendliness rating: ★★★★
Parking: $5 for up to 5 hours
Bar: Full service, including margaritas, tequila sunrise, Lone Star beer, and Mexican brews
Wine selection: Very limited; 3 by the glass
Dress: Very casual; western at home here
Disabled access: Wheelchair accessible; call first
Customers: Families, couples, shoppers, tourists
Lunch/Dinner: Monday–Thursday, 11:30 A.M.–10 P.M.; Friday and Saturday, 11:30 A.M.–midnight; Sunday, 11:30 A.M.–9 P.M.

Atmosphere / setting: Rustic characteristics of a border town, with a full-scale Texas-style chuck wagon and six grazing tables.

House specialities: Enchiladas in several varieties (e.g., Texas chili and cheese); chicken, steak, shrimp, or vegetables and cheese fajitas; Durango burgers; Texas barbecue; combination platters; seafood (e.g., A-1 salmon roast); barbecue baby back ribs; bourbon pecan pie; frozen yogurt float.

Other recommendations: Black bean soup; jalapeño mashed potatoes; sizzling barbecue corn; combination platters; Padre Island shrimp; Texas dirt cake.

Summary & comments: Everything in the Lone Star State is big, and so is this grand, Texas-style, family get-together experience. The chuck wagon and grazing tables, including one of healthy "good for ya grub," offer more than 25 items, complimentary with your lunch or dinner. On smaller entrees, there's a slight charge. The space is mucho grande—seats up to 550—and the private party room accommodates 20–75. This is the heart of Texas in Chicago.

P. S. Bangkok

Thai	★★★	Inexpensive

3345 North Clark Street

(312) 871-7777

Zone 1   North Side

Quality	Value
84	A

Reservations: Recommended on weekends

When to go: Lunch, dinner, and Sunday brunch

Entree range: $5.95–9.95; market price for some dishes

Payment: VISA, MC, AMEX, D, DC

Service rating: ★★★¹/₂

Friendliness rating: ★★★¹/₂

Parking: Street

Bar: Beer and wine only

Wine selection: Extensive list of 30 types, including Italian, French, German, Californian, and Chilean

Dress: Casual

Disabled access: Yes, except no ramps; several steps

Customers: Local, couples, some families

Brunch: Sunday, 11:30 A.M.–4 P.M.

Lunch/Dinner: Sunday–Thursday, 11:30 A.M.–10 P.M.; Friday and Saturday, 11:30 A.M.–11:30 P.M.; Monday, closed.

Atmosphere / setting: Large room with woodwork, filled with plants and ornately decorated with gilded, framed pictures, Thai antiques, art, and other artifacts. A large Thai musical instrument called a lanat is on the windowsill, and there is an unobtrusive Buddhist shrine.

House specialities: The exotic banana blossom salad (with shrimp, chicken, peanuts, roasted garlic, and coconut); steamed fish with fresh Thai herbs; stuffed Pacific langoustine, filled with seafood and topped with crunchy roasted shallots and garlic with a piquant tamarind sauce (all the spices can be savored). Beware of hot peppers!

Other recommendations: Love Me Tender duck over crispy rice noodles with Thai sauce; lotus blossom curry with seafood; Thai-style chicken cashew. From the special menu: buttercup squash-curry patty (appetizer); Siamese red curry noodle (with strips of pork, beef, chicken, or tofu, and spinach noodles); homemade Thai cantaloupe cake.

Summary & comments: The menu lists 115 items plus many specials, and is as ambitious and elaborate as the cooking. The wide array of authentic dishes in many categories spans seafood, poultry, meat, and vegetables often prepared with exotic ingredients. Pay attention to dishes listing hot chilies, or having "fiery" in the title—they may be incendiary. Some are described as mild. The restaurant honors requests for substitutions. If you are a die-hard Thai-food fan, go to their Sunday brunch, which features more than 100 vegetarian, seafood, and meat dishes. Service is courteous and efficient. There also is a Thai garden party room with a waterfall, pond, and private bar. Catering, takeout, and delivery are available.

Palm Restaurant

Steak/Seafood ★★★¹/₂ **Moderate/Expensive**

Mayfair Regent,
  181 East Lake Shore Drive

Quality	Value
87	C

(312) 944-0135
Zone 3   Near North

Reservations: Recommended
When to go: Any time
Entree range: $12.50–29 or market price
Payment: All major credit cards except DC
Service rating: ★★★★
Friendliness rating: ★★★★
Parking: Valet
Bar: Full service
Wine selection: Fairly extensive and on the pricey side; several selections by the glass
Dress: Upscale, mostly business and dressy
Disabled access: Wheelchair access, rest rooms
Customers: Locals, tourists, celebrities
Lunch/Dinner: Monday–Friday, 11:30 A.M.–10 P.M.
Dinner: Saturday, 5–10:30 P.M.; Sunday, 5–10 P.M.

Atmosphere / setting: Speakeasy look; high-back booths; caricatures of famous people and Chicago's movers and shakers; sawdust on floors; fun and comfortable.

House specialities: Jumbo Nova Scotia lobsters, three pounds and more; variety of steaks: prime-aged New York sirloin, 19 ounces; steak a la Stone, 19 ounces; porterhouse, 24 ounces; prime rib, 25 ounces; good selection of sides, such as spinach aglio e olio; hash browns; cottage fries.

Other recommendations: Linguini several ways and pasta of the day; veal in different styles, including Milanese and Piccata; Caesar and other salads. Best known for New York cheesecake; other desserts include key lime pie and deep dish apple cobbler.

Summary & comments: A fun, entertaining place because of the caricatures on the walls and characters at the tables. A great place with great prices for simply prepared quality fare and people-watching, while the attentive staff watches out for your dinner needs.

Pampanga Restaurant

Filipino ★★¹/₂ **Inexpensive**

6407 North Caldwell Avenue
(312) 763-1781
Zone 1   North Side

Quality	Value
77	B

Reservations: Recommended
When to go: 4–7 P.M.
Entree range: $5.95–9.95
Payment: VISA, MC
Service rating: ★★★
Friendliness rating: ★★★★
Parking: Street in front; parking also in back of restaurant
Bar: BYOB
Wine selection: BYOB
Dress: Casual
Disabled access: Yes
Customers: Mixed, local, Filipino, couples, business
Lunch/Dinner: Monday, 3–8:30 P.M.; Wednesday–Sunday, 11:30 A.M.–8:30 P.M.; Tuesday, closed.

Atmosphere / setting: Colorful, tropical decor with bright-hued tablecloths, rattan chairs, light wood tables, tiki lights, and a buri (bamboo screen). Charming artifacts from the Philippines, including wood carvings and paintings depicting life in a farm village; intimate.

House specialities: Lumpia frito (traditional egg roll); lumpianitas (bite-sized spring rolls filled with meat and vegetables); ukoy (fritters of shredded vegetables topped with shrimp and served with garlic-rice vinegar); pancit bihon guisado (rice noodles stir-fried with vegetables and with—or without—pork, fish ball, sausage, and shrimp); Pampanga's fried rice; tocino (Pampanga's homemade, cured, sliced pork marinated in secret spices).

Other recommendations: Pork or chicken adobo (marinated in soy sauce, vinegar, and onion); beef or goat kalderetang (stewed in tomato sauce, red pepper, green olives, and green peas) flavored with brandy. Wonderful dessert (not on menu) is a coconut rice-flour cake baked in a banana leaf. Calamansi (Filipino lemonade—very refreshing); Filipino tea is oolong brewed with toasted rice.

Summary & comments: Pampanga is a province near Manila in the near north section of the Philippine Islands. The owner started this restaurant in 1977, and it's evident there's a lot of family caring and a loyal clientele here. Photos on one wall are of various weddings and parties held in the private room. Although Tagalag is the national language, Filipinos speak Spanish since the islands were under Spanish rule for about 500 years. There's a lot of Spanish influence in the cuisine, but many items are distinctively Filipino, utilizing a lot of tropical fruits and vegetables, seafood, and pork. One fish that is available occasionally is milkfish (sweeter than whitefish), and the owner gets it fresh-frozen from the Philippines. One of the few places serving Filipino food.

Papagus Greek Taverna

Greek ★★★★ Moderate

Embassy Suites Hotel,
   620 North State Street
(312) 642-8450
Zone 3   Near North

Quality	Value
90	**C**

Reservations: Recommended
When to go: Any time for mezedes (little plates);
   lunch or dinner
Entree range: $8.50–19.95
Payment: Major credit cards
Service rating: ★★★★
Friendliness rating: ★★★½
Parking: Valet, $4.75; validated parking in Embassy
   Suites underground lot
Bar: Full service
Wine selection: Expansive; mostly Greek
Dress: Casual
Disabled access: Wheelchair accessible; call first
Customers: Mixed, local, travelers, business
Lunch/Dinner: Thursday, 11:30 A.M.–10 P.M.;
   Friday, 11:30 A.M.–midnight; Saturday, noon–
   midnight; Sunday, noon–10 P.M.

Atmosphere / setting: Comfortable, rustic old-world-style taverna.

House specialities: Mezedes (appetizers) are the centerpiece here: taramosalata (cod or lobster roe salad); spanikopita (spinach pie); saganaki (flambéed cheese); grilled garlic-marinated shrimp. Main courses: Greek roast chicken; spicy lamb and beef meatballs; braised lamb with orzo.

Other recommendations: Roasted eggplant spread; marinated char-grilled octopus; olive bread salad; char-grilled skewer of swordfish.

Summary & comments: Some of the best light renditions of traditional Greek cuisine, served in a colorful, rustic setting. Chef uses a creative license on many items. This may not be in Greektown, but it has brought a good taste of Greece to the downtown area. Even the earlier skeptics have conceded that this place knows its stuff. Greek family-style feast is available.

Honors / Awards: *Chicago Tribune*'s "the best Greek restaurant in Chicago."

Pappagallo's

Italian/American ★★★ Inexpensive/Moderate

246 Greenbay Road, Highwood
(708) 432-6663
Zone 11   Northern Suburbs

Quality	Value
84	B

Reservations: Recommended
When to go: During the week
Entree range: $9.95–20.95
Payment: All major credit cards
Service rating: ★★★½
Friendliness rating: ★★★½
Parking: Lot
Bar: Full service
Wine selection: Extensive; mostly Italian with a few Californian and French
Dress: Casual
Disabled access: Yes
Customers: Local, business, couples
Lunch: Monday–Friday, 11 A.M.–3 P.M.
Dinner: Monday–Thursday, 4–10 P.M.; Friday and Saturday, 4–11 P.M.; Sunday, 4–9 P.M.

Atmosphere / setting: Bright and cozy; green and white tablecloths; canopied front porch for al fresco summer dining.

House specialities: Mama Lena's tortellacci (homemade pasta with three cheeses and spinach—great al forno (baked) with cheese-garlic sauce); award-winning artichoke fritters; grilled Norwegian salmon; camparama dessert (almond cookie, amaretto and hazelnut whipped cream, and a chocolate shell).

Other recommendations: Grilled calamari; fried calamari; steak al forno.

Summary & comments: Formerly Bertucci's, this Highwood restaurant had a recent name change because a pizza chain with the same name built several units in the area and didn't want any confusion. The restaurant otherwise remained the same—known for its steak and seafood with Italian specialties.

Pars Cove

Persian ★★★¹/₂ **Inexpensive/Moderate**

---

435 West Diversey Parkway
(312) 549-1515
Zone 1   North Side

Quality	Value
89	**C**

Reservations: Recommended
When to go: Any time
Entree range: $6.95–19.95
Payment: All major credit cards; if you pay with cash,
  you receive a 30% discount
Service rating: ★★★¹/₂
Friendliness rating: ★★★★¹/₂
Parking: Limited parking behind restaurant, street,
  and garage kitty corner to the restaurant
Bar: Full service
Wine selection: International; several by the glass
Dress: Varied; can range from casual to formal
Disabled access: No, but willing to help those with
  special needs; several steps down
Customers: Diverse, professional, business, ethnic,
  couples, yuppie
Open: Monday–Thursday, 4–11 P.M.; Friday, 4 P.M.–
  midnight; Saturday, 11 A.M.–midnight; Sunday,
  11 A.M.–11 P.M.

Atmosphere/setting: The decor is attractive and
cozy, especially the front non-smoking room. The
restaurant features nice Persian decorative touches and
plants in window alcoves by the stairs. It's dimly lit;
romantic.

House specialities: Chicken fessenjan, a very popular
Persian dish of chicken breast simmered with
pomegranate and walnut sauce; charbroiled kebabs of
lamb, beef, or filet mignon; variety of seasonal fresh
fish, including salmon, whitefish, swordfish, trout, and
red snapper. Seafood degustation for two or more,
$12.95 each, includes appetizers, baked shrimp,
scallops, lobster, fish with vegetables, couscous, and
rice. Vegetarian specialties such as veggie Mediterranean (in split pea tomato-lime sauce) and veggie
fessenjan.

Other recommendations: Appetizers, including baba
ganouj, dolmeh, tabbouleh, and herb yogurt served
with Persian bread. Lentil soup; Pars salad (tomato,

cucumber, and onion with lemon dressing). Zolobia, a fried Persian dessert with yogurt and honey.

Summary & comments: This place has had a following since the owner had his first restaurant in a different location. The fish and seafood have always been its strength, but chicken, meat, and vegetarian items are equally savory and somewhat exotic. Persian cooking uses lots of herbs, citrus marinades, and pomegranate juice, so sauces tend to be fragrant and slightly sweet-tart. Most entrees come with fluffy Persian rice pilaf. Portions are generous, and service is gracious.

The Parthenon

Greek ★★★★½ **Inexpensive/Moderate**

---

314 South Halsted Street, Greektown

(312) 726-2407

Zone 4   The Loop

Quality	Value
95	**B**

Reservations: Recommended for 6 or more

When to go: Weekdays

Entree range: $5–15

Payment: Major credit cards

Service rating: ★★★★½

Friendliness rating: ★★★★★

Parking: Free valet

Bar: Full service

Wine selection: Extensive, mostly Greek; house wines available by the glass, carafe, and bottle

Dress: Casual, moderately upscale

Disabled access: Wheelchair access, rest rooms

Customers: Greek-American, diverse American

Lunch/Dinner: Monday–Thursday, 11 A.M.– 1 A.M.; Friday–Sunday, 11 A.M.–2 A.M.

Atmosphere / setting: Barbecuing lamb on a spit and gyros in the window; enter through the bar area. Several cozy dining rooms; lively Greek setting with waiters' shouts of "Oopa!" as they flambé saganaki with brandy. Everyone seems to have an enjoyable time here, but it's quiet enough to have a private conversation over a meal.

House specialities: Flaming saganaki (kasseri used instead of the saltier kefalotiri) and succulent home-made gyros—both introduced to Chicago here. Great assortment of mezedes (substantial appetizers) such as spinach-feta pies, mini shish kebabs, and homemade sausage; Greek-style whole red snapper or sea bass; top-quality lamb prepared in various ways: rotisserie-roasted, extra thick prime lamb chops, fork-tender lamb with artichokes avgolemono, and tigania (pork tenderloin chunks marinated in wine sauce). Succulent Athenian broiled chicken.

Other recommendations: Kotopitakia (chicken phyllo pie); dolmades (herbed rice- or meat-stuffed vine leaves); broiled octopus; vegetarian moussaka (layered eggplant and potato dish); lamb sweetbreads;

shrimp flambée; ravani (walnut honey cake); crispy walnut-rich baklava; homemade yogurt with walnuts.

Summary & comments: The Parthenon is the oldest restaurant in Greektown, having celebrated its 25th anniversary in July 1993. Of all the Greek restaurants in the Chicago area, this reliable establishment, appropriately named for the majestic structure on the acropolis of Athens, has remained tops for the most comprehensive menu, consistent quality of food, and gracious service. The name carries a deep responsibility for excellence, and the Liakouras family never takes that lightly. Chris Liakouras, who started this second restaurant in Greektown in 1968 with his brother Bill, now runs it with his nephew, Peter. The first Greektown restaurant has since closed. Here, new dishes are always being added to the ambitious menu, which is in English and Greek, and there are daily dinner specials. Except for the family-style dinner, "the menu is a la carte so ordering is more flexible," according to Chris. The mezedes on the menu are offered in two portion sizes and as a combination of four choices. This basic concept is ideally suited to the Greeks' cultural sense of filoxenia (hospitality) and the centuries-old tradition of getting together with friends to eat several little dishes, drink wine, and talk. You couldn't find a better place than here. Everyone has fun. Returning to the Parthenon after just one visit is like coming home. Kaly orczi! (Good appetite!)

Honors/Awards: Much great press over the years, including *Chicago* magazine, the *Chicago Tribune*, the *Chicago Sun-Times,* and various television and radio stations.

Pastiche

Global/Eclectic ★★★½ **Inexpensive/Moderate**

	Quality	Value
4343 North Clarendon Street (mezzanine level)	87	B

(312) 296-4999
Zone 1   North Side

Reservations: Accepted
When to go: Any time
Entree range: $7.95–14.95
Payment: All major credit cards
Service rating: ★★★★
Friendliness rating: ★★★★½
Parking: Available upon request
Bar: Full service, including international beers
Wine selection: 50 international wines, $15–39; 11 by the glass
Dress: Casual
Disabled access: Yes; private elevators
Customers: Diverse, all ages
Brunch: Sunday, 10:30 A.M.–2:30 P.M.
Dinner: Tuesday–Thursday, 5–10 P.M.; Friday and Saturday, 5–11 P.M.; Sunday, 5–9 P.M.

Atmosphere / setting: Private elevator delivers guests to the lounge overlooking the roof-deck, outdoor terrace with a view of the Buena Park neighborhood. Floor-to-ceiling windows in the banquet room. Artistic blend of styles and colors; warm, comfortable, and friendly.

House specialities: Ying Yang soup (two vegetarian soups—one mild, one spicy—swirled in a bowl); plantain polenta, a fusion of Caribbean and Italian cuisines; fish du jour, sometimes Vera Cruz–style, poached in a banana leaf with relish and fragrant sesonings; Polish pierogi (with assorted fillings) and potato pancakes; Jamaican jerk chicken, spicy but not fiery.

Other recommendations: Conch fritters with key lime-mustard sauce; grilled fillet of yellow fin tuna in soy-ginger marinade; grilled-to-order beef tenderloin with Gorgonzola and pistachio; daily flan; staple southern sweet potato pie.

Summary & comments: The colorful decor, international wine list, and menu with a global reach reflect the definintion of pastiche—"an artful harmony of unrelated items, brought together as one." Chef Patti Davids Mockus is a partner in this cafe together with her mother, manager Ursula Davids, and brother, John Davids, who creates the eclectic wine list. Patti's unique talent is to select favorite foods from various foreign lands, blend some of them together in one dish and present them artistically. The menu is limited but its scope is the world, and the large selection of tapas encourages spontaneity and sharing. Many different countries are represented, and most dishes are served with American flair. Several items are traditional American. The animated global cooking together with the international wine list at affordable prices make dining here like a trip around the world.

Pazzo's Pizza and Pasta Kitchen

New Italian ★★½ **Inexpensive**

	Quality	Value
	79	B

NBC Tower, 455 North Cityfront Plaza
(312) 329-0775
Zone 4   The Loop

8725 West Higgins Road
(312) 714-0077
Zone 2   North Central/O'Hare

Yorktown Shopping Center, Lombard
(708) 620-4144
Zone 9   Western Suburbs

Reservations: Suggested
When to go: Off-peak lunch and dinner times
Entree range: All items under $10
Payment: VISA, MC, AMEX
Service rating: ★★★
Friendliness rating: ★★★★★
Parking: Building lots, street
Bar: Full service
Wine selection: Jugs of wine placed on tables (using the honor system) including CK Mondari, chianti, chablis, and rose; $2.50 a glass
Dress: Casual
Disabled access: Yes
Customers: Business, local, family
Lunch/Dinner: Monday–Thursday, 11 A.M.–10 P.M.; Friday and Saturday, 11 A.M.–11 P.M.; Sunday, 4–10 P.M.; times may vary with each location—call first.

Atmosphere / setting: Contemporary, casual, and spacious with an open kitchen. Call each location regarding private parties.

House specialities: Wood-fired pizza selection; pasta; zebra panzottini (striped semolina pasta filled with ricotta and spinach, served on a bed of mixed peppers with a tomato-garlic cream sauce); polenta cup filled with basil pesto and ragout of vegetables, black olives, and spicy tomato sauce; pollo rigatoni (square rigatoni with chicken, roasted peppers, black olives, and spinach in a white cream sauce); dolci, cannoli cake, tiramisu, or gelato.

Other recommendations: Oriental lime chicken, salad with mixed greens, peanuts, sesame seeds, and crispy noodles in a mustard vinaigrette; Pazzo's Caesar with mixed greens, herb croutons, shaved Parmigiano, and Pazzo's creamy Caesar dressing.

Summary & comments: Fun and delicious Italian cuisine, colorful presentations, generous portions, low prices, and friendly staff—these are the key buzz words that spell success for this California-based chain. The first Chicago location debuted in December 1993 under the former name, Milano's Italian Kitchen. The name change for only the Chicago restaurants occurred in spring 1994; the eight other locations around the country will keep the Milano's name. This place wins over first-time customers, and it's not surprising.

Pegasus Restaurant and Taverna

Greek	★★★	Inexpensive/Moderate

130 South Halsted Street, Greektown

Quality	Value
83	**C**

(312) 226-3377

Zone 4   The Loop

Reservations: Recommended
When to go: Weekdays; Friday and Saturday are busy
Entree range: $5.75–19.75
Payment: Major credit cards
Service rating: ★★★★
Friendliness rating: ★★★★
Parking: Valet
Bar: Full service
Wine selection: Mostly Greek (about 98%), with a few French and Californian
Dress: Casual
Disabled access: Yes, including rest rooms
Customers: Diverse, international
Lunch/Dinner: Monday–Thursday, 11 A.M.–midnight; Friday, 11 A.M.–1 A.M.; Saturday, noon–1 A.M.; Sunday, noon–midnight.

Atmosphere / setting: Mediterranean bright with murals of Mykonos. Summer roof garden with white-washed walls, lattice work, small trees, and flowers, in the style of traditional Grecian gardens. Dramatic view of the Chicago skyline.

House specialities: Shrimp Alexander; broiled lamb chops; whole red snapper; chicken Athenian-style; beef tashkebab (beef cubes simmered in wine-tomato sauce with rice pilaf); briami (assorted cooked fresh vegetables); traditional Greek dishes such as pastitsio (baked macaroni and meat with bechamel).

Other recommendations: Grilled marinated baby octopus; Alexander's salad (mixed lettuce, feta, and garlic dressing); swordfish kebab; special walnut-raisin cake; and creamy rice pudding.

Summary & comments: The menu is a blend of authentic and original home-style dishes from several regions, prepared in a light, healthy way. A mezedes (small course) menu was created for the roof garden, which is an especially pleasant experience on a nice summer evening.

Pierogi Inn

Polish   ★★½   **Inexpensive**

5318 West Lawrence Avenue
(312) 725-2818
Zone 2   North Central/O'Hare

Quality	Value
79	B

Reservations: Recommended for large parties
When to go: Any time
Entree range: $4.95–8
Payment: Cash and personal checks; no credit cards
Service rating: ★★★
Friendliness rating: ★★★★
Parking: Street
Bar: None
Wine selection: BYOB
Dress: Casual
Disabled access: Yes, including rest rooms
Customers: Polish-American, other locals
Lunch/Dinner: Every day, 10 A.M.–10 P.M.

Atmosphere / setting: Original store front has a comfortable diner-like setting with a carryout counter and several tables; adjacent dining room has a very simple, no-frills decor with some Polish art.

House specialities: Pierogi (dumplings filled with the traditional mushrooms, cabbage, potato and cheese, and with creative items such as shrimp, whitefish, strawberries, and other seasonal fruits); great soups, especially mushroom, barley, and barszcz with uszka (red beet soup with wild mushroom dumplings).

Other recommendations: Duck or beef goulash; veal cutlet with sauerkraut; golabki (stuffed cabbage rolls); nalesniki (cheese blintzes).

Summary & comments: Pierogi Inn began as a small store front with a large carryout business, and it expanded to the space next door so there could be a dining room. It remains very simple, with a blackboard menu; it's popular because the Polish cooking is authentic, flavorful, and a good value. Chef Richard Anton's mother is in the kitchen and makes all the delicious, time-consuming pierogis—the main attraction here. Catering and carryout. Smacznego!

Prairie

Midwestern ★★★★½ **Moderate/Expensive**

---

500 South Dearborn Street
(312) 663-1143
Zone 5   South Loop

Quality	Value
95	C

Reservations: Recommended
When to go: Monday is the slowest day, but any time is fine
Entree range: Lunch, $9–24; dinner a la carte, $12–24
Payment: All major credit cards
Service rating: ★★★★
Friendliness rating: ★★★★½
Parking: Valet
Bar: Full service
Wine selection: Mostly Californian; some Oregon; 8–10 from the Midwest; several available in smaller bottles
Dress: Summer, casual to formal; winter, business and dressy (suits and ties optional)
Disabled access: Yes, including rest rooms
Customers: Local business clientele, theatergoers, couples, Bears football fans on Sunday morning, some foreign and domestic tourists
Breakfast: Monday–Friday, 6–10 A.M.; Saturday, 7–10 A.M.
Brunch: Sunday, 11 A.M.–2 P.M.
Lunch: Monday–Friday, 11:30 A.M.–2 P.M.; Saturday, 11 A.M.–2 P.M.
Dinner: Sunday–Thursday, 5:30–10 P.M.; Friday and Saturday, 5:30–11 P.M.

Atmosphere / setting: Striking split-level space with tall windows and honey-colored oak cathedral ceiling. The interior is patently a Frank Lloyd Wright design—a fine example of the Prairie School of Architecture. Attractive display case, open kitchen, and comfortable lounge area.

House specialities: Midwestern duck; Wisconsin buffalo; Minnesota wild rice; local corn; crispy sweet potato (side to entrees); Illinois and Wisconsin cheeses; Iowa pheasant and pork chops; Kansas City steak and coho salmon and other heartland products are prepared in seasonal ways (e.g., appetizer: sauté of wild mushrooms in a crispy sweet potato basket with roasted corn and charred red pepper sauces—beautiful presentation); tender Hasselbring buffalo steak with roasted shallot sauce and jerky; baked walleyed pike stuffed with wild rice and vegetables in lemon-dill butter; grilled veal chop with apples, chestnuts, cranberries, and apple jack brandy sauce; warm strawberry-rhubarb tart with apple-cinnamon ice cream (in spring).

Other recommendations: Appetizer: grilled bobwhite quail on braised apples with huckleberry relish and peppercorn cornbread; Prairie field salad with pickled vegetables and sprouts; fillet of sturgeon de Jonghe with smothered bell pepper broth and oven-roasted potatoes; simple soup of chilled summer melons, mint, champagne, and lemon sorbet (in season).

Summary & comments: Chef Stephen Langlois opened this restaurant after avidly combing old heartland cookbooks and unearthing authentic recipes from farm cooks, then imaginatively incorporating such seasonal ingredients as edible flowers into his stunningly visual creations. The result is a refined, contemporary dining experience with historical roots. The only restaurant here devoted exclusively to Midwestern cuisine.

Printer's Row

New American ★★★★½ **Moderate**

---

550 South Dearborn Street
(312) 461-0780
Zone 5   South Loop

Quality	Value
95	**B**

Reservations: Recommended
When to go: Any time; weekdays usually less busy
Entree range: Lunch, $7.50–13.95; dinner, $3.50–24.95
Payment: VISA, MC, AMEX, D
Service rating: ★★★★
Friendliness rating: ★★★½
Parking: Street or lots nearby
Bar: Full service
Wine selection: Big American wine list; numerous fine choices by the glass, bottle, or half bottle; 120–130 bottles
Dress: Casual; comfortable for after work, pre-theater, or business lunch
Disabled access: Yes
Customers: Blend of neighborhood, business, travel, professional, and suburban
Lunch: Monday–Friday, 11:30 A.M.–2:30 P.M.
Dinner: Monday–Thursday, 5–10 P.M.; Friday and Saturday, 5–11 P.M.

Atmosphere / setting: In the historic Printer's Row area, this establishment is both sophisticated and comfortable. Cozy banquettes, warm lighting, artistic fish tiles on a central pillar, and beautiful tablewear on white tablecloths create warmth and intimacy. Seats up to 120 in 3 rooms.

House specialities: Grilled duck breast with smoked tomato sauce, smooth polenta, and balsamic vinegar; weekly menu features a shellfish or wild and farm-raised fish and a venison item (e.g., venison chop with an American-Italian sun-dried blueberry-grappa sauce). Tuna seared with Chinese molasses (not sweet), cucumber, and chili vinaigrette is an example of an Asian influence here. Vegetable paella, mildly spicy with saffron rice, herbs, and a garden variety of veggies, satisfies any Spanish cravings.

Other recommendations: Grilled salmon with prosciutto-pasta cake and whole grain mustard butter;

roasted, custom-cut pork chop; desserts such as homemade ice cream (honey walnut or black currant); coffee crème brûlée (flavors change weekly); pear tart with lemon ice cream.

Summary & comments: Chef/owner Michael Foley opened this restaurant more than a decade ago, when the Printer's Row area was not yet renovated. This pioneer soon received recognition and awards for his innovative, modern American cooking, which is committed to healthful preparations based on fresh, local products and influenced by his travels. A third-generation restaurateur, Foley has much experience, and his unwavering dedication over the years has produced consistent quality here. Chef de cuisine Allen Sternweiler's cooking has counterpoints of sweet and piquant, and often gives a twist to the common items. The menus change weekly and focus on servicing daily diners through a la carte items. One of Chicago's best dining experiences. Can accommodate private functions from 15–120.

Honors / Awards: Among the host of local, regional, national, and international awards are *Travel Holiday Magazine* Good Value Dining Award, 1992–94; *Wine Spectator*'s Award of Excellence, 1988–1993; DiRoNA Award, 1993.

The Pump Room

American/Continental ★★★★ **Expensive**

Omni Ambassador East Hotel, 1301 North State Parkway

Quality	Value
92	C

(312) 266-0360

Zone 3   Near North

Reservations: Required

When to go: Friday or Saturday evenings

Entree range: Breakfast, $4.95–9.95; lunch, $9.50–14.95; dinner, $19.50–35

Payment: All major credit cards

Service rating: ★★★★¹/₂

Friendliness rating: ★★★★¹/₂

Parking: Valet; nearby self-park garage

Bar: Full service

Wine selection: Extensive international list, $16 up; about 8 available by the glass

Dress: Days, business, no jeans or tennis shoes; evenings, dressy; gentlemen required to wear jackets after 4:30 P.M.

Disabled access: Wheelchair acccessible; call for details; some small stairways

Customers: Professionals aged 30-plus, celebrities, couples

Breakfast: Monday–Saturday, 7–11 A.M.

Brunch: Sunday, 11 A.M.–2:30 P.M.

Lunch: Monday–Saturday, 11:30 A.M.–2:30 P.M.

Dinner: Monday–Thursday, 6–10 P.M.; Friday and Saturday, 5 P.M.–midnight; Sunday, 5–10 P.M.

Atmosphere / setting: Formal, elegant, stunning split-level dining room with bar/lounge and a gallery of celebrity photos. Sparkling mahogany-toned room lavishly appointed with crystal chandeliers, lush floral arrangements, and sheer ceiling drapes with tiny lights. This atmosphere and the restaurant's history still cast a spell.

House specialities: World-famous aged prime rib of beef, slow-roasted with rosemary and served with fresh herb jus and horseradish cream; crispy roast duck with braised red cabbage and pinot noir sauce. The Pump Room salad (spinach, bacon, egg, radish, and mustard vinaigrette) and Caesar salad will remain fixtures. Baked Alaska, flamed tableside for two to four. New items include wild mushroom au gratin topped with phyllo pastry, and vodka-cured, smoked salmon and ahi tuna tartar.

Other recommendations: Duck and wild mushroom ravioli; special appetizer of seared ahi tuna, smoked shrimp, pickled ginger, and wasabi sauce; pureed black bean soup; dinner fish special such as grilled swordfish, braised fennel, balsamic glaze, and zinfandel citrus sauce; a la carte creamed spinach, and garlic and horseradish whipped red potatoes.

Entertainment & amenities: Live entertainment nightly in lounge with dancing.

Summary & comments: "Booth One" is a legend made famous by this Chicago landmark, a premier celebrity gathering place since the late 1930s. Sample the complimentary hors d'oeuvre buffet in the lounge during weekday cocktail hours, then browse through the "who's who in entertainment" photo exhibit. Chef Munther Massarweh introduced a new menu at press time. A list of cognacs, sherries, and ports is available for after-dinner sipping. A special place for business meals, celebrity sightings, and romantic dinners with dancing.

Honors / Awards: AAA 4 Diamond Award

R. J. Grunts

| American | ★★★ | Inexpensive |

2056 Lincoln Park West
(312) 929-5363
Zone 1   North Side

Quality	Value
81	A

Reservations: Accepted for 6 or more only
When to go: Any time a craving hits
Entree range: $4.95–14.95
Payment: Major credit cards
Service rating: ★★½
Friendliness rating: ★★★½
Parking: Street
Bar: Full service; several imported, domestic, and on-tap brews
Wine selection: Mostly lower-priced domestic; very limited; 6 choices by the glass or half carafe; 4 by the bottle
Dress: Blue-jean casual
Disabled access: Yes; call first
Customers: Mixed, families, singles, couples, all ages
Open: Monday–Thursday, 11:30 A.M.–10 P.M.; Friday and Saturday, 11:30 A.M.–11 P.M.; Sunday, 3–10 P.M.
Brunch: Sunday, 10 A.M.–2:30 P.M.; $10.95 buffet or order from the menu

---

Atmosphere / setting: Casual with plants and wooden booths. Stucco walls showcase original comical art, including a tribute to the waitresses. The centerpiece salad bar provides plenty of colorful decor.

House specialities: Signature salad bar with 40-plus items from raw veggies and prepared salads to grains and fresh fruit; oversized cheeseburgers or other options, including the turkey burger; award-winning vegetarian chili and steak Terry Yaki; baby back ribs; R.J.'s chop steak.

Other recommendations: Chicken-fried rice; vegetarian items in every menu category: veggie burgers; the "Love Omelette" (brunch); el veggio quesadillas; new vegetable fajitas.

Summary & comments: The original Lettuce Entertain You creation is still alive and well and basically unchanged after 23 years, except for the addition of a front window overlooking Lincoln Park.

Since its inception, this place has recognized the importance of vegetarian cuisine and healthful food choices while also offering burgers and ribs. Throughout the years, the menu has expanded vegetarian offerings in each category, and recently has launched even more, with the new menus for lunch, dinner, brunch, and children, called "Grunts for the Runts." The menu has always been humorous and extensive, covering salad bar options, appetizers, burgers, sandwiches, and entrees. Now there's a Chicago Mex category with South-of-the-border items such as charred shrimp burrito and chicken enchiladas. Under "Flashbacks" is "Sorry hun, no bun," a burger sans bread from the original 1971 menu. Most entrees include the salad bar—a deal. Odd placement of some salad bar items (such as chocolate mousse next to chopped chicken liver) results in occasional suprises in the mouth. In addition to the broad range of foods, even the beverages—fresh-squeezed juices, herbal teas, giant malts and shakes, and espresso—follow the motto of catering to our variable tastes.

Red Tomato

Italian	★★½	**Inexpensive**

3417 North Southport Avenue
(312) 472-5300
Zone 1   North Side

Quality	Value
79	**B**

Reservations: Recommended on weekdays; not accepted on Friday and Saturday
When to go: Early evenings any day
Entree range: $8.95–15
Payment: All major credit cards
Service rating: ★★★
Friendliness rating: ★★★★
Parking: Street
Bar: Full service
Wine selection: Extensive, mostly Italian; most chosen to complement the food, $15–69; several nice choices by the glass, $3.50–5.25
Dress: Casual
Disabled access: Yes, including rest rooms
Customers: Local, professional, couples, business
Lunch/Dinner: Monday–Thursday, 11:30 A.M.–10:30 P.M.; Friday and Saturday, 11:30 A.M.–11:30 P.M.; Sunday, 11:30 A.M.–10 P.M.

Atmosphere/setting: Colorful exterior; near the L tracks in a northwest side neighborhood. Two different sections—one is casual and the other is semiformal; also outdoor dining section.

House specialities: Scallopini al "Red Tomato" (medallions of veal over fresh tomato sauce topped with buffalo mozzarella); lasagnas; pizza ochri; pizzette "Red Tomato" (artichoke, tomato, capers, onion, and pepper); involtini di melenzane (grilled eggplant rolled with spinach and ricotta, topped with Bel Paese cheese and roasted peppers).

Other recommendations: Fresh fish specialties (e.g., salmone al vapore—fillet steamed and served over chianti sauce); beef, veal, and game items.

Summary & comments: The chef is dedicated to creating dishes and adding his mark to regional recipes. The restaurant grew out of the original pizza place next door, and the pizzette is quite good. This is one Italian place without a pasta emphasis; there are many alternatives. The place can be bustling on weekends.

Relish

American   ★★★½   **Inexpensive/Moderate**

2044 North Halsted Street
(312) 868-9034
Zone 1   North Side

Quality	Value
86	C

Reservations: Accepted
When to go: Dinner
Entree range: $9.50–16.50
Payment: VISA, MC, AMEX, DC, CB
Service rating: ★★½
Friendliness rating: ★★★
Parking: Street
Bar: Full service
Wine selection: All American; sold by the glass
Dress: Chic casual
Disabled access: Yes
Customers: Locals, yuppies, couples, business
Dinner: Monday–Thursday, 5:15–10 P.M.; Friday and Saturday, 5:15–11 P.M.; Sunday, 5:15–9 P.M.

Atmosphere / setting: Intimate with colorful, contemporary art. Two dining rooms are separated by a narrow bar area, with French doors opening onto a garden which is available for summer al fresco dining.

House specialities: Annetto-marinated sea scallops, red onion and oranges, and tomatillo relish; barbecued tuna steak and crisp Tabasco onions on painted pony beans with garlic; hickory-smoked pork loin chop stuffed with mozzarella on couscous and "relish tapenade." Award-winning dessert, "chocolate orgasm."

Other recommendations: Spicy Portuguese chicken sausage and charred bread pudding with smoked green tomato relish; balsamic-marinated portobello and radicchio with Gorgonzola biscuit; Maryland lump crab cake, ancho and cilantro aioli, corn, and salsa.

Summary & comments: Charming place with an easy to miss entryway from the street. The hidden garden is lovely for outdoor summer dining. The main dining room is smoke-free. Chef Ron Blazek's cooking is forward in flavor and creative in the combination of ingredients, and his presentations are attractive and often whimsical. On the downside, recent reports have been of great lapses in service, but there's good reason to hope that is being improved.

Reza's

Persian   ★★★   **Inexpensive/Moderate**

5255 North Clark Street
(312) 561-1898
Zone 1   North Side

Quality	Value
84	**C**

432 West Ontario Street
(312) 664-4500
Zone 3   Near North

Reservations: Recommended on Thursday, Friday, and weekends
When to go: Avoid end of week and weekends
Entree range: $8.95–12.95
Payment: No credit cards
Service rating: ★★★½
Friendliness rating: ★★★★½
Parking: Valet (downtown)
Bar: Full service
Wine selection: Extensive; international; fairly priced; several by the glass
Dress: Moderately casual
Disabled access: Yes, including rest rooms, elevators
Customers: Diverse; more local at Clark St.; more business downtown
Lunch/Dinner: Every day, 11 A.M.–midnight

Atmosphere / setting: Modern Persian; spacious, casual look—attractive and comfortable.

House specialities: Vegetarian samplers and seafood dishes Persian-style; eggplant steak appetizer; kebabs (e.g., shrimp and filet with veggies); chicken dishes.

Other recommendations: Variety of appetizers (e.g., dolmeh felfel; grilled skewered mushrooms); duck breast with sweet and sour pomegranate sauce and walnuts; marinated char-broiled quail.

Entertainment & amenities: Wednesday, guitar; other weeknights, piano. Call first. Downtown location has nightly music and a free shuttle bus for lunch to and from Merchandise Mart and other locations.

Summary & comments: The original Reza's has expanded several times and does a brisk business. The huge, newer place on the west side of downtown is in the former Sieben's Brewery, which then became Berghoff Brewery and Restaurant. It's a great place for casual business lunches. Both are large and bustling.

Roditys

Greek   ★★★¹/₂   **Inexpensive/Moderate**

---

222 South Halsted Street, Greektown

(312) 454-0800

Zone 4   The Loop

Quality	Value
89	**B**

Reservations: Recommended
When to go: Weekdays; avoid busy weekends
Entree range: $6.95–14.50
Payment: VISA, MC, AMEX
Service rating: ★★★★¹/₂
Friendliness rating: ★★★★¹/₂
Parking: Lot across the street
Bar: Full service
Wine selection: Mostly Greek (about 16, including Boutari grande reserve; 3 by the glass); 2 American
Dress: Casual
Disabled access: Wheelchair access, including rest rooms
Customers: Diverse, some Greek, mostly American
Lunch/Dinner: Sunday–Friday, 11 A.M.–1 A.M.; Saturday, 11 A.M.–2 A.M.

Atmosphere / setting: Attractive 2-room, 200-seat space that balances classical and modern impressions, from jigsaw-style wooden wall murals, pottery, and other artifacts to tile roof sections and inlaid tile tables. Open and laid back overall.

House specialities: Roditys special platter mixes hot spinach-cheese pie with cold items (e.g., taramosalata, cheeses, and octopus salad); lamb dishes such as unusual village-style cutlets (mini-chops pan-fried and then flambéed with green peppers, onions, garlic, and tomato); and lamb riblets, baked riganato-style.

Other recommendations: Taramosalata; whole fried squid; horta (boiled dandelions with olive oil and lemon); large dolmades with beef and rice; broiled whitefish; rice pudding; nougatina.

Summary & comments: The slightly spicier, home-style traditional cooking here gives this 22-year-old place its large Greek following, especially after church on Sundays. One half of the menu is in Greek, which testifies to the clientele. This place and the Parthenon tend to be where most of the Greeks like to dine.

Rosebud Cafe

Italian　　★★★　　**Inexpensive/Moderate**

1500 West Taylor Street
(312) 942-1117
Zone 5　　South Loop

Quality	Value
83	C

Reservations: Highly recommended
When to go: Before 7 P.M. and after 9 P.M.
Entree range: Pastas, $8.95–12.95; chicken, $14.95; veal, $16.95
Payment: All major credit cards
Service rating: ★★¹/₂
Friendliness rating: ★★★
Parking: Lot, valet
Bar: Full service
Wine selection: Extensive; international; some outstanding bottles among the Italian choices
Dress: Upscale, but no jacket required
Disabled access: Yes, including rest rooms
Customers: Local, international, tourist
Lunch: Monday–Friday, 11 A.M.–3 P.M.
Dinner: Monday–Thursday, 5–10:30 P.M.; Friday and Saturday, 5–11:30 P.M.; Sunday, 4–10:30 P.M.

Atmosphere/setting: Loud, crowded, very "in Chicago." New second floor where 120 can be seated for private dining.

House specialities: Calamari and mussels in either light red wine or white wine broth; chicken Vesuvio; pappardelle (square noodles) marinara; baked cavatelli; special pasta such as tortiglioni arrabbiata (spirals in spicy red sauce).

Other recommendations: Roasted red peppers; veal Parmigiana; lemon ice; and cannoli.

Summary & comments: This Taylor Street mecca of fine, traditional Italian cooking is a true trattoria: service is friendly and knowledgeable, the portions are too generous, and the place is often packed. Waits are common even with reservations. It has been widely recognized by the press, and it maintains a steady customer flow. Not a place to go for a quiet business dinner or romantic evening.

Russian Tea Cafe

Russian ★★★½ Moderate

---

77 East Adams Street
(312) 360-0000
Zone 4   The Loop

Quality	Value
88	**C**

Reservations: Highly recommended
When to go: Quieter time 2–5 P.M.
Entree range: $10–16
Payment: Major credit cards
Service rating: ★★★★
Friendliness rating: ★★★★½
Parking: Lots nearby; hopes to have valet in near future
Bar: Full service, including Russian vodkas
Wine selection: Two dozen selections; mainly French, Italian, California, and Washington wines; several by the glass
Dress: Casual to moderately upscale and dressy
Disabled access: Yes; menus available in braille
Customers: Diverse, Russian-American, symphony and opera crowd, talk-show hosts and guests from television and radio stations nearby
Lunch/Dinner: Monday, 11 A.M.–4 P.M.; Tuesday–Thursday, 11 A.M.–11 P.M.; Friday, 11 A.M.–midnight; Saturday, noon–midnight; Sunday, 1–9 P.M.

Atmosphere / setting: Cozy, old-world atmosphere with a great deal of woodwork, Russian urns, pots, and tablecloths; well-spaced booths and tables; dessert display case.

House specialities: Blini with top-quality Russian caviar; borscht; goriachaya zakuska (appetizer platter for 2-plus including chicken dumplings, stuffed cabbage, and beets); wild game (e.g., stuffed quails with pomegranate sauce); vegetarian dishes (e.g., jumbo stuffed mushrooms with spinach, onion, and cheese); hot farmer's cheese blintzes.

Other recommendations: Elaborate kulebiaka (meat pie) filled with ground beef, cabbage, and onions; blinchiki (crêpes—the beef stroganoff are great; also salmon and cheese); roast pheasant "Erevan" with Armenian brandy, walnut and pomegranate sauce, and brandied prunes; Tashkent carrot salad (named for hometown of owners; a la carte or comes with entrees); chicken croquettes; hearty homemade apricot-plum strudel is the thick-crusted Russian version; Russian tea (blend of three, including black currant).

Summary & comments: The only serious Russian restaurant in town (at press time the Russian Palace opened nearby), this exquisite cafe received rave reviews within the first several months of opening in fall 1993. The Chicago Symphony bought the building the cafe was originally in, and the conductor, former conductor, symphonygoers and operagoers all dine here before or after the event. Owner Vadim Muchnik is the gracious host and kisses ladies' hands, while his partner and mother Klara heads the kitchen. The ambitious menu is about as long as Tolstoy's *War and Peace*, and the menu describes customs and a bit of historical background of dishes and their famous namesakes. This is a fine ethnic experience.

Ruth's Chris Steakhouse

Steaks ★★★★ **Moderate/Expensive**

431 North Dearborn Street
(312) 321-2725
Zone 4   The Loop

Quality	Value
93	**B**

Reservations: Recommended
When to go: Avoid peak times, 6–8 P.M. on weekends
Entree range: $10–27
Payment: All major credit cards
Service rating: ★★★½
Friendliness rating: ★★★★
Parking: Free valet
Bar: Full service
Wine selection: International, especially American, French, and Italian; heavy California bent; several by the glass
Dress: Moderately casual, business
Disabled access: Yes
Customers: Very local; have a following
Lunch: Monday–Friday, 11:30 A.M.–3 P.M.
Dinner: Monday–Friday, 3–11 P.M.; Saturday, 5 P.M.–midnight

Atmosphere / setting: Clubby; plaid carpet; lots of sports memorabilia.

House specialities: All prime cuts here: New York strip steak, 16–18 ounces; 20-ounce T-bone; petite filet of beef tenderloin, 8-ounce; provimi veal chop; veal sweetbreads; barbecued shrimp Orleans; three classic sauces offered with entrees and sides.

Other recommendations: Fish of the day; live Maine lobster; porterhouse for two; Prince Edward's mashed potatoes with garlic; turtle soup served with sherry; gumbo Louisiane; bread pudding with Jack Daniel's whiskey sauce; pecan pie.

Summary & comments: One of the newest among Chicago's steak houses, this New Orleans franchise spot is very successful. Menu pays tribute to its roots with several New Orleans touches. Steaks sizzle appealingly because they get a coating of butter. Juices are sealed into steaks on the hottest 1,800° F grill. One of a fast-growing chain with a good reputation.

The Saloon

Steak	★★★½	**Moderate/Expensive**

200 East Chestnut Street
(312) 280-5454
Zone 3   Near North

Quality	Value
89	**C**

Reservations: Accepted
When to go: Before 8 P.M.
Entree range: $9.95–24.95
Payment: VISA, MC, AMEX, D, DC, CB
Service rating: ★★★★
Friendliness rating: ★★★★
Parking: Doorman parks cars; no valet
Bar: Full service
Wine selection: Extensive, featuring a large meritage and Californian selection
Dress: Casual to jacket-and-tie dressy
Disabled access: Yes
Customers: Business, theatergoers, tourists
Brunch: Saturday and Sunday, 11 A.M.–4 P.M. Santa Fe brunch (served, not buffet)
Lunch/Dinner: Monday–Saturday, 11 A.M.–midnight
Dinner: Sunday, 3–10 P.M.

Atmosphere / setting: Enter through the handsome, contemporary bar with a two-tone wooden floor. Dining room has a warm, comfortable atmosphere, banquettes, and sponge-painted, rusty, salmon-hued walls; tiny candle lamps give soft lighting.

House specialities: Smoked 16-ounce porkchop; 48-ounce porterhouse steak; 18-ounce Kansas bone-in strip with chili corn relish; 13-ounce filet mignon; surf and turf; potato-crusted fish of the day (e.g., walleyed pike); beefsteak tomato and onion with crumbled blue cheese; crispy calamari.

Other recommendations: Appetizer sampler plate (includes jalapeños stuffed with cheddar cheese, house smoked barbecue chicken skewers, and blackened scallops); buffalo mozzarella salad; shrimp cocktail; wood-grilled lobster tail; crispy potato cake; Cajun chips; tuna tartare; jumbo asparagus with vinaigrette; garbage salad. Desserts include banana steak, fresh fruit cobbler, key lime tart, and crème brûlée.

Summary & comments: The Saloon was opened on the Gold Coast in 1991 by the Restaurant Development Group, which also owns Kinzie Street Chophouse. The two places have some similarities besides locations, but more differences. A signature item here is the potato-crusted fish, and it was sampled on several occasions; once, the walleyed pike lacked seasoning and its crust was slightly greasy—the only minor flaw noted. The concept is great and usually works well. To his credit, our well-schooled waiter noticed that the steak we ordered as medium-rare arrived more medium, and he whisked it back for another. Order several items and share, if possible. Save room for good desserts. The same firm just opened Grappa next door.

Santa Fe Tapas

Southwestern ★★★ **Inexpensive/Moderate**

	Quality	Value
1962 North Halsted Street (312) 404-9168 Zone 1 North Side	**82**	**C**

Reservations: Recommended
When to go: Less crowded after 7:30 P.M.
Entree range: $2.95–19.95, mostly tapas size
Payment: VISA, MC, AMEX, D, DC
Service rating: ★★★½
Friendliness rating: ★★★★
Parking: Valet, lot nearby
Bar: Full service; one of the best lists, including specialty drinks such as sangria, a variety of margaritas (e.g., passion fruit), infused spirits, and good beers; large tequila and rum collection
Wine selection: International; selective; mostly Spanish; from $10.50 a bottle; also selections from New Mexico, Baja, Chile, Italy, Portugal, and California; several by the glass
Dress: Casual
Disabled access: Yes, including rest rooms
Customers: Diverse, local, yuppie, couples, all ages
Dinner: Monday–Thursday, 5–11 P.M.; Friday and Saturday, 5 P.M.–midnight; Sunday, 5–10:30 P.M.

Atmosphere/setting: Very Southwestern/Mexican; "cowboyish" with tiles and earth tones. Long, narrow store front with a substantial bar; dining alcove streetside.

House specialities: Blue corn crêpes with smoked salmon and cilantro cream cheese; chicken fritters; alligator fritters with good sauce; game specialties; grilled shrimp with pecan pancake; herb-grilled salmon; farm-raised, sautéed catfish with spicy peanut and asparagus salsa. The only entree (non-tapas item) is fajitas.

Other recommendations: Mushrooms filled with spinach and crabmeat; seafood casuales; barbecue pork tenderloin with spicy peanut sauce and cucumber salsa; torta de pollo; crispy duck with chipotle and fruit relish. Desserts: pumpkin cheesecake and cappuccino flan.

Summary & comments: The tapas concept was adapted to innovative Southwestern fare here, and it's doing well in this attractive, fairly new store front on Halsted Street's "restaurant row." Because of the tapas (smaller plates), more food can be sampled— especially fun with the margaritas or some nice wine. Spices vary, but none are too hot; all flavors are fresh and distinctive. You won't find these dishes in Santa Fe, New Mexico, because many are unique creations by chef/co-owner Daniel Castro.

Santorini

Greek ★★★½ **Inexpensive/Moderate**

---

800 West Adams Street, Greektown
(312) 829-8820
Zone 4   The Loop

Quality	Value
89	**C**

Reservations: Recommended
When to go: Weekdays
Entree range: $8–16
Payment: Major credit cards except DC
Service rating: ★★★★
Friendliness rating: ★★★★
Parking: Free valet
Bar: Full service
Wine selection: International: Greek, American, French, and Italian
Dress: Varies from casual to formal
Disabled access: Yes, including rest rooms
Customers: Diverse, about one-third Greek
Lunch/Dinner: Sunday–Thursday, 11 A.M.–midnight; Friday and Saturday, 11 A.M.–1 A.M.

Atmosphere/setting: Cozy with fireplace in room's center. Lovely authentic interior decorated with plates and baskets; art depicts the hilly island, Santorini.

House specialities: Seafood is the showcase: charcoal-grilled octopus; shrimp ala Santorini; charcoal-grilled swordfish steak with Santorini sauce; bacalao and garlic sauce; broiled red snapper fillet (unique here, instead of whole fish); shrimp Tourkolimano (butterflied jumbos baked in tomato and feta sauce); baked fish ala spetsiota; Santorini salad; sokolatina (semisweet chocolate mousse cake) with "Santorini" written over each slice.

Other recommendations: Appetizer spreads such as eggplant, fish roe, and spicy feta; tzatziki (cucumber-yogurt dip); chicken ala Santorini; lamb scharas (thin slices charcoal-grilled and prepared the original Greek way); seafood platter (shellfish and fish); homemade yogurt with honey and nuts; nougatina (rich crème and nut cake).

Summary & comments: This fairly recent addition to Greektown is upscale, refined, and probably the most expensive. Many inexpensive items are on the menu, but there is an absence of the traditional dishes, which tend to be less costly. Seafood, steaks, and chops draw a higher price. Daily specials are creative and enticing, and some are repeated several times weekly, such as the lamb stamnas (crêpe filled with lamb, vegetables, cheeses, and pine nuts). Service is attentive and knowledgeable.

Sayat Nova

Armenian	★★★½	**Inexpensive/Moderate**

20 West Golf Road, Des Plaines
(708) 296-1776
Zone 10   Northwest Suburbs

Quality	Value
88	**C**

Reservations: Recommended on weekends
When to go: Weekdays
Entree range: $10.50–15
Payment: All major credit cards
Service rating: ★★★★
Friendliness rating: ★★★★½
Parking: Lot
Bar: Full service
Wine selection: Limited, about 22 selections; mostly American, a few Italian, 15–16 Californian; 3 by the glass
Dress: Casual, some dressy
Disabled access: Yes
Customers: International, diverse, business, couples, families
Lunch: Tuesday–Friday, 11:30 A.M.–2 P.M.
Dinner: Tuesday–Thursday, Sunday, 4–10 P.M.; Friday and Saturday, 4–11 P.M.

Atmosphere / setting: Middle-Eastern decor with tile inserts in wall alcoves; white tablecloths, red napkins, and candles. Very romantic and cozy; comfortable private booths; dimly lit.

House specialities: Spinach boereg (pastry); baba ganouj (eggplant-tahini appetizer); yalanji sarma (rice and pine nut–stuffed grape leaves); hummus and tahini with toasted pita bread; jajic (minted yogurt and cucumber dip); Boghossian combination: lamb chop, lamb and chicken shish kebab, lula kebab (ground beef and lamb), rice pilaf, broiled green pepper and tomato—a nice sampler.

Other recommendations: Various lamb specialties including sautéed lamb and chops; shrimp kebab. Pastries: cheese and pear strudel, paklava (pastry rolls more delicious than they look); cheesecake with raspberry sauce—not Armenian, but a creamy, light version; Armenian coffee.

Summary & comments: Sayat Nova is well established in this northwest suburb and has a steady

clientele. It's reliable for delivering authentic Armenian cuisine—one of the only restaurants that offers
this cooking. The gracious hospitality extended by this
family-owned business, now into the second generation, invites return visits. One of the nicest places for a
romantic evening or quiet business dinner.

Seasons Restaurant at the
Four Seasons Hotel

American   ★★★★½   **Moderate/Expensive**

**120 East Delaware Place at
Michigan Avenue**

Quality	Value
97	**C**

(312) 280-8800, Ext. 2134
Zone 3   Near North

Reservations: Recommended
When to go: Any time
Entree range: $22–34
Payment: VISA, MC, AMEX, DC, D
Service rating: ★★★★★
Friendliness rating: ★★★★★
Parking: Valet at the hotel entrance or self-parking on
Rush or Walton streets with covered access to
hotel's seventh-floor lobby; lunchtime parking is $5
with validation; dinnertime is $3 at the self-park
garage with validation
Bar: Full service
Wine selection: 320 selections of domestic and
imported wines including California sparkling wines
and French champagnes; many fine selections by the
glass
Dress: Jacket required for men; upscale casual; dressy
Disabled access: Yes
Customers: Traveler, business, local
Breakfast: *Seasons Restaurant:* Monday–Satur-
day, 6:30–10:30 A.M.; Sunday, 6:30–10 A.M.
Seasons Cafe: Sunday–Thursday, 8–11:30 A.M.;
Friday and Saturday, 8 A.M.–12:30 P.M.
Brunch: Sunday, 10:30 A.M.–1:30 P.M.
Lunch: Monday–Saturday, 11:30 A.M.–2 P.M.
Dinner: Sunday–Saturday, 6–10 P.M.

Atmosphere / setting: Opulent carpeted dining room
with drapes, crystal sconces, and white tablecloths;
lovely floral arrangements; elegant; artwork on walls;
nice view from tables near windows.

House specialities: Menu changes each season. Some
examples: grilled portobello mushroom with foie gras
and balsamic syrup; organic field greens, raspberry
vinaigrette, and goat cheese crouton; naturally farmed
veal chop, pickled corn relish, and arugula whipped
potatoes; specials such as pan-seared Gulf snapper
with basil oil, vegetable-potato Napoleon, and
Japanese buckwheat noodles; desserts such as warm

fig and blueberry compote; orange-Drambuie ice cream with wild honey-cabernet sauce; Seasons chocolate marjolaine.

Other recommendations: Lunch: Maine lobster salad with Southwestern flavors; seared ahi tuna salad with cooling papaya-ginger relish; steamed Atlantic salmon fillet on cucumber semolina; beef vinaigrette; scallopini of chicken on fennel-potato pancake with spring morel-port wine sauce; grilled prime minute steak, Dijon mustard béarnaise, and shoestring fries. Dinner: roast Casco cod fillet with smoked cod-scallop hash; roasted free-range chicken and pearl barley–sweet corn pilaf; prime rib-eye steak, rustic onion baked potato, and garlic-mustard and rosemary grits; Atlantic salmon fillet braised in chardonnay with fennel-herb risotto and shallot-wine reduction.

Entertainment & amenities: Jazz in the adjacent Seasons Lounge Friday and Saturday evenings can be heard in the dining room.

Summary & comments: Seasons specializes in innovative American cuisine made from fresh—often unusual—regional ingredients served in a simple style. Executive chef Mark Baker, who is from Boston, loves working with New England seafood, and it shows. He completely changes the menu the first day of spring, summer, and autumn, and changes it partially mid-winter to utilize the freshest local products. Seasons has worked with the Department of Agriculture in several different states to hand pick the highest caliber regional suppliers. The restaurant also offers alternative cuisine which is low in calories and cholesterol. Baker's cooking overall avoids rich sauces; his creations evolve with richness of flavor from prime ingredients cooked together and from reductions and vinaigrettes. One of the most splendid hotel dining rooms anywhere.

Honors / Awards: Hotel is Chicago's only 5-star and 5-diamond hotel; it has won numerous awards, which include the restaurant; the chef has received much recognition in the press.

Shaw's Crab House and Shaw's Blue Crab Lounge & Oyster Bar

Seafood ★★★★½ **Moderate**

21 East Hubbard Street
(312) 527-2722
Zone 4   The Loop

Quality	Value
95	**C**

Reservations: Main dining room, suggested; Blue Crab Lounge, not accepted

When to go: Any time

Entree range: $12.95–18.95; Blue Crab Lounge, blackboard items a la carte and a bit cheaper

Payment: All major credit cards

Service rating: ★★★

Friendliness rating: ★★★★

Parking: Valet, $5

Bar: Full service

Wine selection: Largely Californian, several international; good selection by the glass; list chosen for seafood

Dress: Main dining room, dressy; Blue Crab Lounge, dressy or casual

Disabled access: Wheelchair accessible; call first

Customers: Business, travelers, couples, singles

Lunch: *Main dining room:* Monday–Friday, 11:30 A.M.–2 P.M.

Lunch/Dinner: *Blue Crab Lounge:* Monday–Thursday, 11:30 A.M.–10 P.M.; Friday, 11:30 A.M.–11 P.M.; Saturday, 5–11 P.M.

Dinner: *Main dining room:* Monday–Thursday, 5:30–10 P.M.; Friday and Saturday, 5–11 P.M.; Sunday, 5–10 P.M.

Atmosphere / setting: Two restaurants in one, with the main dining room (325 seats) reminiscent of an old New England seafood house, and the Blue Crab Lounge essentially a raw bar with high tables and stools, serving a limited blackboard menu with some hot, simple dishes.

House specialities: Shaw's crab cakes; a great variety of oysters; sautéed sea scallops; Shaw's seafood platter.

Other recommendations: Shaw's seafood stew; lobster bisque; seasonal specialties such as Maryland soft-shell crabs, Dungeness crab, Columbia River spring chinook salmon, and stone crab. Daily desserts:

popular refreshing key lime pie, pecan pie, and rich truffle cake.

Entertainment & amenities: Blue Crab Lounge, jazz or blues, Tuesday–Thursday, 7–10 P.M.

Summary & comments: Pristinely fresh products, a variety of preparations, an extensive list of seafood-friendly wines, and knowledgeable service make Shaw's one of the best seafood places around. An on-staff seafood buyer constantly monitors products and storage temperatures. Oyster, Swedish crayfish, and other promotions keep the crowds coming. Overall, simple preparations fare better than the more elaborate dishes. Chef Yves Roubaud's crab cakes rate as the best. The bread basket items are addictive.

Shaw's Seafood Grill

Seafood	★★★	Moderate

---

660 West Lake Cook Road, Deerfield

Quality	Value
80	**C**

(708) 948-1020

Zone 11   Northern Suburbs

Reservations: Accepted and suggested

When to go: Any time

Entree range: Lunch, $6.95–9.95; early evening menu, $8.95–11.95; dinner, $11.95–19.95

Payment: All major credit cards

Service rating: ★★★

Friendliness rating: ★★★

Parking: Lot

Bar: Full service

Wine selection: Selected for seafood; largely Californian; several international; good selection by the glass

Dress: Casual or business

Disabled access: Wheelchair accessible; call first

Customers: Mostly business, travelers, couples, singles

Lunch: Monday–Friday, 11:30 A.M.–2:30 P.M.

Dinner: Early evening menu, Sunday–Friday, 5–6 P.M.; Monday–Thursday, 5–9:30 P.M.; Friday and Saturday, 5–10:30 P.M.; Sunday, 4:30–9 P.M.

Atmosphere / setting: Resembles a 1940s East Coast seafood house with seating for 250.

House specialities: Shrimp pot stickers and plum sauce; grilled seafood salad; regional oyster specials; grilled flatbread with various toppings (as an appetizer for dinner or as a main course for early dinner and lunch); Lake Superior whitefish, garlic crusted.

Other recommendations: Pan-seared walleyed pike, smashed potatoes, julienned vegetables, roasted tomato relish; grilled seafood skewer; seasonal specialties such as Maryland soft-shell crabs, Dungeness crab, grilled Copper River king salmon (available only 2–3 weeks each summer). Daily desserts: popular key lime pie and pecan pie.

Summary & comments: Although similar to Shaw's Crab House in Chicago, this place has some menu differences and is fashioned more like Blue Crab

Lounge in the city. The same care is given to pristinely fresh products prepared in a variety of ways. Together with knowledgeable service and a good wine list and atmosphere, this is one of the best seafood restaurants in the suburbs. Seafood promotions keep the crowds coming. Overall, simple preparations fare better than more elaborate dishes.

Sher-A-Punjab

Indian	★★★	**Inexpensive**

2510 West Devon Avenue
(312) 973-4000
Zone 1   North Side

Quality	Value
82	**B**

Reservations: Recommended
When to go: Any time
Entree range: $8–11.75; lunch buffet, $5.95; dinner buffet, $7.95
Payment: VISA, MC, D, DC, CB
Service rating: ★★
Friendliness rating: ★★★¹/₂
Parking: 2 city lots nearby
Bar: None, BYOB
Wine selection: None
Dress: Moderately casual
Disabled access: Yes
Customers: Diverse, including many ethnic families
Lunch/Dinner: Every day, 11 A.M.–11 P.M.

Atmosphere / setting: Clean and modern looking with pink tablecloths, plastic covers, candles, and plants.

House specialities: Saag paneer (homemade cheese cooked in spiced spinach); dal (spiced lentil dip); mixed vegetable curry; chicken tandoori (not on buffet); delicate chicken biryani; lamb curry.

Other recommendations: Butter chicken; bharvan kulcha (stuffed bread); paneer jalfrazie (cheese cubes sautéed with vegetables and spices); eggplant bhartha, cooked in spicy yogurt.

Summary & comments: The extensive buffet here is a very nice way of sampling the menu, except for certain items such as the tandoori specialties, which must be made to order. The buffet is replenished frequently and includes two breads. Make several trips to sample a group of items at a time, starting with appetizers such as crispy samosas; return for entrees (some spicy); finish with the refreshing desserts, such as the carrot "cake" and khee (sweet milk with the tiniest thread noodles). Spiced tea settles all. Service can have lapses. The proprietor also owns Bundoo Khan, a Pakistani restaurant on the same block. It's small, casual, cozy, and also a very good value.

Shilla

Korean/Japanese ★★★½ **Moderate**

5930 North Lincoln Avenue
(312) 275-5930
Zone 1   North Side

Quality	Value
86	**C**

Reservations: Recommended, especially Thursday, Friday, and Saturday; call a day or 2 in advance to reserve private room, minimum of 4

When to go: Any time, but Thursday and weekends are busier

Entree range: $7.95–28.95; lunch buffet, $6.99

Payment: VISA, MC, AMEX, DC

Service rating: ★★★

Friendliness rating: ★★★

Parking: Free lot

Bar: Full service, including OB beer and Asian products

Wine selection: Very limited: Californian, French, and Asian; 3 each whites and reds listed (bottle and glass) but they're sometimes out of 2; house wine by the glass; saké and sweet plum wine appropriate for some foods

Dress: Mostly dressy, some casual

Disabled access: Yes

Customers: Korean, family, business

Open: Monday–Saturday, 11 A.M.–10:30 P.M.; Sunday, 11 A.M.–9:30 P.M. Bar area, every day, 6 P.M.–2 A.M. Lunch buffet, 11:30 A.M.–3 P.M. Saturday and Sunday buffet, 50 different Korean, Japanese, and Chinese items and unlimited sushi, noon–4 P.M. and 5:30–9:30 P.M., $14.99. Children 12 and under, $1.50 per year over age 2

Atmosphere / setting: Large, upscale restaurant centered around an attractive, 50-seat main dining hall with 7 rooms surrounding it. The most picturesque room is the central one with lacquered chairs, colorful upholstery, and aquariums separating it from the sushi bar. The back room, although a bit dated and pale in decor, is outfitted with grills in tables at booths; ventilation could be improved—it can get a bit smoky. Smaller private dining rooms, some with grills in tables, are popular with business people who book them for lunch or dinner meetings.

House specialities: Chap chae (Korean pan-fried shredded pork and vegetables); mung bean noodles; nakji bogeum (stir-fried octopus and vegetables in spicy sauce); kalbi (broiled, marinated short ribs). The owners are proud of their homemade doenchang jige (chopped beef, vegetables, hot pepper, and bean paste in a pot with rice); most places buy the six-month fermented paste. Try the Korean barbecue, a variety of marinated meats and chicken grilled at the table; eat them wrapped in lettuce with bean paste. Sik hae (off the menu) is honeyed cinnamon broth, sweet rice, and pine nuts.

Other recommendations: Pajun (scallion pancake with chopped octopus); buffets (giant clams with black bean sauce, snow crab, steamed fish, Korean specialties, maki rolls, and more).

Summary & comments: Experience this place with several people if possible, since it's fun to share a variety of specialties, some of which are quite generous. The Korean menu is the one Asian cuisine that's least exotic for the American palate, since it's based on grilled meats and barbecue-style sauces. A flotilla of side dishes is served as an accompaniment to dinner, including kim chee (spiced fermented cabbage or radish, bean sprouts, and cucumber). Dessert comes with dinners.

Siam Cafe

Thai	★★★	Inexpensive

4712 North Sheridan Road
(312) 769-6602
Zone 1   North Side

Quality	Value
84	**A**

Reservations: Accepted
When to go: Any time; evenings and lunchtime can
   be busy
Entree range: $4.75–6.75
Payment: VISA, MC, AMEX, DC
Service rating: ★★★¹/₂
Friendliness rating: ★★★¹/₂
Parking: Street
Bar: Beer and wine
Wine selection: American
Dress: Casual
Disabled access: Yes
Customers: Local
Lunch/Dinner: Wednesday–Monday, 11:30 A.M.–
   9 P.M.; Tuesday, closed.

Atmosphere / setting: Attractively decorated with
Thai furnishings; dressier than many Thai places.

House specialities: Hot and spicy seafood soup (one
version is just shrimp; another is beef and chicken);
spring rolls; mee krob (crispy rice noodle, fried tofu,
shrimp, and sweet-and-sour sauce); yum nam tok
(beef-onion salad with hot-sour sauce); pad thai (rice
noodles, peanuts, bean sprout, and egg sauce); curry
fried rice with choice of meat or shrimp.

Other recommendations: Kai yang (marinated
charcoal chicken); kra tiem prik Thai (chicken, beef, or
pork with garlic) without rice; red snapper with ginger
or hot sauce.

Summary & comments: Large menu with many
good choices for rock-bottom prices. Hot items on the
menu are starred, and one column of dishes is called,
"original hot and spicy." Some of the ingredients
include red and green curry paste, red chili sauce,
jalapeño pepper, and red-hot spicy sauce! These are for
the veteran hot food lovers—novices beware. There
are numerous intriguing rice dishes and variations
without rice.

The Signature Room at
the Ninety-Fifth

New American   ★★★★   Moderate/Expensive

	Quality	Value
875 North Michigan Avenue, atop the John Hancock Center	**90**	**C**

(312) 787-9596
Zone 3   Near North

Reservations: Recommended
When to go: Any time
Entree range: $19–29; Sunday brunch buffet, $25
Payment: VISA, MC, AMEX, DC
Service rating: ★★★★
Friendliness rating: ★★★★½
Parking: Self-park garage
Bar: Full service
Wine selection: Award-winning, all-American list with 120 selections; most are moderately priced, from $20 a bottle to expensive vintages at $250 a bottle; several good selections by the glass
Dress: Chic casual, business, semiformal to dressy; at dinner, jackets suggested but not required
Disabled access: Yes
Customers: Locals, business, couples, travelers
Brunch: Sunday, 10:30 A.M.–2 P.M.; extensive buffet of hot and cold foods, large assortment of desserts
Lunch: Monday–Friday, 11 A.M.–2 P.M.; cold and hot buffet available for $6.95
Dinner: Sunday–Saturday, 5–10 P.M.

Atmosphere / setting: The view from the top of the city on the 95th floor of the John Hancock Center is spectacular on a clear day. The breathtaking panorama is a beautiful, majestic backdrop for dining. Elegant, contemporary, sleek interior with lovely chandeliers and wrap-around windows.

House specialities: Honey- and ginger–glazed salmon with napa cabbage, shiitake mushroom and daikon salad, and ginger-lime vinaigrette; cappellini with shrimp and scallops, roasted tomatoes and black truffles, white wine, garlic, and olive oil; signature sweetbreads; homemade ice cream.

Other recommendations: Appetizer: roasted portobello mushroom glazed with goat cheese, sun-dried tomatoes, and black olives, with basil pesto; chilled scallop sausage with blue corn tortilla chips and smoked caviar gazpacho; wild mushroom terrine with feta cheese, eggplant, roasted garlic puree, and tomato croutons; fettuccini sautéed with wild mushrooms, tomato, parsley, and garlic; roasted eggplant curry and tomato soup. Entrees: marinated and grilled swordfish with avocado sorbet, cilantro, and grapefruit oil; sautéed duck breast glazed with dried cherries and cranberries, and anaheim and ancho chili sauce. A vegetarian main course: roasted eggplant, zucchini, peppers, and portobello mushrooms in phyllo with two cheeses, with vegetable coulis. Lovely, feathery raspberry bombe and a beautiful fruit tart made more delicious by a chocolate layer on the pastry.

Entertainment & amenities: Live music (often piano, violin, or saxophone) Saturday, 7–11 P.M.; Sunday, 11 A.M.–2 P.M. and 7–10 P.M.

Summary & comments: Healthful, contemporary American cuisine based on organically grown produce and chemical-free ingredients overall. The light cuisine is flavored a great deal with infused oils. The greatest 360-degree panoramic view of Chicago and its lakefront is from this restaurant, atop the John Hancock Center. The management, in its vision statement on the menu, makes its commitment to excellence in products, service, and atmosphere with an environmental conscience. It donates 10% of profits to a chosen charity each month.

Honors / Awards: *Wine Spectator* Grand Award; Top Ten Most Distinguished Restaurants in North America

Skadarlija

Serbian/Continental ★★★ Moderate

4024 North Kedzie Avenue
(312) 463-5600
Zone 1   North Side

Quality	Value
84	**B**

Reservations: Accepted
When to go: Dinner
Entree range: $10.95–15.95
Payment: AMEX
Service rating: ★★★★½
Friendliness rating: ★★★★½
Parking: Street
Bar: Full service, including the aromatic slivovitz
(plum brandy)
Wine selection: Limited; Californian
Dress: Casual, but no shorts; dressy, depending on
time
Disabled access: Yes
Customers: Local, ethnic, family, couples
Open: Wednesday–Sunday, 6 P.M.–2 A.M.;
Saturday, 6 P.M.–3 A.M.; Monday and Tuesday,
closed.

Atmosphere / setting: Restaurant has two levels of
seating, an outdoor terrace, a bar area, and a dance
floor. Dimly lit, comfortable dining room; seats about
100.

House specialities: Ajvar (appetizer spread of green
and red sweet peppers with oil and vinegar); kjamak
(fermented milk spread); Serbian cold plate (mixture
of homemade sausage, cheese, olives, and peppers); a
special appetizer of batter-fried, cheese-stuffed sweet
peppers; raznici (shish kebab); tender Wiener
schnitzel; roast veal.

Other recommendations: Homemade cheese strudel
appetizer; cevapcici (national specialty of well-
garnished ground veal and beef, sometimes
cheese-filled); gypsy plate (combination of several
specialties for two); karadjordjeva (national specialty
of veal steak wrapped around Bulgarian cheese, lightly
breaded and baked). Palacinke (crêpes with preserves,
chocolate, and walnuts) and apple strudel are desserts
to try. Serbian tea (flambéed slivovitz).

Entertainment & amenities: Live gypsy music every night—violinist, accordionist, keyboardist, and vocalist. Serbian and Russian musicians. Owner Zvonko plays the accordion and the synthesizers.

Summary & comments: Skadarlija is a well-known street in Belgrade frequented by musicians, artists, and writers, and paintings of this street are on the walls. Appropriately, an evening at this namesake restaurant is a cultural experience. Traditional Serbian fare is prepared well here and served in a most gracious style. There's a preponderance of meat in this cuisine, especially pork and veal, but a couple of fish items are offered. The atmosphere is warm and friendly, and the authentic ethnic entertainment enlivens the evening.

Song Huong

Vietnamese/Chinese ★★★¹/₂ **Inexpensive**

5424 North Broadway
(312) 271-6702
Zone 1   North Side

Quality	Value
86	**A**

Reservations: Accepted but not needed
When to go: Any time
Entree range: $3.95–17.95
Payment: VISA, MC, AMEX, D
Service rating: ★★★
Friendliness rating: ★★★★
Parking: Street
Bar: None
Wine selection: BYOB
Dress: Casual
Disabled access: None; 1 step up to door
Customers: Local, Vietnamese, Chinese
Lunch/Dinner: Sunday and Monday, Wednesday–
Thursday, 11 A.M.–10 P.M.; Friday and Saturday,
11 A.M.–11 P.M.; Tuesday, closed.

Atmosphere / setting: Nondescript looking store front
in older building. Ultra-simple decor, but pleasant and
comfortable; glass tops over tablecloths; casual.

House specialities: Chicken cole slaw (tender
poached breast slivers and cabbage-carrot slaw in
lemongrass-cilantro vinaigrette with chopped peanuts);
spring roll; Vietnamese pancake (rice flour, crêpe-like
pancake holds marinated shrimp and bean sprouts);
sour shrimp soup; catfish simmered in a clay pot;
coconut curries with frog legs or venison; noodle
dishes with choice of meat or seafood.

Other recommendations: Lemongrass pork
(tenderloin slices and sweet onion in a sauce redolent
of lemongrass, cilantro, and pepper spices over rice);
lime beef; fried catfish in ginger sauce (whole, deep-
fried, marinated fish with ginger and peppers).

Summary & comments: Bare bones decor belies the
consistently top-notch kitchen effort, very true to
Vietnamese cuisine—evident with tables of Vietnamese businessmen enjoying dinner. The menu of 15
appetizers, 17 soups, 12 rice and rice noodle dishes, 18
house specialties, plus an array of 38 chicken, pork,

vegetable, beef, and seafood preparations, and 6 fried rice offerings is very impressive for a small store front. Each dish is sophisticated, fresh tasting, and very carefully prepared to emphasize its particular flavors. For instance, corn and crab soup is a bowl of fresh summer corn simmered with choice crab and seductive spices. Sour shrimp soup is packed full of crisp-cooked vegetables and fresh pineapple in a spicy broth, topped with fresh, perfectly cooked shrimp. American customers might be steered away from the chef's specialties, because those tend to be ordered by the ethnics, but they certainly are worth it. Although Vietnamese cuisine prevails, the Chinese food also is well prepared; the audible sizzling chicken, pork, beef, or shrimp creations are delicious attention-getters. Vietnamese ice coffee (with condensed milk) is a perfect ending, although rich. Desserts include the strange but good mixtures of mung beans, coconut milk, and crushed ice.

Spiaggia

Italian   ★★★★   **Moderate/Expensive**

---

980 North Michigan Avenue
(312) 280-2750
Zone 3   Near North

Quality	Value
93	**C**

Reservations: Recommended
When to go: Any time
Entree range: $9.95–28.95; per person total, $50–60
Payment: All major credit cards
Service rating: ★★★
Friendliness rating: ★★½
Parking: Underground city facility on Walton
Bar: Full service
Wine selection: Extensive, Italian, $18–90 a bottle
Dress: Business, some semiformal and formal
Disabled access: Yes
Customers: Local, national, international, business travelers, North Shore, northwest and other suburbanites, celebrities from entertainment and political arenas (The Rolling Stones, Placido Domingo, Elton John, Robert Duvall, Norman Mailer, Alice Cooper, Dustin Hoffman, former Illinois Governor James Thompson, Mayor Richard Daley, Robert De Niro, Paul Newman, Itzhak Pearlman, Zubin Mehta, and Daniel Barenboim)
Lunch: Monday–Saturday, 11:30 A.M.–2 P.M.
Dinner: Monday–Thursday, 5:30–9:30 P.M.; Friday and Saturday, 5:30–10:30 P.M.; Sunday, 5:30–9 P.M.

Atmosphere / setting: Contemporary, rather formal dining setting overlooking Lake Michigan and Oak Street Beach.

House specialities: Faraona alle verze (wood-roasted guinea hen with savoy cabbage, pancetta, and porcini); gauzzetto di cozze (mussels steamed with white beans in an aromatic garlic-tomato broth); ravioli di ricotta con caciotta toscana; wood-roasted thin-crust gourmet pizzas (e.g., duck sausage, sage, goat cheese).

Other recommendations: Pastas (e.g., stracci con ragu di funghi—rags of fresh pasta with wild mushrooms); dentice in acqua pazza (literally "red snapper in crazy water").

Entertainment & amenities: Piano every evening at 6:30 P.M.

Summary & comments: Named because it's possible to see Oak Street Beach from the restaurant's windows, this very chic restaurant, one of the Levy Restaurants, has had ups and downs. Under the talented direction of chef Paul Bartolotta, the food has been elevated to a new plateau. He's rescued it from the earlier experimental and creative Italian fare and brought it back to regional roots. And the sometimes inconsistent, reserved service appears to have gotten on track. The casual Cafe Spiaggia offers light fare for lower prices, (312) 280-2764.

Honors / Awards: Chef Paul Bartolotta is the recipient of the James Beard Award; *Chicago* magazine's Critics Choice Award.

St. Germain Restaurant/Bakery Cafe

French Bistro ★★★¹/₂ **Inexpensive/Moderate**

1210 North State Parkway
(312) 266-9900
Zone 3   Near North

Quality	Value
88	**C**

Reservations: Not necessary on weekdays, but suggested on weekends
When to go: Any time; less busy 3–5 P.M.; great for breakfast, lunch, dinner, or late-night supper
Entree range: Lunch, $7–12; dinner, $9.50–18
Payment: All major credit cards
Service rating: ★★★¹/₂
Friendliness rating: ★★★¹/₂
Parking: 3 hours validated in lot across the street
Bar: Full service
Wine selection: French and Californian
Dress: Casual
Disabled access: Yes
Customers: Local, French, tourist
Lunch/Dinner: Monday–Thursday, 8 A.M.–10 P.M.; Friday and Saturday, 8 A.M.–11 P.M.; Sunday, 8 A.M.–9 P.M.

Atmosphere / setting: Charming; très Parisienne in style. One section similar to a French outdoor cafe; beautiful bakery display of breads, rolls, and pastries is the centerpiece. Central bistro room is elevated; dimly lit bar room in rear.

House specialities: Change weekly. Some top choices include namesake pizza with mixed bell peppers, mushrooms, asparagus, and mozzarella; escargot de Bourgogne; grilled double breast of chicken; rib-eye steak grille; salmon grille; breads and pastries from the bakery. You're offered a choice of bread as well as french fries, rice, St. Germain potatoes, or fresh vegetables with your meal.

Other recommendations: Soup du jour (e.g., onion or potato-leek); crêpe du jour (crêpes Bretonnes such as spinach and cheese); grilled goat cheese sandwich; croque-monsieur (French bistro classic of ham and melted Swiss cheese on toasted pain de mie).

Entertainment & amenities: Pianist on Saturday.

Summary & comments: A nice vicarious escape to France—the setting transports you, whether you just carry out baked goods, have a snack, or enjoy an entire meal. Sandwiches can be made with your choice of bread or croissant. This is a relaxing, fun place. Owners opened a petite bakery cafe on Michigan Avenue on the Gold Coast in 1993.

Stanley's Kitchen & Tap

Southern	★★½	Inexpensive

1970 North Lincoln Avenue
(312) 642-0007
Zone 1   North Side

Quality	Value
79	**A**

Reservations: Accepted for 8 or more
When to go: Any time
Entree range: $4.95–8.95
Payment: All major credit cards
Service rating: ★★★
Friendliness rating: ★★★★
Parking: Street, lot nearby
Bar: Full service; extensive American bourbon and whiskey list
Wine selection: All American; everything available by the glass; good pinot grigio, chardonnay and merlot choices
Dress: Casual
Disabled access: Yes
Customers: Locals, couples, families, some business
Dinner: Monday–Friday, 5 P.M.–2 A.M.; Saturday, noon–3 A.M.; Sunday, noon–2 A.M.

Atmosphere / setting: Entryway through 100-seat saloon with 32-foot mahogany bar. Very homey, like the inside of a house. White and green wooden porch where you can play checkers, chess, dominoes, or backgammon in rocking chairs; 80-seat dining room resembles a stage set depicting a family kitchen 50 years ago. Nostalgic decor designed by Kathryn Kozan includes 1940 white enamel stove, garish figurine lamps, wicker chairs, and print tablecloths, including one whimsically depicting ants.

House specialities: Kentucky-fried tomatoes; blackened catfish, tender and coated with well-balanced Cajun seasonings; Stan's vegetarian lasagna, a nice layering of wide noodles with ricotta cheese, spinach, mushrooms, zucchini, and carrots, topped with mozzarella and flavorful marinara sauce; creamy chicken shortcake (resembles chicken pot pie on sourdough biscuits).

Other recommendations: Fried catfish strips, blackened or buffalo-style; black bean chicken chili, served with corn tortilla chips and spiced with cumin (thick with chicken); chicken-fried steak made with pounded sirloin, preferred over the usual cube steak; jalapeño Jack sticks. Suppers are served with side dish of choice. Exceptional side dishes: southern spaghetti (tossed) and wet fries (with gravy). Desserts such as apple pie with cinnamon ice cream and bread pudding served with warm vanilla sauce are good.

Entertainment & amenities: Playing backgammon or one of the games on the porch.

Summary & comments: This fairly new restaurant is part of the trend offering what our fast-paced, high-stressed lives require—comforting food in a nurturing atmosphere. This is as close to Mom's cooking as you can get. The food is simple and good, served in generous portions in a caring environment, and the bargain prices add to the comfort factor.

Szechwan House

Chinese	★★★★	Moderate

600 North Michigan Avenue

	Quality	Value
	92	C

(312) 642 3900

Zone 4   The Loop

Reservations: Recommended
When to go: Any time
Entree range: $7.95–31.95; average $11–14
Payment: All major credit cards
Service rating: ★★★★
Friendliness rating: ★★★★★
Parking: Street; lots nearby
Bar: Full service, incuding Mandarin cocktails and imported beers
Wine selection: Regular list offers about 2 dozen international selections, including Harvest Moon chardonnay private label and several Oriental choices (2 served in jars); mostly affordable; bottle, $13–120; several by the glass; upscale wine list for gourmet menu
Dress: Casual, but most people are in business attire
Disabled access: Yes, but rest rooms are down a set of stairs
Customers: Mixed, largely business and convention, tourists
Lunch/Dinner: Sunday–Thursday, 11:30 A.M.–10:30 P.M.; Friday, 11:30 A.M.–11 P.M.; Saturday, noon–11 P.M.

Atmosphere / setting: Attractive, spacious dining room divided into sections; bar/lounge; Chinese decor.

House specialities: Appetizers: fire pot satay beef; Szechuan noodle salad. Entrees: black bean salmon (fillets); steamed fish (fillet); veal Mongolian-style. Vegetable dishes: Szechuan string beans; festival of mushrooms; steamed vegetable delight with tofu and garlic dipping sauce. Items from new "gourmet menu": three jewels in a nest (scallops, escargot, and filet mignon chunks with Chinese vegetables, in a potato bird's nest). Chef's specialities: new Hwa Shee Jeer Surprise (chicken and escargot in spicy hot sauce with mushrooms and vegetables); Governor's Chicken, a best-seller.

Other recommendations: Assorted hot appetizers; hot and sour soup; new Taiwanese escargot rice (healthier than fried rice); moo shi crêpes with chicken, vegetables, shrimp, beef, pork, or duck. Desserts: rich Chinese crêpes with dates, banana in flaming rum, or light almond tofu.

Summary & comments: This has long been one of the top Chinese restaurants because of the comprehensive menu, excellent cooking, and attentive service from the friendly staff. Managing partner Alfred Hsiu is always adding new menu items, and to celebrate the Szechwan House's 13th anniversary, he made additions to his already large 12-page menu: a gourmet menu and a new wine list to complement it; a strictly vegetarian menu; some healthy options, new chef's specialties, assorted new appetizers, and a dessert. The restaurant is capable of turning out some wonderful banquets. You'll never be bored dining here on a regular basis—the food is exciting and the menu tempts return visits. Note: The building is scheduled to be wrecked; the restaurant will move to another undetermined downtown location.

T'ang Dynasty

Chinese	★★★	Moderate

100 East Walton Street
(312) 664-8688
Zone 3   Near North

Quality	Value
86	C

Reservations: Recommended
When to go: Any time
Entree range: $8.50–32.95; average $9.50–12.95
Payment: VISA, MC, AMEX, DC, Transmedia, JCB
Service rating: ★★★★
Friendliness rating: ★★★★½
Parking: Valet, dinner only, $4.50
Bar: Full service
Wine selection: International, including Californian and Asian; several by the glass
Dress: Casual, but mostly business attire
Disabled access: Yes
Customers: Mixed, mostly business and convention, tourists
Lunch: Monday–Saturday, 11:30 A.M.–2 P.M.; Sunday, 11:30 A.M.–2:30 P.M.; buffet with over 20 items, Wednesday–Friday, $8.95
Dinner: Sunday–Thursday, 3–10:30 P.M.; Friday and Saturday, 3–11 P.M.

Atmosphere / setting: Exquisite interior with aquariums and lovely artifacts; lower level from sidewalk; attractive bar/lounge in front; large, elegant dining rooms in back with beautiful Chinese screens.

House specialities: Chef's special won ton soup; rolls for two seasons (spring roll, chicken filling; autumn roll, shrimp stuffing); beggar's hen; jade prawns in bird's nest; dragon and phoenix (prawns, chicken, macadamia nuts, and honey-garlic); T'Ang Dynasty scallops (crêpe packages filled with scallop-mushroom mixture); king crab delight; glazed orange beef.

Other recommendations: T'Ang Dynasty soong (sautéed minced ingredients wrapped in lettuce leaf: lobster, chicken, vegetable); smoked tea duck; Peking duck (One hour preparation); four-color sizzling steak; Maine lobster or catch of day prepared in your choice of Chinese cuisine–style; Shanghai-style abalone; velvet shrimp.

Summary & comments: T'Ang Dynasty has always offered a lighter style of Chinese cooking and has done numerous exquisite banquets, complete with carved vegetable garnishes and pastries shaped like birds and fastened to a vegetable tree. The buffet lunch is a nice way to taste several dishes, and other specialties from the regular menu are prepared with skill. Service is professional, and the atmosphere is sophisticated.

Tallgrass Restaurant

New French   ★★★★¹/₂   **Very expensive**

1006 South State Street, Lockport
(815) 838-5566
Zone 8   Southern Suburbs

Quality	Value
95	**C**

Reservations: Necessary
When to go: Thursday or Sunday evening
Entree range: $37–42
Payment: Personal checks (local), VISA, MC
Service rating: ★★★★¹/₂
Friendliness rating: ★★★★
Parking: Street
Bar: Full service
Wine selection: Fairly priced list with extensive
   French and American choices
Dress: Upscale casual to business and dressy
Disabled access: Yes
Customers: Diverse
Dinner: Thursday–Sunday, 6–9 P.M.

Atmosphere / setting: In a lovely historic building with an interior of handsome wood, mirrors, tin ceiling, crystal, and silver antiques. Victorian, eclectic setting; colorful Portuguese service plates.

House specialities: Potato sandwich of duck breast, candied onions, chutney, and port sauce; foie gras and coddled eggs in truffle sauce; walnut-sorrel pesto-coated rack of lamb with Gorgonzola hollandaise; grilled Atlantic salmon and jumbo prawn with mint-ginger, udon noodles, and sesame-soy sauce.

Other recommendations: Lobster, mango, basil salad, and Parmesan tile; veal sweetbreads Provençal, ratatouille, and Mediterranean vegetable au jus; architectural desserts (e.g., chocolate-cherry tour d'Eiffel, and Tallgrass white and dark chocolate tower with raspberries and two sauces); the savory of poached pear, spiced nuts, and blue cheese. For a sensuous finish, try the soufflé of dark chocolate mousse and raspberries.

Summary & comments: One of the best restaurants in the Chicago area and certainly a shining star in the southwest suburbs. Chef Robert Burcenski mixes techniques and great ingredients in compatible creations such as lobster-shrimp soufflé lasagna and a salad of stir-fry crispy capon, sugar snap peas, radicchio, and cashew-peanut sauce. The service is knowledgeable and accommodating, and altogether Tallgrass is a great dining experience if you can pay the bill without wincing.

Honors / Awards: DiRoNA, *Conde Nast.*

Tania's

Cuban/Spanish   ★★★½   Moderate

2659 North Milwaukee Avenue
(312) 235-7120
Zone 2   North Central/O'Hare

Quality	Value
86	**B**

Reservations: Accepted
When to go: Any time
Entree range: $9.95–21.95
Payment: Major credit cards
Service rating: ★★★★
Friendliness rating: ★★★★
Parking: Free valet, dinner only
Bar: Full service
Wine selection: Exceptional list: Spanish, French, Chilean, and Californian
Dress: Well-dressed business and casual; dancing attire late at night
Disabled access: Yes
Customers: Local; popular with the Cuban community; many couples in late evening
Open: Sunday–Friday, 11 A.M.–4 A.M.; Saturday, 11 A.M.–5 A.M.

Atmosphere / setting: Spacious, beautiful interior resembles a courtyard complete with a fountain filled with flowers and two colorful parrots overhead. Big glass windows; lovely balcony; wrought iron accents and colorful art. Very romantic. Big bar area with dance floor.

House specialities: Cuban black bean soup; croquetas de jamón; Estoril shrimp in sherry-garlic sauce; Cuban-style seafood paella for two (more liquid than Spanish version) requires one hour; red snapper, Caribbean-style; shrimp in Creole sauce; lechon asado (Cuban roast pork slices cooked with yucca).

Other recommendations: Empanadillas vegetarianas (foldovers with ricotta and spinach); octopus Galician-style with Spanish paprika; palomilla steak cut Cuban-style. And for the grand finale, great guava flan, moist Cuban cake, or apple cheesecake. Caribbean coffee is a showy production done tableside; when the waiter flambées the rum and cinnamon, sparks fly.

Entertainment & amenities: Wednesday–Sunday, 10:30 P.M.–4 A.M., live, 12-piece band plays Cuban and Caribbean music.

Summary & comments: Menu is devoted mostly to Cuban specialties, which have a strong Spanish influence. Some Mexican and Puerto Rican dishes, as well. Very gracious service with flair. Menu changes twice a year, but certain signature items remain. Although the music can be loud, the overall cultural dining/dancing experience is fun.

Taylor Street Bistro

French Bistro ★★★ **Inexpensive/Moderate**

1400 West Taylor Street
(312) 829-2828
Zone 5   South Loop

Quality	Value
81	B

Reservations: Recommended, especially on weekends

When to go: Any time; walk-ins usually have to wait up to 15 minutes

Entree range: $8.50–15.95

Payment: VISA, MC, AMEX, DC

Service rating: ★★★

Friendliness rating: ★★★★

Parking: Lot

Bar: Full service, including a nice selection of beer and ale (e.g., bistro beer and nonalcoholic), waters, and sparkling cider

Wine selection: Well-balanced list of French and American; several half bottles and a selection of about 8 by the glass, $3.50 up; fair pricing, $15–175 a bottle

Dress: Casual

Disabled access: Yes

Customers: Local, city, and suburban

Lunch: Monday–Friday, 11:30 A.M.–2 P.M.

Dinner: Monday–Saturday, 5:30–10:30 P.M.

Atmosphere / setting: Attractive, lively decor; very "bistro" with red and white tablecloths.

House specialities: Angelhair pasta with shrimp, sun-dried tomatoes, and saffron butter; pizza ala Taylor Street Bistro (wide choice of ingredients); creative salads (e.g., beignet salad, honey mustard vinaigrette, and spinach with goat cheese); roasted chicken with French fries.

Other recommendations: Assorted pâtés ala maison; escargot simmered in tarragon; French onion soup; medallions of veal with mushrooms.

Summary & comments: The only French restaurant in the midst of the legendary Taylor Street Italian neighborhood. Chef/owner Joseph Doppes produces some nice examples of French bistro fare as well as one or two Italian pasta items, and his wife, Ann, is responsible for the wine list and managing the place.

Thai Borrahn

Thai	★★★★	Inexpensive

247 East Ontario Street
(312) 642-1385
Zone 3   Near North

Quality	Value
90	**B**

Reservations: Accepted only for large groups
When to go: Any time
Entree range: $6.25–18
Payment: VISA, MC, AMEX
Service rating: ★★★★
Friendliness rating: ★★★★½
Parking: Street
Bar: Full service, including Thai beer
Wine selection: Limited international, including Japanese saké and selections from Brazil, France, and Italy; mostly American; 11 by the glass, affordable
Dress: Business, well-dressed; no T-shirts
Disabled access: No; restaurant on second floor—no elevator
Customers: Local
Open: Monday–Thursday, 11 A.M.–10 P.M.; Friday, 11 A.M.–11 P.M.; Saturday, 4–11 P.M.; Sunday, 4–10 P.M.

Atmosphere / setting: "Borrahn" in Thai means "ancient times," so a lot of the furnishings are antiques. The lovely authentic Thai decor includes a raised dais for in-floor Thai dining, complete with cushions—a most tranquil setting. In that area, diners remove their shoes and sit on the platform at low tables with cushions in a sumptuous fashion. The owners keep adding to the decor and remodeling.

House specialities: Ieuu chicken (chicken with fried noodles and broccoli); the famous pad thai (thin rice noodles, sweet turnip, bean sprouts, tofu, and egg stir-fried in sweet-sour tamarind sauce with a choice of meat or vegetables); tom yum chicken (hot and sour soup with lemongrass, cilantro, lime, chili, and mint); wonton soup with fried cheese; Thai Borrahn jan ront (sesame beef in a hot plate with oyster sauce and vegetables).

Other recommendations: Borrahn spring roll (unusual with avocado, cream cheese, and more);

seaweed spring roll; house garden salad with mild curry peanut sauce; pad talay (seafood combination in sauce with vegetables, basil, and ginger); catfish red curry.

Summary & comments: This relative newcomer on the downtown dining scene offers affordable gourmet Thai cuisine. The setting is beautiful and sophisticated, hidden among the treetops on the second floor in the Gold Coast area. There's a seafood focus to the varied menu, and several vegetarian items and options are offered. The food is artfully decorated. A great place for Thai food when you're in the North Michigan Avenue area, or make it a destination.

Thai Touch

Thai ★★★★ **Inexpensive**

3200 West Lawrence Avenue
(312) 539-5700
Zone 1   North Side

Quality	Value
91	B

Reservations: Recommended weekends and for 8 or more
When to go: Any time; weeknights less busy
Entree range: $5.95–12.95
Payment: VISA, MC, DC
Service rating: ★★★½
Friendliness rating: ★★★★½
Parking: Lot nearby
Bar: Full service, including Thai beer
Wine selection: Limited; some appropriate selections for this spicy cuisine
Dress: Casual
Disabled access: Yes
Customers: Mixed, local American and ethnic, suburbanites
Lunch/Dinner: Tuesday–Saturday, noon–10 P.M.

Atmosphere / setting: Attractive split-level room with Thai touches such as carved wooden tables and gilded native artwork; Thai music tapes.

House specialities: Appetizers: chicken satay; delicate crab-in-the-bag (deep-fried crispy bundles of crab-shrimp mixture served with plum sauce); coconut chicken soup with galanga (a ginger-like root). Entrees: chicken pad thai (rice noodles, tofu, and ground peanuts).

Other recommendations: Grilled pork on a stick; green papaya salad; drunken shrimp with bamboo shoots, bean sprouts, eggs, and hot peppers.

Summary & comments: This established gem on the mid-Northwest Side serves classic Thai cuisine as stunning as the restaurant's interior. Owner/chef Art Lee is masterful at creating specialties with well-balanced flavors and textures and beautiful presentations. The servers, some of them Art's relatives, are helpful and accommodating. Ask for advice on ordering a well-balanced meal with your choice of spicy hotness. Most dishes can be prepared meatless as well. This is some of the best Thai food for the price.

That Steak Joynt

Steak/Seafood   ★★★¹/₂   **Moderate/Expensive**

1610 North Wells Street
(312) 943-5091
Zone 1   North Side

Quality	Value
85	**C**

Reservations: Recommended
When to go: Any day, 5–7 P.M.; may be early
  theatergoers dining before curtain
Entree range: $12.95–28.95
Payment: All major credit cards
Service rating: ★★★¹/₂
Friendliness rating: ★★★★
Parking: Valet, garage
Bar: Full service
Wine selection: Mostly American and French; several
  selections by the glass
Dress: Casual
Disabled access: No, but willing to help individuals
  that need special care
Customers: Diverse, business, couples
Dinner: Monday–Friday, 5 P.M.–1 A.M.; Saturday,
  5 P.M.–2 A.M.; Sunday, 4 P.M.–1 A.M.

Atmosphere / setting: Victorian mansion with lavish
decor and winding staircase; elegant and comfortable;
piano lounge.

House specialities: Steaks: New York strip, rib eye,
T-bone, and filet mignon; award-winning barbecue
ribs; strawberries zabaglione; hot fudge sundae;
cheesecake.

Other recommendations: Great creamed spinach;
fresh fish (e.g., swordfish or whitefish) broiled to order;
combinations of steak and lobster or chicken and ribs.

Entertainment & amenities: Gary Phillips on piano
Wednesday–Saturday night.

Summary & comments: This Old Town cornerstone
has been around a long time, and owner Billy Siegel's
watchful eye and presence keep the clientele satisfied.
He's added more fish to the menu recently and has
rolled back prices for anniversary celebrations. Lovely
setting for a romantic dinner.

---

302 West

New American   ★★★¹/₂   **Moderate**

---

302 West State Street, Geneva
(708) 232-9302
Zone 9   Western Suburbs

Quality	Value
87	**C**

Reservations: Recommended
When to go: Any time
Entree range: $16.50–25
Payment: VISA, MC, AMEX, DC, CB, D
Service rating: ★★★¹/₂
Friendliness rating: ★★★★
Parking: Street
Bar: Full service; premium labels
Wine selection: Very extensive American list with emphasis on California and other West Coast selections; several French champagnes; many unique, sometimes eccentric styles from some of America's most adventurous winemakers. Some of the best of different styles from different regions in each price range, and some "cost-is-no-object" bottles; arranged in escalating price order in each category; several $18–30, but most more expensive. Ask for list of ports, sherries, and madeiras. Chef/owner Joel Findlay selects the wines and gives educational descriptions of grape varieties
Dress: Casual; no dress code
Disabled access: Yes
Customers: Business, couples, wine lovers
Dinner: Tuesday–Thursday, 6–9 P.M.; Friday and Saturday, 6–10 P.M. Bar: Tuesday–Saturday, 5 P.M.–1 A.M.

Atmosphere / setting: Elegant, spacious white tablecloth restaurant on the second level of a historic bank building, built in 1924. It's a powerful structure with heavy, imposing 30-foot palladium windows and high ceilings. Effort is made here to have relaxed fine dining; never intimidating.

House specialities: Menu changes daily. Typical offerings: appetizers of roasted beefsteak tomato stuffed with goat cheese and herbs on angelhair pasta; grilled, sliced southern-style barbecue rabbit tenderloin with little corn pancakes. Entrees: grilled Hawaiian moonfish steak with roasted pineapple vinaigrette and toasted macadamias; grilled, tequila-honey-lime marinated half free-range chicken on spiced red beans; roasted sablefish fillet in smoked salmon cream; roasted, sliced pork tenderloin with Cajun gravy and southern-style "goober peas." Desserts: homemade mascarpone ice cream with intense, dark mocha sauce; malted-milk chocolate mousse cake on dark chocolate sauce; peach-almond ice cream cake on raspberry sauce; granita of wildly fruity Barbera wine. All entrees include a marinated cucumber-Vidalia onion salad on Boston lettuce.

Other recommendations: Appetizer of grilled jumbo sea scallops tossed with baby lettuces and chardonnay vinaigrette. Entrees: fresh Canadian walleye fillet sautéed in ground pecans and light orange beurre blanc; grilled buffalo rib-eye steak with horseradish mashed potatoes and natural juices. Desserts: fresh mission figs marinated in sweet muscat wine with mascarpone cheese; key lime cheesecake on raspberry sauce.

Entertainment & amenities: Regularly scheduled piano, harp, and vocal entertainment.

Summary & comments: The daily menu is a single page, whereas the wine list is 13 pages (not counting the extensive list of ports, sherries, and madeiras and an additional list of wines by the glass). Truly a wine-oriented restaurant, and the list is well worth scrutinizing before ordering, since this is a chance to try some very unusual selections. Chef/owner Joel Findlay's personality definitely shines through his menu and wine lists. About 20 daily desserts—some quite sweet, especially those with caramel sauce or brown sugar.

Honors / Awards: *Wine Spectator* Award of Excellence; Best Seafood Chef Award by Illinois Seafood Association; DiRoNA.

Trattoria Gianni

Italian   ★★★¹/₂   **Inexpensive/Moderate**

1711 North Halsted Street
(312) 266-1976
Zone 1   North Side

Quality	Value
87	C

Reservations: Requested
When to go: After-theater crowd leaves at 7:30 P.M.
Entree range: Pastas, $8.95–12.95; entrees, $10.95–16.95
Payment: VISA, MC, AMEX, DC, CB
Service rating: ★★★★
Friendliness rating: ★★★★★
Parking: Valet in front of restaurant
Bar: Full service; all Italian beers
Wine selection: All Italian regional wines; several by the glass
Dress: Chic casual
Disabled access: Yes
Customers: Appeals to all ages, including families
Brunch: Sunday, noon–3 P.M., Italian buffet brunch
Lunch: Tuesday–Friday, 11:30 A.M.–2:30 P.M.
Dinner: Tuesday–Thursday, 5–11 P.M.; Friday and Saturday, 5–11:30 P.M.; Sunday, 4–10 P.M.

Atmosphere / setting: Typical authentic Italian trattoria setting—warm, friendly, and bright.

House specialities: Polpo (grilled octopus); grilled portobello mushroom; calamari vino blanco; rigatoni Nocerina (sun-dried tomatoes, mushrooms, olive oil, garlic, and basil in cream sauce); conchili del mercante (crumbled Italian sausage, mushrooms, fresh tomato sauce, scamorza cheese, peas, and a touch of cream); spaghetti Portofino (scallops, scampi, cherry tomatoes, olive oil, and garlic); vitello alla Gianni (scallopini sautéed in brandy sauce with mushrooms, cherry tomatoes, and artichoke hearts); pollo Toscana (boneless chicken breast marinated with fresh herbs, with vegetables); salmone al vino bianco (fillet of fresh Norwegian salmon grilled first, then sautéed with white wine, lemon, capers, and butter); lombata (veal chop) Vesuvio. Desserts: homemade cannoli; tartufo; mandarino (sorbet inside frozen orange shell); tiramisu, a cloud of lady fingers soaked in marsala and espresso with mascarpone, whipped cream, and cocoa powder (voted best in Chicago).

Other recommendations: Insalata alla Lipare (mixture of lentils and grilled and marinated calamari on a bed of arugula with chopped plum tomatoes, garnished with fresh basil and thyme)—this item is not on the menu; gamberi alla Napolitana (mussels in marinara sauce and grilled vegetables); saltimbocca al sorrentina (tender veal scallopini topped with prosciutto and mozzarella, sautéed with white wine and tomatoes).

Summary & comments: Chef-owned place is comfortable and shows caring, and offers some excellent innovative cooking. One of the best trattorias in town without the high noise level and crowds of some "in" spots. It's possible to have a relaxed dinner here even on a busy night. Chef Gianni Delisi has plans to install a ten-seat bar, move the kitchen from the middle to the rear of the room, and extend the dining room with a more open, airy feeling. Buon appetito!

Trio

Fusion ★★★★★ **Expensive/Very Exp.**

1625 Hinman Avenue, Evanston
(708) 733-8746
Zone 11   Northern Suburbs

Quality	Value
98	**C**

Reservations: Highly suggested; weekends often booked weeks in advance; accepted up to 3 months in advance

When to go: Tuesday–Thursday

Entree range: $18–30; some specialties are higher

Payment: VISA, MC, AMEX, D, DC

Service rating: ★★★★★

Friendliness rating: ★★★★★

Parking: Valet, $5

Bar: Full service; international beers; extensive single malt scotches; infused grappas

Wine selection: Fairly extensive; French, American, Italian, and several other international; many lesser known quality wines; good range of style and price, from $22 a bottle; slanted toward seafood-friendly choices; 10–12 by the glass; wine flight tastings (e.g., 4 half-glasses); willing to open almost any bottle to serve a glass; reserve list

Dress: Jackets suggested; dressy overall

Disabled access: Yes; need assistance up 2 steps for rest rooms

Customers: All types, all ages, except children (a few); business, couples

Dinner: Tuesday–Thursday, 5:30–9:30 P.M.; Friday and Saturday, 5:30–10:30 P.M.; Sunday, 5–9 P.M.

Atmosphere / setting: Housed in The Homestead, designed in Williamsburg Inn-style. Country estate-type living room is a waiting lounge. Welcoming entryway with display of kitchen-made specialty items; wine rack room dividers. Comfortable, warm main dining room and a brighter, more intimate porch room overlooking a garden. A subtle, rustic courtyard decor with antique weathered wood paneling and carved alabaster wall sconces, with earthy purples and greens and dried flowers. The kitchen, with one table in an alcove, is a bit more than half of the 3,500 square feet of restaurant space.

House specialities: Porcini "cappuccino" with Parmesan tuille; antipasto misto (chef's seasonal selections such as prosciutto, fresh figs, cherries, asparagus, baby vegetables, and lemon aioli); wild rice risotto with asparagus, wild mushrooms, and pecorino romano chips; trio of fish tartares; caviar service on a painter's palette (mostly local; slightly higher with Beluga). Specials: lobster bisque; roasted squab with garlic, dauphinoise potatoes, morels, squab jus, and 50-year-old balsamic vinegar glaze; shellfish blanquette with lobster, sea scallops, mussels, monkfish, chanterelles, leeks, and fennel poached in vermouth and cream; grilled veal chop and crispy sweetbreads with three-bean ragout, escarole, and pearl onions, in a rosemary-infused veal reduction. Desserts: triple chocolate malted marquis with dried cherries and hazelnut almond praline; lemon tart Nico with white pepper ice cream and dried figs.

Other recommendations: Wok-charred beef carpaccio rolled in red flower pepper and truffle potato salad with Tramonto's red wine vinegar and basil oil; sautéed foie gras with caramelized orange, mixed lettuces, and dried figs, with organic hazelnut vinaigrette; herb-crusted rack of lamb with ratatouille risotto, roasted shallot, and black olive aioli; crispy tuna in katiafi with Chinese greens, copper well noodles, and Szechuan oil.

Summary & comments: By far, one of the finest, most spectacular restaurants to open here in some time. It made culinary waves immediately after opening on October 1, 1993, the fifth wedding anniversary of the owner/chefs. Trio is named for the three cuisines it represents and for the talented partnership of proprietor Henry Adaniya and his partners, executive chef Rick Tramonto and pastry chef Gale Gand. The cooking is built on classic French and Italian foundations with Asian influences, and the finished dishes are avant garde. Stunning presentations—some whimsical—are arranged on unusual surfaces such as marble, granite, and mirrors. An entire dinner parade of such spectacular menu items is definitely culinary theater. There are those who prefer the subtleties of dining and consider this theatrical display a bit ostentatious. However, there's no disagreement on the culinary expertise here and the passion and energy exhibited on every level. Informed servers anticipate diners' needs, but are never doting. Bursts of enthusiasm are transported from the kitchen to your plate—or whatever substance holds your food. The joy of cooking here has rejuvenated even the most jaded, worldly diner. The degustation menu is a great spontaneous tasting opportunity. Kitchen table must be reserved weeks in advance.

Honors / Awards: Gale Gand is the winner of 1994 Robert Mondavi Award for Culinary Excellence. Rick Tramonto received many awards as well when he was a chef in England, including "Country Restaurant of the Year." The couple have a long list of impressive credits, including the "Red M" in the prestigious Michelin Guide, 1991, after only one year at Stapleford Park Hotel, England.

Tucci Milan

Italian	★★★	**Inexpensive/Moderate**

6 West Hubbard Street
(312) 222-0044
Zone 4   The Loop

Quality	Value
82	**C**

Reservations: Recommended for lunch and dinner
When to go: Any time
Entree range: Lunch, $9–13; dinner, $14–20
Payment: Major credit cards
Service rating: ★★★
Friendliness rating: ★★★½
Parking: Valet after 5 P.M., $4
Bar: Full service
Wine selection: Italian and American; some nice selections at good value; about a dozen by the glass
Dress: Casual
Disabled access: Yes
Customers: Mixed; business, couples
Lunch/Dinner: Monday–Thursday, 11:30 A.M.–10 P.M.; Friday, 11:30 A.M.–11 P.M.; Saturday, noon–11 P.M.; Sunday, 5–10 P.M.

Atmosphere/setting: Open kitchen, high ceilings, bustling bar, seating for 210.

House specialities: Daily rotisserie items featuring seasonal game such as half duck with balsamic coriander glaze, red Swiss chard, grappa-soaked cherries, and polenta; ravioli del giorno and mezzaluna alla salsiccia (half-moon ravioli stuffed with Italian sausage, with tomato sauce).

Other recommendations: Daily antipasto platter; lasagna; herb-roasted chicken; caramelized shallot mashed potatoes; homemade desserts, especially the sensuous chocolate budino.

Summary & comments: The rustic, cosmopolitan atmosphere together with the earthy cuisine featuring creative pizzas, robust salads, freshly made pastas, and rotisserie game and chicken are enticing. The fair prices for wine and food are an added bonus. Another Lettuce Entertain You Enterprises success.

Tufano's (Vernon Park Tap)

Italian ★★½ **Inexpensive/Moderate**

1073 West Vernon Park Place
(312) 733-3393
Zone 5   South Loop

Quality	Value
76	B

Reservations: Not accepted; walk-ins wait about half
 an hour on weekends
When to go: Weekdays
Entree range: $6–12
Payment: Cash, personal checks (local); no credit
 cards accepted
Service rating: ★★★
Friendliness rating: ★★★★
Parking: Valet
Bar: Full service
Wine selection: Limited, mostly Italian
Dress: Moderately casual
Disabled access: Limited; handicapped stall in ladies
 rest room
Customers: Diverse
Lunch/Dinner: Tuesday–Thursday, 11 A.M.–
 10 P.M.; Friday, 11 A.M.–11 P.M.
Dinner: Saturday, 5–11 P.M.; Sunday, 3–9 P.M.

Atmosphere / setting: Casual and cozy.

House specialities: Lemon chicken; eggplant
Parmigiana; Tufano special salad.

Other recommendations: Other pasta dishes (e.g.,
lasagna; mussels with angel hair, your choice of red or
white sauce; tortellini Alfredo); veal marsala.

Summary & comments: Also known as Vernon Park
Tap, this is a cornerstone of the old Taylor Street
Italian neighborhood, founded by the Tufano family
over 60 years ago. It's hidden among a row of older
buildings, and the restaurant is behind a bar room. This
is bare-bones decor with blackboards listing the daily
selections. The menu offers choices of red or white
sauce, charges a bit extra for meatballs or sausage, and
has the old traditional Friday fish specials. The place is
a time warp, and that's why it's especially fun. Chef
Joey Di Buono turns out respectable versions of the
old-guard Italian fare in large servings. Everyone who
eats here seems to walk out happy.

Tuscany

Italian	★★★	Moderate

1014 West Taylor Street
(312) 829-1990
Zone 5   South Loop

Quality	Value
84	C

Reservations: Recommended; walk-ins wait about half an hour on weekdays, 1–2 hours on weekends
When to go: 5:30 or 9 P.M.
Entree range: $10–30, average $20
Payment: All major credit cards except DC
Service rating: ★★★
Friendliness rating: ★★★¹/₂
Parking: Valet
Bar: Full service
Wine selection: American and Italian
Dress: Moderately casual
Disabled access: Yes
Customers: Local, diverse
Lunch: Monday–Friday, 11 A.M.–3:30 P.M.
Dinner: Monday–Thursday, 5–11 P.M.; Friday and Saturday, 5 P.M.–midnight; Sunday, 2–9:30 P.M.

Atmosphere / setting: Cozy, Italian, with green and white tablecloths.

House specialities: Eleven dinner specials such as macaroni cippriani (freshly made square noodles with light cream-tomato sauce); rotisserie chicken; stuffed veal chop. All items deftly prepared rustic-style.

Other recommendations: Mainstream antipasto and pastas with good sauces.

Summary & comments: Newest restaurant in Little Italy on Taylor Street. Owned by restaurateur Phil Stefani of Stefani's, this location has an open kitchen with a wood-burning oven and grill to produce typical Tuscan fare. Very popular and bustling.

Honors / Awards: 1993 Silver Platter Award.

Tuttaposto

Mediterranean ★★★★ **Inexpensive/Moderate**

---

646 North Franklin Street
(312) 943-6262
Zone 3   Near North

Quality	Value
91	**C**

Reservations: Recommended
When to go: Any time
Entree range: $6–21
Payment: All major credit cards
Service rating: ★★★★
Friendliness rating: ★★★★½
Parking: Valet
Bar: Full service; attractive bar
Wine selection: Fairly extensive, especially Mediterranean; free wine samples on Wednesdays; wine list gives descriptions and offers many by the glass
Dress: Moderately casual
Disabled access: Yes
Customers: Diverse
Lunch: Monday–Friday, 11:30 A.M.–2 P.M.
Dinner: Monday–Thursday, 5–10 P.M.; Friday and Saturday, 5–11 P.M.; Sunday, 5–9 P.M.

Atmosphere/setting: Loft-type setting; welcoming, with warm Mediterranean touches, such as murals and beautiful bottles and vases. Can be bustling.

House specialities: Couscous with mussels, shrimp, scallops, calamari, clams, and halibut in a spicy tomato broth baked in a Portuguese cataplana; shrimp and kamut; Tuttaposto's Mediterranean vegetable platter; potato gnocchi with portobello mushrooms; double-decker pizza; grilled calamari with spicy Portuguese piri piri sauce, grilled polenta, and Sicilian olive salad.

Other recommendations: Charcoal-grilled lamb chop with tzatziki and Greek-style potatoes; roast salmon with creamy polenta and watercress; Mediterranean plate, a tasting of Middle Eastern salads; wood-roasted scallops with smoked tomato and arugula.

Summary & comments: One of the few restaurants devoted exclusively to the cuisines of all the Mediterranean countries with a desire to educate diners. There's a glossary on the menu and many promotions and tastings. The wine list is user-friendly, with many offerings by the glass and descriptions of the wines.

Twisted Lizard

Southwestern/Mexican   ★★★½   **Inexpensive**

1964 North Sheffield Avenue
(312) 929-1414
Zone 1   North Side

Quality	Value
87	B

Reservations: Not accepted
When to go: Less crowded before 7 P.M. and after 9 P.M.
Entree range: $6.75–8.75
Payment: VISA, MC, AMEX
Service rating: ★★★½
Friendliness rating: ★★★★½
Parking: Valet weekends
Bar: Full service, including 6 types of margaritas; good selection of beers, including Mexican
Wine selection: Small list: Spanish, Chilean, Mexican, and Californian
Dress: Casual
Disabled access: Yes, call first
Customers: Diverse, many young professional
Brunch: Sunday, 11 A.M.–3 P.M.
Lunch/Dinner: Monday–Saturday, 11:30 A.M.–midnight; Sunday, 11 A.M.–10 P.M.

Atmosphere / setting: Cozy, subterranean cantina with bar. Rustic white cedar furniture; copper-top bar; colorful, wooden lizards; collection of dolls strung across the walls.

House specialties: Seafood queso fundido (sautéed shrimp and scallops baked and broiled with Chihuahua cheese, served with homemade flour and corn tortillas); barbecue chicken wings sprinkled with sesame seeds; flautas (three crispy corn tortillas rolled with choice of chicken or beef, topped with guacamole, sour cream, and Anejo cheese); key lime pie; flan; good coffee.

Other recommendations: Enchiladas (three corn tortillas filled and baked with choice of meats, topped with choice of sauce and Chihuahua cheese); barbecue chicken breasts; fajitas (sizzling peppers, onions, and tomatoes with choice of beef, chicken, or seafood with guacamole, pico de gallo, sour cream, rice, and beans).

Summary & comments: This is one of the best places for flavorful, top-flight southwestern and

Mexican food, prepared by Mexican-born co-owner/ chef Sergio Sanchez. The kitchen is so small that daily deliveries are essential, ensuring freshness. The interior is charming—although some people can't accept the lizard motif and are turned away by the name. Thriving catering business and carryout.

Un Grand Cafe

French Bistro   ★★★★   Moderate

2300 North Lincoln Park West

Quality	Value
92	**C**

(312) 348-8886

Zone 1   North Side

Reservations: Recommended

When to go: Early weeknights; late weekends

Entree range: Appetizers, $3.50–7.95; entrees, $12.95–21.95

Payment: All major credit cards

Service rating: ★★★¹/₂

Friendliness rating: ★★★

Parking: Valet, $4

Bar: Full service; cocktail lounge for customers

Wine selection: 50 selections, Beaujolais and American; affordable at $10–35 a bottle; 5 by the glass, $4–7

Dress: Casual

Disabled access: Wheelchair accessible; call ahead for special accommodations

Customers: Casual crowd, local, media, city people; low-key after opera and art gallery crowd

Dinner: Monday–Thursday, 6–10:30 P.M.; Friday and Saturday, 6–11:30 P.M.; Sunday, 5–9:30 P.M.

Atmosphere / setting: Continental flair and unique style in an elegant, renovated old hotel with high ceilings and French doors. Feels like a bistro on the West Bank of Paris; chic; intimate outdoor garden; view of Lincoln Park Conservatory and gardens; seats 120.

House specialities: Onion soup, crock-baked with croutons and Gruyère; World Cup Tart (caramelized onions, Manchego cheese, and oven-dried tomatoes); steak frites; herb-roasted chicken with pearl onions, mushrooms, and cafe frites.

Other recommendations: Duck confit with eggplant and shiitake, baked in phyllo with tomato coulis (appetizer); bouillabaisse (steamed fish and shellfish with tomato-saffron broth and aioli); plats du jour: Friday's special of seafood cassoulet (lobster, scallops, shrimp, fish, and white beans).

Entertainment & amenities: Taking in the stately architecture and charming atmosphere, including the Lincoln Park Conservatory across the street.

Summary & comments: The grand architecture, classic Gallic bistro cuisine, and very competent service here combine to make this restaurant live up to its name. The cooking is directed by Lettuce Entertain You Enterprises managing partner, Gabino Sotelino, who recently hired Gregg Flisiak as executive chef. Expect some innovative dishes amidst the culinary anchors.

Uncle Tannous

Lebanese   ★★★   **Inexpensive/Moderate**

2626 North Halsted Street

(312) 929-1333

Zone 1   North Side

Quality	Value
84	**B**

Reservations: Recommended
When to go: Weekends, although busier then
Entree range: $8–15
Payment: All major credit cards
Service rating: ★★★★
Friendliness rating: ★★★★¹/₂
Parking: Valet
Bar: Full service
Wine selection: Fairly extensive, including French and Californian; several excellent choices by the glass
Dress: Moderately casual to business
Disabled access: Yes, including rest rooms
Customers: Local, North Shore, celebrities
Lunch/Dinner: Tuesday–Sunday, noon–11 P.M.
Dinner: Monday, 5–10:30 P.M.

Atmosphere / setting: Exotic and romantic, with tin ceiling, alcoves, upper level, ceiling fans, and plants; photos of Danny Thomas (who would bring big parties here) and actor Hans Conreid, who played Uncle Tannous on the Danny Thomas Show. Old photos of stars.

House specialities: Lamb chops; kafta kebabs; broiled red snapper Uncle Tannous. Vast array of appetizers and vegetarian plates: falafel, hummus with tahini, baba ganouj-mtabal, grape leaf rolls, chunky eggplant imam bayeldi, and kibbeh muklieh (superb chopped meat and cracked wheat balls stuffed with spiced meat and pine nuts).

Other recommendations: Mediterranean mazza (sampler) for two. Dessert of the day; baklava; Turkish coffee.

Entertainment & amenities: Belly dancing on Saturday, 7:30–9:30 P.M. Viewing the photos on the walls.

Summary & comments: Dependable over the years for maintaining good quality in Lebanese cooking and service. Owner Joseph Skaff is visible most of the time and cares about details. Complimentary relish tray precedes dinner. A great cafe atmosphere for a business dinner (except Saturday) and for a casual evening of enjoyment. Catering for all occasions.

Va Pensiero

Italian   ★★★★½   **Moderate**

Margarita European Inn,
   1566 Oak Avenue, Evanston

Quality	Value
95	**C**

(708) 475-7779
Zone 11   Northern Suburbs

Reservations: Recommended
When to go: Any time
Entree range: $12.50–19.25
Payment: VISA, MC, AMEX, D, DC
Service rating: ★★★★½
Friendliness rating: ★★★★½
Parking: Valet, Monday–Saturday evening
Bar: Full service
Wine selection: All Italian regional list; $18–55;
   excellent selections; 12 by the glass, $5–8.50
Dress: Moderately casual
Disabled access: Yes
Customers: Mostly upscale, sophisticated North
   Shore Italian food lovers; many city business people
   and couples
Lunch: Monday–Friday, 11:30 A.M.–2:30 P.M.
Dinner: Monday–Thursday, 5:30–9 P.M.; Friday
   and Saturday, 5:30–10 P.M.

Atmosphere / setting: Housed in the historic
Margarita European Inn, with arched French doors,
vintage period molding, and antiques. Very Roman-
esque portico. Dining room has a Tivoli Garden look
with plaster-like reliefs, peach-hued walls, candela-
bras, and white tablecloths. Main dining room seats up
to 85; cafe area, open weekends, seats about 90.

House specialities: Roasted Atlantic salmon with a
mustard mascarpone glaze; sautéed shrimp on crispy
onion risotto cake, topped with pistachio pesto; budino
al cioccolato (warm bittersweet chocolate cake with a
creamy center, served with an almond milk sauce).

Other recommendations: Homemade pastas (e.g.,
spinach ravioli stuffed with creamy artichoke filling);
veal dishes (e.g., osso bucco: sautéed escarole and
white bean-garlic purée in a red wine-rosemary sauce);
herb- and Gorgonzola-crusted lamb chops, natural
juices, and potato and walnut gratin in fennel cup; soft
polenta topped with slowly caramelized onions and
fontina cheese sauce; rhubarb ice cream (in season).

Summary & comments: Chef Peggy Ryan's refined, earthy cooking sings out in this quiet, rather formal dining room and shows great harmony in flavors and textures. People often ask her how a chef named Ryan can cook Italian so well. Her instincts are on target in all the dishes sampled on several occasions. The upscale setting in the vintage building is charming—a soothing environment with good jazz background music for enjoying fine Italian cuisine and regional wines.

Honors / Awards: Rated Number One Italian restaurant in Chicago, 1993–94, by *Zagat Guide*.

Via Veneto

New Italian	★★★¹/₂	Inexpensive

3449 West Peterson Avenue
(312) 267-0888
Zone 1   North Side

Quality	Value
85	**B**

Reservations: Recommended weekends
When to go: Any time: weekdays less busy
Entree range: $6.95–12.95
Payment: Major credit cards
Service rating: ★★★¹/₂
Friendliness rating: ★★★¹/₂
Parking: Street, small lot in rear
Bar: Full service
Wine selection: Mostly Italian (various regions),
   Californian, several French; many affordable at $15
   a bottle; Riserva and champagne/sparkling are
   higher, at $52 a bottle; several by the glass
Dress: Casual, business
Disabled access: Yes, including rest rooms
Customers: Diverse, local, business, couples
Open: Monday–Friday, 11:30 A.M.–10 P.M.;
   Saturday, 11:30 A.M.–11 P.M.; Sunday, 3–11 P.M.

Atmosphere / setting: Cozy, bright, rather elegant;
Italian-style with display case of food; white tablecloths; sidewalk cafe with umbrella tables.

House specialities: Antipasto: melenzane stuzzicante
(eggplant with tomato, garlic, olive oil, and mozzarella); shrimp sautéed with garlic; grilled octopus with
balsamic vinegar. Pastas: pumpkin ravioli in tomato–
goat cheese sauce; penne Bolognese. Fish of the day;
vegetarian dishes made from home-grown vegetables.

Other recommendations: Stuffed calamari; risotto
with porcini mushrooms or four cheeses; the namesake
chicken breast with mushrooms in white wine;
homemade tiramisu.

Summary & comments: Several years ago this was a
hidden gem on the Northwest Side; it has since grown
in popularity. Chef/owner Tony Barbanente's penchant
for healthy, light dishes results in fresh, cooked-to-
order items such as the specialties listed. The care
shows both in the attentive cooking and accommodating service. An excellent value off the beaten
restaurant track.

Viceroy of India

Indian   ★★★   **Inexpensive/Moderate**

2520 West Devon Avenue	Quality · Value
(312) 743-4100	**84** · **B**
Zone 1 North Side	

2520 West Devon Avenue
(312) 743-4100
Zone 1   North Side

Quality	Value
84	**B**

19 W. 555 West Roosevelt Road, Lombard
(708) 627-4411
Zone 9   Western Suburbs

104-1/2 West Roosevelt Road, Villa Park
(708) 834-3105
Zone 9   Western Suburbs

Reservations: Recommended
When to go: Any time; weekends are busy
Entree range: $6.50–13; lunch buffet, $5.95
Payment: Major credit cards
Service rating: ★★★
Friendliness rating: ★★★
Parking: Street, lots nearby
Bar: Full service
Wine selection: Limited
Dress: Casual
Disabled access: Yes
Customers: Local, ethnic, tourist
Lunch: Every day, noon–3:30 P.M.; buffet
   available
Dinner: Sunday–Thursday, 5–10 P.M.; Friday and
   Saturday, 5–10:30 P.M.

Atmosphere/setting: Formal, large dining room
highlighted with mauve, burgundy, and white shades.
Each white tablecloth is accented with a red carnation.
A small part of the wall is carved to resemble the
intricate, delicate Mughal art often seen in ancient
Indian Muslim architecture. Dim lights and breezy
sitar music evoke a romantic mood. There's a self-
service room with lighter fare and a cheaper menu.

House specialities: Chicken tandoori (chicken
marinated in yogurt, garlic, ginger, and vinegar) is
deliciously juicy; butter chicken (cooked in tandoor
and marinated in ginger, garlic, yogurt, vinegar, butter,
and spices) is rich and creamy; light peas pulao (fried
long-grain rice with peas) has the perfect taste balance
with spicy bhuna gost (lamb cubes cooked in a spicy

tomato-onion gravy) and tender sheekh kebab (spiced and herbed minced lamb cooked on skewers).

Other recommendations: Chutneys are heartier than most; appetizers such as the steam cheese pakora (steam cheese fritters in graham flour batter) and samosa (flour patties stuffed with delicately spiced potatoes and peas) are light, golden, and crisp; onion kulcha (bread stuffed with onion, dry mango, and spices); kulfi, a homemade Indian-style pistachio and saffron ice cream; satisfy any tropical, fruity craving with the mango lassi (an icy yogurt-mango drink).

Summary & comments: This is one of the nicest Indian restaurants on the famed Devon Avenue, which has a string of Indian shops, cafes, and restaurants. Banquet facility for up to 400 people; restaurant can seat up to 150.

Vivere (Italian Village)

Italian   ★★★★½   **Moderate**

---

71 West Monroe Street
(312) 332-4040
Zone 4   The Loop

Quality	Value
95	**C**

Reservations: Recommended always
When to go: Any time
Entree range: Lunch, $8.75–12.75; dinner, $11.50–22.50
Payment: Major credit cards
Service rating: ★★★★½
Friendliness rating: ★★★★½
Parking: Valet, $5
Bar: Full service
Wine selection: Regular list, "Current Wine Selections," is extensive and well balanced; mostly Italian; good American and French selection; several German and Portuguese; also, an award-winning, 36-page, 950-selection reserve list
Dress: Chic casual, dressy
Disabled access: Yes
Customers: Diverse, business, couples, operagoers, theatergoers
Lunch: Monday–Friday, 11:15 A.M.–2:15 P.M.
Dinner: Monday–Thursday, 5–10 P.M.; Friday and Saturday, 5–11 P.M.; Sunday, closed.

Atmosphere / setting: Award-winning decor is a unique "modern Italian baroque," a blend of the elements of a Medieval castle with futuristic fantasy—burgundy velvet chairs mix with peach hues and black accents, mirrors, and marble and shell-shaped light fixtures. Intimate open mezzanine area.

House specialities: Wild mushroom soufflé; duck crêpes with light Parmesan sauce; daily risotto; pastas (e.g., pheasant-filled pasta with sage; Parmesan eggless pasta); veal (e.g., great stuffed veal chop with garlic, spinach, and fontina cheese). Seafood of the day: charcoal-grilled, broiled, or ai ferri (seared on a hot iron griddle).

Other recommendations: Tortellini alla frutta di mare (baked seafood-filled pasta with fresh seafood sauce); marinated rabbit tenderloin with rosemary, garlic, and tomato sauce. Desserts: chocolate eggplant creation and panna cotta (timbale of sweet cream, caramel sauce, and nougat).

Summary & comments: Vivere means "to live" in Italian, and indeed, this is the way to do it Italian-style. Celebrating its 68th anniversary in 1995, the Italian Village is a city landmark. Vivere is part of a triad of restaurants that make up the Italian Village, launched in 1927 by Alfredo Capitanini and now run in part by three grandchildren. They replaced the previous gourmet Florentine Room with this successful, new restaurant concept several years ago. Chef Peter Schonman prepares exciting contemporary, regional Italian food. The wine lists are dazzling and the prices overall spell good value. The heart-of-downtown location makes this a perfect place for an early dinner before the opera or theater. Vivere is on the main floor; the Village, upstairs (a charming recreation of a town in Italy); and Cantina Enoteca (a great Italian seafood restaurant), downstairs. The same wine lists are available in all three.

Honors / Awards: Wine list has received a *Wine Spectator* "Grand Award" annually since 1984. *Interiors* magazine award for design.

Walker Bros. Original Pancake House

American ★★★½ **Inexpensive**

	Quality	Value
	88	**B**

153 Greenbay Road, Wilmette
(708) 251-6000
Zone 11   Northern Suburbs

1615 Waukegan Road, Glenview
(708) 724-0220
Zone 10   Northwest Suburbs

825 Dundee Road, Arlington Heights
(708) 392-6600
Zone 10   Northwest Suburbs

Reservations: Not accepted
When to go: Breakfast, brunch
Entree range: $3.75–6.50
Payment: VISA, MC, D
Service rating: ★★½
Friendliness rating: ★★★
Parking: Free lot
Bar: No
Wine selection: None
Dress: Casual
Disabled access: Yes
Customers: Locals, families
Open: Sunday–Thursday, 7 A.M.–10 P.M.
   (10:30 P.M. in Wilmette); Friday and Saturday,
   7 A.M.–11 P.M.

Atmosphere / setting: Comfortable and casual with stained-glass decor. The original place in Wilmette was the set for the film, "Ordinary People."

House specialities: Huge baked German pancake—the apple version is great topped with melted butter and cinnamon sugar; puffy omelet; French crêpes with strawberries and cheese.

Other recommendations: Waffles; spinach crêpes; corned beef hash.

Summary & comments: This is an old standby in several Chicago-area locations. The newest outlets are in Highland Park (with an expanded menu serving soups, salads, and sandwiches) and in Lincolnshire (also serving salads and sandwiches). The quality of food exceeds the sometimes uneven service. A great family place for breakfast or brunch, and a fine place for a light supper—or late snack after a movie.

Wild Onion

American ★★★½ **Inexpensive/Moderate**

3500 North Lincoln Avenue
(312) 871-5113
Zone 1   North Side

Quality	Value
85	**B**

Reservations: Accepted
When to go: Any time
Entree range: $8–15
Payment: All major credit cards
Service rating: ★★★
Friendliness rating: ★★★½
Parking: Street
Bar: Full service
Wine selection: American, French, Italian
Dress: Casual
Disabled access: Yes
Customers: Locals, professionals, yuppies, couples
Open: Monday–Saturday, 11:30 A.M.–5 P.M.;
Sunday, brunch 10:30 A.M.–2:30 P.M., dinner 3–10 P.M.

Atmosphere / setting: Loft-style building with high ceilings, exposed brick walls, hardwood floors, lovely outdoor patio dining area.

House specialities: Southwestern shrimp; crab cakes; duck enchiladas with mole sauce; spinach pie with two cheeses; grilled rosemary chicken salad; smoked chicken chili. Vegetarian entrees (e.g., eggplant with goat cheese).

Other recommendations: Baked brie and shrimp; baked heart of artichokes with blue cheese and a lemon-butter sauce; seafood dill angel hair with garlic-tarragon cream sauce; soft shrimp tacos in Creole sauce; mouth-puckering key lime pie.

Summary & comments: Out of the way in an unlikely neighborhood, this place, named for Chicago (the Indian name for "wild onion"), has always been rather creative with its food. The chef has a penchant for artichokes, and there's a good foreign infusion in the menu. The food is well prepared, portions are ample, and the service and atmosphere are pleasant—and the bonus is the pricing. Well worth a visit.

Honors / Awards: Many good reviews from local newspapers, magazine, and radio.

Winnetka Grill

New American   ★★★★   **Moderate**

---

64 Green Bay Road, Winnetka
(708) 441-6444
Zone 11   Northern Suburbs

Quality	Value
90	**C**

Reservations: Strongly recommended
When to go: Weeknights less busy
Entree range: $17.50–25
Payment: All major credit cards
Service rating: ★★★★
Friendliness rating: ★★★½
Parking: Street; valet on weekends
Bar: Full service
Wine selection: Extensive selection of American
   wines: 38 bottles, 12 of which are also available by
   half bottle, glass, or half glass; additional reserve list
   of 65-plus fine wines; user-friendly, allowing more
   tasting options
Dress: Jackets customarily worn; very casual in
   outdoor tent in summer
Disabled access: Limited
Customers: Professional, executives, couples
Brunch: October 1 through mid-May, Sunday
   brunch, 11 A.M.–2:30 P.M.
Dinner: Monday–Thursday, 5:30–9 P.M.; Friday,
   5:30–10 P.M.; Saturday, 5–10 P.M.; Sunday,
   5–9 P.M. (summer)

Atmosphere / setting: Sophisticated, stylish, intimate.
Postmodern 90-seat interior by John Cannon with
geometric columns, painted hardwood floor, dramatic
lighting, and draped fabric panels. Outdoor dining in
climate-controlled tent in view of garden.

House specialities: Seasonal menu with an emphasis
on fresh ingredients and a variety of preparation
methods. Soft-shell crab in season in early summer;
one special appetizer offered three choices, excellent
with basil and balsamic vinaigrette. Other starters:
rich, velvety seared foie gras with nectarines, caramelized black pepper, and colorful sautéed crawfish tails
with a corn waffle and crawfish cream. Pistachio-
crusted halibut fillets, and red and yellow tomato
vinaigrettes; flourless chocolate cake, crème Anglaise,
macadamia ice cream, and edible flowers; homemade
sorbets and ice creams.

Other recommendations: Rock crab and artichoke salad, colorful with Belgian endive, lemon balm, and fennel vinaigrette; grilled selections such as special coho salmon with wild boar bacon and capers in lemon sauce, with gratin potatoes; grilled loin of lamb; eggplant-pesto lasagna; braised rabbit tamale, chanterelles, and roasted loins; crème brûlée with Michigan sun-dried cherries.

Summary & comments: This North Shore restaurant is into its second decade and has adapted its cooking over the years to customers' needs. Owner Henry Markwood said, "When we opened, nouvelle cuisine was the rage with heavily reduced sauces and beurre blanc. And Paul Prudhomme–style blackened red fish, popular then, has given way to more delicate Atlantic salmon—today chef Paul Larson 'blackens' it with an inventive mixture of pumpernickel crumbs. Our sauces emphasize natural juices and flavors." The chef grills over oak and hickory woods and in summer grows herbs and edible flowers on the roof-top garden. Popular before summer concerts at nearby Ravinia Park is the $25 prix fixe, three-course dinner. Available for private parties.

Honors/Awards: *Wine Spectator* Award of Excellence

Yoshi's Cafe

New French ★★★★½ **Moderate/Expensive**

3257 Halsted Street
(312) 248-6160
Zone 1   North Side

Quality	Value
96	**C**

Reservations: Recommended, especially for
  weekends
When to go: Weekend nights are busiest
Entree range: $17–25
Payment: All major credit cards except DC
Service rating: ★★★★½
Friendliness rating: ★★★★½
Parking: Valet, $3.50
Bar: Full service; small full bar separate from dining
  room
Wine selection: About 80 selections, mostly French
  and American; $25 and up per bottle; good
  collection of house wines; by the glass, $6
Dress: Nice, casual; jacket and tie not required
Disabled access: Yes
Customers: Diverse, local, visitors, European,
  couples, business, family
Dinner: Tuesday–Thursday, 5:30–10 P.M.; Friday
  and Saturday, 5:30–10:30 P.M.; Sunday, 5–
  9:30 P.M.; Monday, closed.

Atmosphere / setting: Very romantic, intimate dining
room with print wallpaper, white linen tablecloths, and
lots of silver; very cozy and small, seating only 48
patrons.

House specialities: Unusual fish and seafood
prepared to enhance their individual flavors and
textures, including fluke, sea urchin, and domestic fugu
(blowfish—the Japanese type is poisonous if not
prepared properly, but rest assured that domestic fugu
is non-poisonous). Items change due to availability.
Tuna tartare with guacamole and toast; crêpe filled
with snow crab, smoked salmon, and mushrooms,
topped with sour cream; mixed grill with three
different fishes and sauces: hamachi (yellow tail) with
sweet miso sauce, skate wing with tomato caper sauce,
and salmon with pesto sauce; gourmet salad and mixed
fowl plate with quail, squab, duck breast, and lettuce
with balsamic vinaigrette and foie gras garnish;
medallions of veal stuffed with California goat cheese

and wrapped in prosciutto, with pesto cream sauce, on a bed of buckwheat pasta. Homemade desserts are worth the calories: chocolate cone filled with white and dark chocolate mousse; apricot tart baked in a pastry shell with milk chocolate and apricot preserve bottom, and an almond meringue top.

Other recommendations: Grilled seared tuna with tomato garlic sauce; sautéed chicken breast with apricot-orange sauce and grilled vegetable garnish; grilled beef tenderloin with zinfindel sauce; apple tart with Granny Smith apples in puff pastry.

Entertainment & amenities: An advantage here is that Yoshi owns a seafood wholesale business and gets supplies of Japanese and other fish rarely found otherwise; he also supplies some Japanese sushi places.

Summary & comments: Yoshi Katsumura and his wife, Nobuko, have operated this Franco-Japanese gem on Halsted for more than a decade, and it seems to only get better. His superb French food with Oriental influences is beautifully presented on colorful Japanese plates, and is enhanced by the professional, accommo- dating service and the lovely intimacy of the dining room.

Honors / Awards: DiRoNA Award (distinguished restaurant in North America since 1992, 4 diamonds).

Yvette

New French   ★★★¹/₂   **Inexpensive/Moderate**

1206 North State Parkway
(312) 280-1700
Zone 3   Near North

Quality	Value
85	**C**

Reservations: Recommended
When to go: Any time; weekdays less busy
Entree range: Lunch, $8.50–10.50; dinner, $5.95–17.50
Payment: VISA, MC, AMEX, DC
Service rating: ★★★¹/₂
Friendliness rating: ★★★★¹/₂
Parking: City lot across the street (discounted)
Bar: Full service; attractive bar/lounge in front
Wine selection: More than 50 selections from France and California; about 7 by the glass, $5
Dress: Informal, tastefully casual, some dressy
Disabled access: Yes
Customers: Upscale, largely professional, couples, all ages
Brunch: Saturday and Sunday, 11 A.M.–3 P.M.
Dinner: Monday–Thursday, 5 P.M.–midnight; Friday and Saturday, 5 P.M.–1 A.M.; Sunday, 5–11 P.M., 365 days a year

---

Atmosphere / setting: Sophisticated cabaret ambiance in lounge area, set to accommodate musicians; dining room in back is comfortable, with white, paper-covered tables. Chic Gold Coast bistro with al fresco sidewalk cafe.

House specialities: Fresh oysters on the half shell with sauce mignonette; escargots bourguignons; baked goat cheese salad with baby greens, bacon, and house vinaigrette; pasta of the day (e.g., farfelle with shrimp and garlic); grilled filet mignon, potatoes, and natural juices; freshly made desserts, including signature chocolate oblivion and lemon tart with raspberry sauce.

Other recommendations: Yvette crab cakes served with basil oil; grilled salmon with a honey mustard glaze, julienne of vegetables, and sauce beurre blanc; grilled steak au poivre with ratatouille and roasted potatoes. Daily specials such as grilled veal sweetbreads with whipped potatoes, Bordelaise, and béarnaise sauces.

Entertainment & amenities: Every night, live music (jazz, cabaret) and dancing; no cover.

Summary & comments: Unique French bistro with a cabaret atmosphere and nightly entertainment and dancing. Owner Bob Djahanguiri's hallmark with all his restaurants is designing them himself and blending live music with good French food and ambiance. In addition to this, he owns Yvette Wintergarden, and Toulouse On the Park, 2140 North Lincoln Park West, Chicago, (312) 665-9071. Yvette North is scheduled to open in Wheeling in late 1994. Chef Corey Gerber, who took the kitchen reins here at Yvette in spring of 1994, has put forth some very respectable cooking. A very romantic place for a special occasion or any time you're yearning for a taste of France.

Yvette Wintergarden

New French   ★★★¹/₂   **Inexpensive/Moderate**

---

311 South Wacker Drive
(312) 408-1242
Zone 4   The Loop

Quality	Value
85	**C**

Reservations: Recommended
When to go: Lunch or for a different ambiance at
  dinner with music; before theater or opera
Entree range: $10.50–16
Payment: VISA, MC, AMEX, DC
Service rating: ★★★★
Friendliness rating: ★★★★
Parking: Adjacent lot, $5 after 5 P.M.
Bar: Full service
Wine selection: 50 from France, America, and Italy;
  $15–350 a bottle; many in $20–35 range; half
  bottles, $8; 6 by the glass
Dress: Informal, casual; tends to be dressier in the
  evening for dancing
Disabled access: Yes
Customers: Upscale, professional, all ages
Lunch: Monday–Friday, 11 A.M.–2 P.M.
Dinner: Monday–Thurday, 5–9 P.M.; Friday and
  Saturday, 5–10:30 P.M.; complimentary hors
  d'oeuvres, Monday–Friday, 5:30–7 P.M.; pre-
  theater menu, Monday–Saturday, 5–7 P.M.

Atmosphere / setting: Spectacular tropical atrium
entrance; dining room is intimate and dimly lit; seating
in one dining room designed to view live performances.

House specialities: Classic French onion soup;
lobster and artichoke fritters; sautéed striped sea bass
served with green olive, pistachio, and arugula pesto,
and mushroom and roasted tomato ragout.

Other recommendations: Grilled lamb served with
tomato and garlic confit and crispy potato; seasonal
terrine of the day; salade Niçoise; paillard of chicken
breast; grilled pork tenderloin en cassoulet; freshly
made desserts of the day.

Entertainment & amenities: Monday–Saturday, live
music—large dance floor; no cover.

Summary & comments: Owner Bob Djahanguiri has
a particular talent for creating romantic French bistros,
restaurants, and cabarets with appropriate live music.

This place developed after his Yvette. It's larger and a great downtown spot for before the theater or for relaxing for dinner and dancing. Yvette Wintergarden does private parties for 10–1,500; call catering, (312) 408-1247.

About the Author

Camille Stagg is a food and travel writer and editor with more than 25 year's experience in the journalism and consulting profession. Her work for over 12 years as food editor for the *Chicago Sun-Times* won awards for excellence in food journalism. She was also food editor of *Cuisine* magazine, has appeared regularly on television and radio, and is the author of several books, including the current culinary troubleshooting reference, *The Best of The Cook's Advisor.* Ms. Stagg appeared on leading television and radio shows during several national media tours as a spokesperson with her first best-selling book, *The Cook's Advisor.* She has directed a cooking school, and continues teaching numerous seminars and classes, and conducts food and wine tastings.

Ms. Stagg has served as dining critic for the *Chicago Sun-Times, Pulitzer-Lerner Newspapers, Inside Chicago* magazine, *Talking To the Boss,* and currently for *Chicago Social.* Her travel assignments focusing on cuisine and culture have been extensive: Europe, Australia, North Africa, Hong Kong, Canada, the Caribbean, Mexico, and most of the United States. She holds a B. S. in food science and journalism from the University of Illinois and has studied cooking with experts here and abroad.